BLUEPRINTS

Maths Key Stage 2 Teacher's Resource Book

Second edition

David and Wendy Clemson

Stanley Thornes (Publishers) Ltd

First published in 1992 by:
Stanley Thornes (Publishers) Ltd
Ellenborough House
Wellington Street
CHELTENHAM GL50 1YW
England

Reprinted 1993

Second edition 1995

Reprinted 1995

A catalogue record for this book is available from the British Library.

ISBN 0–7487–2205–X

Typeset by Tech-Set Ltd., Gateshead, Tyne & Wear.
Printed and bound in Great Britain at The Bath Press, Avon..

CONTENTS

Resourcing your mathematics

Most of the resources you and the children need for mathematics are commonly and readily available. In the Activities in every Section we assume the existence of such things as pots and containers, collections of objects and so on, and these general resources are listed below. At the beginning of each Section of the book you will find suggestions for additions to the general resources that will help in working in that particular Section.

In addition to the children themselves, you will need a resource bank, in the classroom, easily accessible to you, the teacher, and preferably also accessible to the children. There are supplies of things like pencils, crayons, books, rulers and the like in most classrooms. Some of these can be set aside as mathematics resources, for the time that they are needed. Some commercially-produced counting aids, such as Unifix©, Colour Factor©, Cuisenaire©, Multilink© and Centicubes©, are commonly available in most schools and are extremely useful. The other kinds of things you might include as mathematics resources are infinite, but here are some suggestions:

- beads, conkers and other nuts, shells, marbles, sticks, timber offcuts, wooden blocks, cotton reels, pressed and mounted leaves, seeds, feathers, egg cups, spoons, soft toys, model farm animals, dolls' house furniture and dolls, model cars, socks, balls of wool, spent matches, elastic bands, pebbles and pieces of string, a heavy rope, a skipping rope;
- containers, cartons and boxes of all kinds, including jugs, beakers, jars and plastic bottles, tins, yogurt pots, margarine tubs, matchboxes, food boxes, egg boxes and boxes big enough for children to get into;
- marbles, beads, dice and spinners;
- building bricks, Duplo©, Lego©, Plasticine©, clay, Play-Doh© and 'play food' or other items made with this, drinking straws and Artstraws©;
- pictures from magazines and catalogues, old greeting cards and postcards;
- number lines, play money, metre sticks, a card-board clock-face, rubber stamps with pictures, numbers, coins or shapes on them, number games, calculators;
- fabrics, metal objects and samples of natural materials;
- a wide variety of art materials, including a range of varieties of paper, cardboard, gummed shapes, scissors, sticky tape, chalks, brushes, paints, inks.

In addition to these general resources we have found the following very useful:

- blank dice, obtainable through educational suppliers, which can be written on with washable felt-tip pen or have stick-on, removable numerals attached;
- many-sided dice, obtainable from shops selling elaborate board games.

Books are necessary too. There are many fiction books which have mathematical ideas as an integral part of the story. Hunting for treasure, deciphering codes, descriptions of room layouts in buildings, journeys made and routes taken are common examples. In choosing non-fiction books we would urge you to consider your mathematics as in need of resourcing in just the same way as you might buy for art and design. Mathematics does not need to appear in the title. Include books on needlepoint, quilts, architecture, printing, desk-top publishing and 'facts'. By 'facts' we are thinking of the data source opportunities given, for example, by *The Guinness Book of Records, Pears Cyclopaedia* and W H Smith's *Factfile*. Good encyclopaedias and atlases should also be available.

Finally, we should like to recommend these books for teachers:

Clemson, D. and Clemson, W. (1994) *Mathematics in the Early Years*, Routledge.

Daintith, J and Nelson, R D (1989) *The Penguin Dictionary of Mathematics.*

Deboys, M and Pitt, E (2nd edn 1980) *Lines of Development in Primary Mathematics,* Blackstaff Press.

Hughes, M (1986) *Children and Number,* Basil Blackwell.

Jones, L Ed (1991) *Teaching Mathematics and Art,* Stanley Thornes.

Merttens, R (1987) *Teaching Primary Maths,* Edward Arnold.

Mottershead, L (1985) *Investigations in Mathematics,* Basil Blackwell.

Williams, E and Shuard, H (3rd edn 1982) *Primary Mathematics Today,* Longman.

Woodman, A and Albany, E (1988) *Mathematics through Art and Design,* Unwin Hyman.

Preface

In order to be able to extract meaning from the world around us it is essential that we become numerate, just as we need to be literate and able to deploy language in a variety of ways. Both the natural and man-made worlds are explicable in some respects only through mathematics. To be deprived of the skills necessary to grapple with a better understanding of the constants and variables in the world is to be both intellectually and practically disadvantaged. It is therefore vitally important that all of our children are exposed to the challenge, beauty, relevance and breadth of mathematics. But to communicate all this demands enlivened teaching.

Mathematicians in the making need enthusiastic mathematicians as teachers. If you, yourself, find mathematics the most irksome part of the curriculum, please give it another go! Mathematics is about pattern and therefore unites language and science. Human beings seem to search for patterns in experience in order to understand. Mathematics is not a 'way of thinking' independent of language, but a realisation that it is about pattern enriches our thinking and understanding.

Whatever the economic and political future of the nation, simply by giving children confidence and competence in doing mathematics you will certainly have influenced the course of some of their lives. You will have empowered them for cognisant adulthood and citizenship. What better ambition is there for a teacher? Never underestimate the capabilities of children, the power of mathematics or the influence of the teacher!

Introduction

What is Blueprints Maths?

Blueprints Maths is a practical, teachers' resource specifically written to fulfil the requirements of the National Curriculum in mathematics for primary schools. It is intended for all teachers, particularly those who are not mathematics specialists, and provides comprehensive coverage in an easy-to-follow format. *Blueprints Maths* is a rich resource of practical ideas to use alongside other materials within your scheme of work. It gives children meaningful, relevant things to do. *Blueprints Maths Key Stage 1* provides Activities for 5 to 7-year-olds; *Blueprints Maths Key Stage 2* provides Activities for 7 to 11-year-olds. For each Key Stage there is a Teacher's Resource Book and a book of Pupils' Copymasters.

Blueprints and the National Curriculum

The *Teachers Resource Book* and the accompanying *Pupils' Copymasters* follow closely the structure of *Mathematics in the National curriculum* (1995). The *Teacher's Resource Book* is arranged in sections, each corresponding to part of the National Curriculum Programme of study. The *Pupils' Copymasters* match the Activities in the *Teacher's Resource Book*.

Blueprints Maths Key Stage 2

The *Teacher's Resource Book* provides dozens of lively Activities through Key Stage 2. The book is arranged in three main sections. The sections relate to the work expected of children through this Key Stage, covering Attainment Targets 2, 3 and 4 at Levels 2–5. A discussion about how to cover Using and applying mathematics appears at the front of the book. At the start of each part of the book there is an extract from the Statutory Orders, comprising the appropriate programme of study point.

The *Teacher's Resource Book* will prove an invaluable resource, even without the use of the *Pupils' Copymasters*. You can, in developing your own schemes of work, choose Activities to fit those aspects on which you are focusing. There is a record sheet at the back of the book, on which you can identify Activities the children have tried, and also note work done contributing to Using and applying mathematics.

The *Pupils' Copymaster Book* provides 114 photocopiable worksheets. C1–C105 are linked specifically to many of the Activities in the *Teacher's Resource Book*. RC1–RC9 are resource copymasters and are for use again and again across all Sections of the book. When completed, the copymasters can be added to children's workfiles or used as exemplar material in pupil profiles. They may also be seen as a resource for teacher assessment. There is a tick list at the back of the book, on which you can note the copymaster sheets the children have used.

Attainment Targets 2–4
Across all these Attainment Targets *Blueprints Maths Key Stage 2* provides coverage of Levels 2–5. It is expected that most children should master Level 4 but Level 5 work is provided for those children who require work beyond Level 4. There are also banks of further extension activities at the ends of sections of the book.

The *Pupils' Copymasters* are provided as support for busy teachers and to provide frameworks for children's recording.

Using and applying mathematics
Using and applying mathematics, has been treated differently from the other parts of the Programme of study. At the beginning of the book you will find a brief summary of how you can incorporate work on Using and applying mathematics into the Activities the children do.

Record keeping
There are photocopiable record sheets at the back of the *Teacher's Resource Book* and the *Pupils' Copymaster Book*. Photocopy one *Teacher's Resource Book* record sheet per child and write in comments on the Levels of the appropriate Attainment Targets the child has worked at. Photocopy one *Pupils' Copymaster* record sheet per child and tick the photocopy sheets each child has worked on.

How to use this book

This book has been tied to the National Curriculum Programme of study so that you can access the Activities easily. Within each of the Sections, namely:

- *Number*
- *Shape, space and measures*
- *Handling data*

the Activities have been arranged to match points in the Programme of study, with Level 2 Activities first, and so on. At the beginning is a discussion of how to achieve coverage of Using and applying mathematics, which demands different treatment in that it 'threads through' the other parts of the Programme of study.

Our general intention is not that the Activities should be worked on in linear fashion, through there are a few places where we have recommended the children do one Activity before another. We hope that you will dip into the book and use the Activities where you consider them appropriate. We would favour an approach where, for a period of time (a day or weeks), you involve all the children in Activities in, for example, Number, at whatever Levels they are working. The Activities will also support thematic work where a number of curriculum areas are involved at the same time, and we have indicated these links where they are particularly potent. For example, some Shape and space Activities would enhance, and themselves be enhanced by, work in art, PE and music.

At the end of the book you will find a record sheet which will enable you to register a child's contact with work on each Attainment Target at Levels 2–5.

If you also have the *Key Stage 2 Pupils' Copymasters* use them to support learning and help with consolidation, assessment and evaluation where appropriate. You will find the copymasters referred to in this book with the symbol:

Copymasters 1–105 are tied to activities in Number, Shape, space and measures and Handling data. Resource copymasters RC1–RC9 can be used again and again as general resources across all the Sections of the book.

Key Stage 2 Programme of Study

The sections of the programme of study interrelate. Developing mathematical language, reasoning and skills in applying mathematics should be set in the context of the other areas of mathematics. Measurement should be associated with handling data and shape and space. Calculating skills should be developed in number and through work on measures and handling data. Algebraic ideas of pattern and relationships should be developed in all areas of mathematics.

LINKS WITH OTHER BOOKS IN THE BLUEPRINTS SERIES

You will find that the maths work in this book can be supported by activities and copymasters in other **Blueprints** books. The index below references related books which you have or may wish to acquire. References are given by copymaster number. All references refer to the 1995 editions of books. References are made to the areas of the programme of study and their numerical subdivisions.

Number

2. Developing an understanding of place value
Maths Investigations: Copymasters 3, 9, 17, 38, 41, 50, 79, School maths day (whole school investigations).

3. Understanding relationships between numbers
Maths Investigations: Copymasters 4, 6, 24, 30–37, 43, 46, 47, 51, 56–59, 64, 68–72, 77.

4. Solving numerical problems
Maths Investigations: all the activities involve problem-solving strategies, for example copymaster 49.

Shape, Space and Measures

2. Understanding and using properties of shapes
Maths Investigations: Copymasters 7, 8, 11, 19, 20–23, 26, 27, 40, 42, 52–55, 60, 61, 71, 74, 76, 78.

3. Understanding and using properties of position and movement
Maths Investigations: Copymasters 16, 25, 32, 44, 45, 81–85.

4. Understanding and using measures
Maths Investigations: Copymasters 1, 28, 29, 31, 62, 63, Doing time (Whole school investigations).

Handling Data

2. Collecting and interpreting data
Maths Investigations: Copymasters 2, 10, 18, 39, 48, Data day (Whole school investigations); **Science Key Stage 2:** Life processes and living things 4, Materials and their properties 1; **Science Investigations:** copymasters 21, 37–39, 44, 48, 50, 52, 54, 59, 63, 65.

3. Understanding and using probability
Maths Investigations: Copymasters 65–67, 72, 75, Games bonanza (whole school investigations).

COVERAGE OF THE CURRICULUM FOR SCOTLAND, WALES AND NORTHERN IRELAND

Blueprints Maths Key Stage 2 covers nearly all the different maths curriculum requirements in place for 7–11 year olds in Wales, Scotland and Northern Ireland. We have set out below the key curriculum content for the relevant stages for Scotland and Northern Ireland.

SCOTTISH NATIONAL GUIDELINES FOR MATHS 5–14

We have correlated the activities in this book against the attainment targets for Information Handling, Number, Money and Measurement, and Shape, Position and Movement Levels B, C and D. References are made to the numbered areas of study in this book for Handling Data (pages 91–117, marked D), Number (pages 1–53, marked N) and Shape, Space and Measurement (pages 54–90, marked SSM).

INFORMATION HANDLING ATTAINMENT TARGET

Level B	Level C	Level D
Collect		
Obtain information (pictures, diagrams) D10 Conduct a class survey D12	Obtain information (variety of sources) D15, 18 Conduct a survey beyond the class D12	Select information sources D12, 17, 18
Organise		
Use a tally sheet D4 Use a simple database D7	Use a grouped tally sheet D4 Enter data in a table D3 Use a database D7, 8, 11	Use diagrams and tables Use database or spreadsheet D8
Display		
Use labels, charts or diagrams D3, 5, 10 Construct a bar graph D6, 9	Construct table or chart D3, 10 Construct a bar graph with multiple units D13	Construct graphs D13, 16
Interpret		
From displays, asking specific questions	From displays and databases D11	From a range of displays and databases D14, 21

NUMBER, MONEY AND MEASUREMENT ATTAINMENT TARGET

Level B	Level C	Level D
Range and type of numbers		
Whole numbers up to 100 then 1000 N1, 54 Quarters N13	Whole numbers up to 10 000 N2, 3, 5, 7, 33, 54 Thirds, fifths, eighths, tenths, and simple equivalences N14 Decimals to two places N9, 10	Whole numbers to 100 000, a million N7, 33 Fractions N17 Percentages, decimals to 2 places N7, 15, 16, 48
Money		
Use coins to £1 N4, 50	Use coins/notes to £25 N4	Use all UK coins/notes N4, 48
Add and subtract		
Mentally 0–20 N30, 35 2 digits (without calculator) N36 2 digit numbers added to or subtracted from 3 digit numbers (with calculator) Money applications up to £1 N50	Mentally one digit to or from numbers up to 3 digits N53 Subtraction by 'adding on' N53, 36 Without calculator, whole numbers with 2 digits added to or subtracted from 3 digits N53, 38 With calculator, for 3 digit whole numbers N53, 49 Money applications up to £20 N53	Mentally, 2 digit whole numbers Without calculator for 4 digits with 2 decimal places (easy) With calculator for 4 digits, 2 decimal places
Multiply and divide		
Mentally 2, 3, 4, 5, 10 N31, 42, 43 Without calculator, 2 digits multiplied by 2, 3, 4, 5, 10 N44 With calculator for 2 digit numbers multiplied/divided by any digit Money applications up to £1 N51	Mentally all tables to 10 N32 Mentally 2 or 3 digit numbers by 10 N4, 6 Without calculator, 2 digit numbers by 1 digit With calculator 2 or 3 digits by 1 or 2 digit numbers by 1 or 2 digits N41, 49 Money applications up to £20	Mentally, whole numbers by single digits (easy) N40, N58 Mentally for 4 digit numbers including decimals by 10 or 100 N58 Without calculator for 4 digits with up to 2 decimal places by a single digit N58 With calculator for 4 digits with up to 2 decimal places, by 2 digits N58 Applications in money

Level B	Level C	Level D
Round numbers		
Round 2 digit whole numbers to nearest 10 N55	Round 3 digit whole numbers to nearest 10 N55	Round any number to nearest whole number N56–58
Fractions, percentages and ratios		
Find halves and quarters N13	Find simple fractions N14, 15	Work with simple fractions N15, 16, 18, 19
Patterns and sequences		
Even and odd numbers N21 Whole number sequences within 100 N37 More complex sequences with shapes	Patterns within multiplication tables N34	More complex sequences N23
Functions and equations		
Find missing numbers N45	Use simple 'function machines' for doubling, halving, adding and subtracting N22, 46, 47	Recognise and explain simple relationships between two sets of numbers or objects N24, 25, 39
Measure and estimate		
Length: m, $\frac{1}{2}$m, $\frac{1}{4}$m, cm SSM24 Weight: kg, $\frac{1}{2}$kg Place objects in order of length and weight Use abbreviations: m, cm and equivalences Length conservation when shapes change SSM32 Read scales SSM24	Weight: accuracy up to 20 kg SSM26 Volume: litre, $\frac{1}{2}$litre, $\frac{1}{4}$litre SSM26 Area: shapes composed of different shapes or grids SSM34, 35 Estimate length and weight in standard units SSM25, 28 Select appropriate measuring devices and units N52, SSM26, 32, 33 Read scales SSM32, 33 Weight and area conservation when shapes change SSM32	Length: small/large N11, SSM29 Weight: extended range of articles SSM29, 31 Volume: accuracy extended to small units SSM29, 36 Area: right-angled triangles SSM35 Temperature Estimate small weights, areas and volumes Kilometres Select appropriate measuring devices and units N52, 33 Imperial units of measurement SSM30

Level B	Level C	Level D
Time		
Place events in time sequence Tell time using analogue display SSM27 Tell time using digital display SSM27	Use 12-hour timetables SSM27 Conventions for recording time Work with hours, minutes SSM27 Use calendars	Use 24-hour times and equate with 12-hour times Calculate duration in hours/minutes Time activities in seconds Calculate speeds
Perimeter, formulae, scales		
		Calculate perimeters SSM34

SHAPE, POSITION AND MOVEMENT ATTAINMENT TARGET

Level B	Level C	Level D
Range of shapes		
Respond to written/oral descriptions of shapes SSM4 Identify and name triangular/square pyramids Shapes that will tile SSM16, 17 Make 3D shapes SSM9	Identify 2D shapes within 3D shapes Draw circles SSM8 Recognise 3D shapes within 2D drawings SSM10	Discuss 3D/2D shapes SSM12 Recognise pentagon, hexagon SSM7 Identify and name equilateral and isosceles triangles Radius, diameter, circumference SSM37, 38 Create or copy a tiling using a shape template SSM16, 17 Make 3D models: cube and cuboid. Rigidity properties of triangles
Position and movement		
Turning through right angles SSM20 Recognise and name the four compass points Grid references SSM18 Create a square or rectangle SSM6	Describe features of a journey or route Create paths on squared paper	Directions of route or journey Use an 8-point compass rose Use a co-ordinate system to locate a point on a grid N26, 27, 28, SSM19 Create patterns by rotating a shape SSM16, 17

Level B	Level C	Level D
Symmetry		
Recognise symmetrical shapes SSM11	Find lines of symmetry	Draw lines of symmetry SSM11, 13, 15
	Complete a symmetrical shape	Create symmetrical shapes SSM 11, 13, 14, 15
Angles		
Draw right angle SSM11, 3	Know that a right angle = 90° SSM20	Draw, copy and measure angles accurately within 5 degrees SSM22
	Use 'right, acute, obtuse' to describe angles SSM20, 21	Use standard notation 060, 150, 300, to express bearings SSM42
	Know that a straight line = 180° SSM7	

THE NATIONAL CURRICULUM FOR NORTHERN IRELAND

Because the programme of study for the National Curriculum for Northern Ireland is under review at the time of going to press, we have correlated the activities in this book against the Key Stage 2 statements of attainment for the maths content attainment targets (Number, Algebra, Shape and Space, Measures and Data Handling) as set out in the 1990 document. This book is correlated against Levels 2–5 of that document by level and lettered statement of attainment. Numbers refer to areas of study in this book.

Attainment Target N: Number

All the activities in this AT are contained within the programme of study for Number on pages 1–53 of this book.

Level 2
a: 1; **b:** 13; **c:** 20, 29, 35; **d:** 35, 50; **e:** —.

Level 3
a: 1, 2; **b:** 9; **c:** 14; **d:** 30; **e:** 50; **f:** 31, 42; **g:** 22, 42, 43, 49, 51; **h:** 54, 55; **i:** 44.

Level 4
a: 3; **b:** 5, 54; **c:** 4, 6; **d:** 7, 10, 11; **e:** 8, 12; **f:** 15, 16; **g:** 32; **h:** 35–38; **i:** 38–41; **j:** 49; **k:** 48, 53; **l:** —; **m:** 55, 56; **n:** 49; **o:** 49.

Level 5
a: 33; **b:** 14, 17, 18; **c:** 19; **d:** 18; **e:** —; **f:** 38; **g:** 41; **h:** 48; **i:** 12; **j:** —; **k:** 56; **l:** 54, 55, 58.

Attainment Target A: Algebra

All the activities in this AT are contained within the programme of study for Number on pages 1–53 of this book.

Level 2
a: 20; **b:** 20, 29, 38; **c:** 20, 29, 38; **d:** 21; **e:** 45.

Level 3
a: 36, 37; **b:** 36, 37; **c:** 6, 42; **d:** 46, 47.

Level 4
a: 22; **b:** 23; **c:** 31, 32; **d:** 47 **e:** 45–47; **f:** 26–28.

Level 5
a: 33–34; **b:** 23, 24; **c:** 23, 24; **d:** 25 **e:** 25, 60, 62; **f:** 26–28.

Attainment Target M: Measures

All the activities in this AT are contained within the programme of study for Shape, Space and Measures on pages 54–90 of this book, apart from those marked N, which are from the Number section on pages 1–53.

Level 2
a: 23; **b:** N50; **c:** 24, 25, 27.

Level 3
a: 26; **b:** 32, 33; **c:** 25, 28.

Level 4
a: 29; **b:** 34; **c:** 34; **d:** 25, 28; **e:** 27.

Level 5
a: —; **b:** 30; **c:** 31; **d:** 20–22; **e:** 36–38.

Attainment Target S: Shape and Space

All the activities in this AT are contained within the programme of study for Shape, Space and Measures on pages 54–90 of this book.

Level 2
a: 1, 2, 3, 4, 5; **b:** 6, 20; **c:** 6, 20; **d:** 43.

Level 3
a: 40; **b:** 20; **c:** 11.

Level 4
a: 7, 20, 21, 22; **b:** 8, 9, 16, 17; **c:** 18; **d:** 18, 19; **e:** 6, 20; **f:** 15.

Level 5
a: 12; **b:** 43; **c:** 14, 15; **d:** 13, 15; **e:** 18.

Attainment Target D: Handling Data

All the activities in this AT are contained within the programme of study for Handling Data on pages 91–111 of this book.

Level 2
a: 1; **b:** 4; **c:** 3, 6; **d:** 2, 5; **e:** 22–25; **f:** 22–25.

Level 3
a: 3; **b:** 7, 8, 11; **c:** 9; **d:** 10; **e:** 24–25 **f:** 25.

Level 4
a: 12; **b:** 19, 20; **c:** —; **d:** —; **e:** 13; **f:** —; **g:** —; **h:** 26; **i:** 26–29.

Level 5
a: 15; **b:** 30; **c:** —; **d:** 32; **e:** 16; **f:** 31; **g:** 27; **h:** —.

Covering Using and applying mathematics

Using and applying mathematics 'threads through' other parts of the Programme of study. We are absolutely confident that if the children with whom you are working have experience of a wide variety of the Activities in this book, they will embrace the demands of Using and applying mathematics. To illustrate this we discuss, under the relevant level descriptions, the key aspects which should be regularly in evidence while children are engaged in mathematical tasks in your classroom and school, and set down example activities from within the book which will meet requirements in Using and applying mathematics.

Using and applying mathematics

■ 1. Pupils should be given opportunities to:

a use and apply mathematics in practical tasks, in real-life problems and within mathematics itself;	Shape, space and measures 27 Handling data 13
b take increasing responsibility for organising and extending tasks;	Number 11 Handling data 15
c devise and refine their own ways of recording;	Shape, space and measures 33 Handling data 1
d ask questions and follow alternative suggestions to support the development of reasoning.	Number 52 Handling data 2

■ 2. Making and monitoring decisions to solve problems

Pupils should be taught to

a select and use the appropriate mathematics and materials;	Number 47 Shape, space and measures 22
b try different mathematical approaches; identify and obtain information needed to carry out their work;	Number 22 Shape, space and measures 18
c develop their own mathematical strategies and look for ways to overcome difficulties;	Number 38 Number 56
d check their results and consider whether they are reasonable.	Number 55

■ 3. Developing mathematical language and communication

a understand the language of number, the properties and movements of shapes, measures, simple probability, relationships, including 'multiple of', 'factor of' and 'symmetrical to';	Shape, space and measures 2 Handling data 22
b use diagrams, graphs and simple algebraic symbols;	Handling data 10 Handling data 13
c present information and results clearly, and explain the reasons for their choice of presentation.	Handling data 4

■ 4. Developing mathematical reasoning

a understand and investigate general statements, *eg 'wrist size is half neck size', 'there are four prime numbers less than 10'*;	Number 24
b search for pattern in their results;	Number 15
c make general statements of their own, based on evidence they have produced;	Number 37 Number 39
d explain their reasoning.	Handling data 21

LEVEL DESCRIPTIONS AND OUR COMMENTARY

Attainment target 1: Using and applying mathematics

■ Level 2

Pupils select the mathematics for some classroom activities. They discuss their work using familiar mathematical language and are beginning to represent it using symbols and simple diagrams. They ask and respond appropriately to questions including 'What would happen if...?'.

LEVEL 2

There is much talk, under the National Curriculum, of the 'independent learner'. This is the Level at which the independent mathematician begins to emerge. Give the children choices and chances to resource their own work and they will soon be able to do so with confidence. The key principles both you and the children should operate are to do with access and 'finishing off'. All that is necessary for a task must be readily accessible and everyone must agree on the procedures for putting away resources when they have finished using them.

At this Level the children should not only be given opportunities to talk about their work, both while they are doing it and after they have completed it, but with your help they should know how to begin to write down what the outcomes are.

With increased breadth of experience of practical mathematical activity the children will begin to speculate about extending the Activities they are trying. When they say, for example, 'I wonder what would happen if I put another ball of Plasticine on the balance?' or... 'another four in this set?' or... 'another +2 into the calculator?', they are stating the problem. They can go on to solve the problem with your guidance and say whether what happened matched what they expected.

■ Level 3

Pupils try different approaches and find ways of overcoming difficulties that arise when they are solving problems. They are beginning to organise their work and check results. Pupils discuss their mathematical work and are beginning to explain their thinking. They use and interpret mathematical symbols and diagrams. Pupils show that they understand a general statement by finding particular examples that match it.

LEVEL 3

This is the Level at which children's practice in estimation will support their learning. Such practice will have helped them to understand that if we know roughly 'what to expect' in terms of an answer we can say whether our answer is likely to be correct. Now the children should not only be adept at resourcing their mathematical Activities, but also at making judgements about answers, outcomes and progress so far, in the light of their own notions of what should happen.

With the practice in talking about their mathematics that they have had at Levels 1 and 2, they should be ready and able to begin reporting orally what happens in their Activities and to write down outcomes in a way that makes these easy for everyone to understand.

You can now help the children to develop their capacity to make mathematical hypotheses and carry through tests of these, by letting them carry their investigations beyond the end of a 'session', and continuing a line of work until they are ready to take on a new problem.

■ Level 4

Pupils are developing their own strategies for solving problems and are using these strategies both in working within mathematics and in applying mathematics to practical contexts. They present information and results in a clear and organised way, explaining the reasons for their presentation. They search for a pattern by trying out ideas of their own.

LEVEL 4

This is the Level at which the children are beginning to decide how to tackle an Activity and planning the order of doing things. They will be able to make decisions about the sort of mathematics that is needed. When they are recording you can encourage them to develop their own 'codes' in collecting and collating data. They will be moving beyond anecdotal evidence to the idea that we can test our mathematical solutions, and be ready to devise ways of testing them and explaining the outcomes.

From their own evidence they can begin to make generalisations.

■ Level 5

In order to carry through tasks and solve mathematical problems, pupils identify and obtain necessary information; they check their results, considering whether these are sensible. Pupils show understanding of situations by describing them mathematically using symbols, words and diagrams. They make general statements of their own, based on evidence they have produced, and give an explanation of their reasoning.

LEVEL 5

Now the children are able to see through a mathematics task by judicious planning. They can break the work required into 'bites' to be done one at a time and in a given order, and they can review and preview their work along the way. They will by now be adopting strategies for extracting meaning from mathematics data, no matter how it is conveyed, and they can begin to use their knowledge in creating generalisations that they themselves can test. This is the Level at which the virtually independent mathematician emerges.

Note that at the ends of the sections on Number, Shape, space and measures and Handling data there are a number of further extension activities intended to challenge those children who require them.

Number

INTRODUCTION

Number

Number is one of the two major building blocks of mathematics, the other being Shape and space. Without a sense of number and an appreciation of the power of number children cannot make progress into areas of mathematics such as Algebra, Measures and Handling data.

In one sense it could be argued that number has been, and continues to be, the major preoccupation of primary school mathematics for it partly matches the old arithmetic of the 'three Rs'. Indeed even a cursory glance into many primary schools would provide ample evidence that children's mathematical experience can be directly linked to the doing of sums.

What the National Curriculum offers, though, is a much broader definition of mathematics than pages of sums, for the requirements in relation to number work are themselves much broader than what has been traditionally offered. In order to grapple with number work in the context of the National Curriculum, children and teachers are going to have to embrace a wide range of activities, many of them not suited to pencil and paper operations. For example, where an exploration of, and an appreciation of, number patterns may once have been seen by some as recreational mathematics – not proper maths at all – these areas are now seen as an essential part of the way children can come to understand number. To manipulate number, to use it rather than be its servant, is the aim. In this Section of the book we offer a range of practical Activities and, where appropriate, paper and pencil opportunities through which children can start on the road to using numbers for their own purposes; and, hopefully, to do so with a sense of enjoyment and achievement.

Resourcing Number

In addition to a selection of the resources we have listed at the beginning of this book, the following will prove useful in carrying through some of the Activities in this Section:

- Playing cards, dominoes, snakes and ladders, ludo.
- Small toys and stationery items for a class 'shop'.
- Biscuit cutters, ingredients and cooking facilities.
- Maps, including aerial, local, world, motorway and weather.
- Plastic money and play papernotes.

Algebra

Algebra can conjure up experiences, for some, which have to do with learning tricks using numbers and letters whilst they are not aware of the purpose of the manipulations. It is one of those areas of mathematics that provoke strong feelings. This is a pity because the purpose of Algebra is really to simplify understanding through the creation of sets of generalisations about such things as number patterns or the path of a line on a graph. In tackling early work in Algebra we need to keep in mind that it is about generalising from the particular and that for children really to make sense of the purpose of Algebra they have to have the opportunity to work with lots of numbers before they can see a generalisable pattern.

There are two main ways in which the foundations of some aspects are commonly found in classrooms. Children often encounter 'sums' which invite them to state what is the missing number. These are often of the form $4 + ? = 6$. Whilst there are clear connections, here, with algebraic ideas it must not be assumed that Algebra is just about handling equations. It is most important to appreciate that equations represent formulations of general statements derived from sets of real data and as such are just one way of making such statements. In other words, it is important to understand what it is that equations and formulae are actually representing and to do so the children should make full use of real data and be able to relate their general statements to practical cases.

The other encounter many children have with Algebra is oral, for example, when teachers ask for a general statement of the kind 'What sort of a number/sequence of numbers is that?' We believe that it is important to maintain oral questioning of this sort. Using appropriate language, describing relationships logically and clearly, and explaining a relationship that you have detected to others who may not have done so, is at the heart of genuine development. Rushing to the formula or equation must be avoided.

The foundations of Algebra, as set out in the National Curriculum, pay particular attention to relationships and sequences as well as patterns and the creation of generalisations.

Resourcing Algebra

The resource bank that we mention at the front of the book is appropriate for work in this Section. Additional resources that may help include:

- resources about ancient number systems;
- resources about classical art and architecture, and examples of pattern in the natural world.

You may wish to pursue pattern-making ideas in art and technology. These will demand a variety of materials and media, including all those we have mentioned in the general resource bank.

Good use can be made of the most recent technologies. Computers and good software, and, if possible the acquisition of 'robot' devices will reap rewards in both understanding and motivation.

Programme of study: Number

■ 1. Pupils should be given opportunities to:

a develop flexible and effective methods of computation and recording, and use them with understanding;

b use calculators, computers and a range of other resources as tools for exploring number structure and to enable work with realistic data;

c develop the skills needed for accurate and appropriate use of equipment.

For this part of the Programme of study we have set down examples drawn from the body of the book.

a Area of study 38

b Area of study 48

c Area of study 49

Attainment target 2: Number and algebra

Level descriptions

■ Level 2

Pupils count sets of objects reliably, and use mental recall of addition and subtraction facts to 10. They have begun to understand the place value of each digit in a number and use this to order numbers up to 100. They choose the appropriate operation when solving addition and subtraction problems. They identify and use halves and quarters, such as half of a rectangle or a quarter of eight objects. They recognise sequences of numbers, including odd and even numbers.

■ Level 3

Pupils show understanding of place value in numbers up to 1000 and use this to make approximations. They have begun to use decimal notation and to recognise negative numbers, in contexts such as money, temperature and calculator displays. Pupils use mental recall of addition and subtraction facts to 20 in solving problems involving larger numbers. They use mental recall of the 2, 5 and 10 multiplication tables, and others up to 5×5, in solving whole-number problems involving multiplication or division, including those that give rise to remainders. Pupils use calculator methods where numbers include several digits. They have begun to develop mental strategies, and use them to find methods for adding and subtracting numbers with at least two digits.

■ Level 4

Pupils use their understanding of place value to multiply and divide whole numbers by 10 or 100. In solving number problems, pupils use a range of mental and written methods of computation with the four operations, including mental recall of multiplication facts up to 10×10. They add and subtract decimals to two places. In solving problems with or without a calculator, pupils check the reasonableness of their results by reference to their knowledge of the context or to the size of the numbers. They recognise approximate proportions of a whole and use simple fractions and percentages to describe these. Pupils explore and describe number patterns, and relationships including multiple, factor and square. They have begun to use simple formulae expressed in words. Pupils use and interpret co-ordinates in the first quadrant.

■ Level 5

Pupils use their understanding of place value to multiply and divide whole numbers and decimals by 10, 100 and 1000. They order, add and subtract negative numbers in context. They use all four operations with decimals to two places. They calculate fractional or percentage parts of quantities and measurements, using a calculator where appropriate. Pupils understand and use an appropriate non-calculator method for solving problems that involve multiplying and dividing any three-digit by any two-digit number. They check their solutions by applying inverse operations or estimating using approximations. They construct, express in symbolic form, and use simple formulae involving one or two operations.

Number

How the Areas of study in this book fit the Programme of study and Attainment target 2: Number and Algebra level descriptions. Points in the Programme of study		Areas of study and 'best fit' with level descriptions			
		Level description 2	Level description 3	Level description 4	Level description 5
■ 2. **Developing an understanding of place value and extending the number system**	**a** read, write and order whole numbers, understanding that the position of a digit signifies its value; use their understanding of place value to develop methods of computation, to approximate numbers to the nearest 10 or 100, and to multiply and divide by powers of 10 when there are whole-number answers;	1	2	3, 4, 5	6,'7
	b extend their understanding of the number system to negative numbers in context, and decimals with no more than two decimal places in the context of measurement and money;		8, 9	10, 11	12
	c understand and use, in context, fractions and percentages to estimate, describe and compare proportions of a whole.	13		14, 15	16, 17, 18, 19
■ 3 **Understanding relationships between numbers and developing methods of computation**	**a** explore number sequences, *eg counting in different sizes of step, doubling and halving, using a multiplication square,* explaining patterns and using simple relationships; progress to interpreting, beneralising and using simple mappings, *eg* $C = 15n$ *for the cost of n articles at 15p*, relating to numerical, spatial or practical situations, expressed initially in words and then using letters as symbols;	20, 21		22	23, 24, 25
	b recognise the number relationship between co-ordinates in the first quadrant of related points on a line or in a shape, *eg the vertices of a rectangle, a graph of the multiples of 3;*			26	27, 28
	c consolidate knowledge of addition and subtraction facts to 20; know the multiplication facts to 10×10; develop a range of mental methods for finding quickly from known facts those that they cannot recall; use some properties of numbers, including multiples, factors and squares, extending to primes, cubes and square roots;	29	30, 31	32, 33, 34	

Number

How the Areas of study in this book fit the Programme of study and Attainment target 2: Number and Algebra level descriptions.

Points in the Programme of study		Level description 2	Level description 3	Level description 4	Level description 5
■ 3. **Understanding relationships between numbers and developing methods of computation – continued**	**d** develop a variety of mental methods of computation with whole numbers up to 100, and explain patterns used; extend mental methods to develop a range of non-calculator methods of computation that involve addition and subtraction of whole numbers, progressing to methods for multiplication and division of up to three-digit by two-digit whole numbers;	35	36, 37	38	39, 40, 41
	e understand multiplication as repeated addition, and division as sharing and repeated subtraction; use associated language and recognise situations to which the operations apply;		42, 43, 44		
	f understand and use the relationships between the four operations, including inverses;	45	46	47	
	g extend methods of computation to include addition and subtraction with negative numbers, all four operations with decimals, and calculating fractions and percentages of quantities, using a calculator where appropriate;				48
	h understand and use the features of a basic calculator, interpreting the display in the context of the problem, including rounding and remainders.			49	
■ 4 **Solving numerical problems**	**a** develop their use of the four operations to solve problems, including those involving money and measures, using a calculator where appropriate;	50	51	52	
	b choose sequences of methods of computation appropriate to a problem, adapt them and apply them accurately;			53	
	c check results by different methods, including repeating the operations in a different order or using inverse operations; gain a sense of the size of a solution, and estimate and approximate solutions to problems.		54	55	56, 57, 58

Areas of study and 'best fit' with level descriptions: Level description 2–5 columns above.

Programme of study: Number

Pupils should be taught to:

■ 2. Developing an understanding of place value and extending the number system

a read, write and order whole numbers, understanding that the position of a digit signifies its value; use their understanding of place value to develop methods of computation, to approximate numbers to the nearest 10 or 100, and to multiply and divide by powers of 10 when there are whole-number answers;

Area of study 1 | P of S 2a | LD 2

NUMBERS TO 100

RC1,2 C1–7

Commentary
Do make sure all the children have achieved basic numeracy and have mastered Number at Level 1. Too many children underachieve in mathematics because they are 'put off' at an early age. If the groundwork is not substantial they will simply not have the conceptual understanding to progress. This does not mean you should let children repeat Level 1 work 'just to make sure'. Unnecessary repetition of work done before is just as de-motivating as work that seems too difficult.

Place value is only grasped by some children after copious practical experience with 'real' numbers and counting aids. There is no benefit in trying to get children to compute in their heads, when their error rate is high or when they prefer to use counting aids. With your help the children will use the resources to come to an understanding of place value, and then manipulate the numbers without counters.

Activity 1: Numbers we know
Assemble a bank of numbers that are important to the children. Include, for example, some of the following:

- ages;
- birthdays;
- house numbers;
- lucky numbers;
- ages of the children's brothers and sisters;
- the number of days in a week, weeks in a year, months in a year;
- classes or teachers in school, choices at dinnertime;
- numbers used in advertising (Heinz 57®, 7 Up®).

Draw a display line from 1 to 100 on a long strip of paper and record the important information attached to each number.

Copymaster 1 allows children to make their own personal number collection.

Activity 2: Number games
To reinforce the children's number recognition and counting skills, give them plenty of opportunity to play number games. A pack of ordinary playing cards offers the possibility of *Snap*, sets games and sequencing. Bought-in games like *Dominoes*, *Snakes and Ladders*, *Ludo* and other track games are fun. Home-made games can enable the children to rehearse just those numbers they seem unsure about. Home-made dice and spinners, or blank dice marked up, can have the numerals or dots on them that the children playing need to practice.

There are two unmarked track games on **copymasters 2** and **3**; 100 square games appear under Activity 4 below.

Activity 3: Number quiz
To alert the children to the fact that there are numbers everywhere, compile a number quiz around the school. Remember to keep the vocabulary simple and use picture clues where possible. You could include questions like the following:

- How many windows are there in Mr Colcot's room?
- How many pet hamsters are there in school?
- How many children are in class Y2?

1	2	3	4	5	6	
Rian's lucky number. 1 April is April Fool's Day.	Pair. Twins. Marcel's lucky number.	Lucky for Ira. 3 June is Tamara's birthday.	4 July is Independence Day in the USA.	Fingers, toes. Lucky for Ben and Kamil.	Philippa's cat born 6 May.	

Let the children follow up this Activity with the chance to set each other questions, to which they have determined the answers.

Activity 4: 100 square
Using 10 by 10 grids of squares, let the children each make their own 100 square, numbering from left to right across the grid. Use these grids to look for number patterns. (You do not need to expose the idea of patterns of 10, unless the children find out themselves.) The children will enjoy ringing all the numbers, for example, with a three in them, and this should fuel discussion of place value.

Now using another 10 by 10 grid let the children make it into a base board for a track game (like the base board used for *Snakes and Ladders*). Remember that the numerals usually 'trail' on such a board, going from left to right on one row and then right to left on the next. They can draw on their own snakes and ladders, alligators and trees or whatever they choose. Let the children play their games in school, declare everyone a '100 champ' and let the children take their games home.

Resource copymaster 1 is a 10 by 10 grid of squares, while **copymaster 4** is a half grid of rectangles. Two copies of the latter, stuck side by side on strong card, will make a good game board. **Copymaster 5** is a sample game for children to use, called 'Up the aliens and down the bats!' **Resource copymaster 2** presents two 100 squares with numerals entered in, for the children's use.

Activity 5: Place value
Collect a number of resources before you have a discussion with the children. Some things you could find invaluable are:

- 100 1p coins and 10 10p coins;
- Colour Factor© or Cuisenaire© 1s and 10s;
- squared paper strips, some just one square long, and others ten squares long;
- spent matches and elastic bands which can be put into bundles of ten.

Taking only one of these resources for each session, or other resources of your own devising, show how you can set out a small given number, for example, 15.

Explain the exchange of ten 1s for one 10. Lay the number out quite deliberately so that all the children can see it the right way up, with the one 10 on the left and the 'odd ones' on the right. Do this action with a series of numbers and then let the children have goes. Then transfer the setting out to a piece of paper divided lengthwise into two halves. Finally, do some numbers and record how many tens and odd ones or units there are, on the paper.

Set up an interactive display of numbers from 11 to 99. Change the tasks each day, and either let one child present the display each day or let children use it freely during their spare moments. If you allow the latter, you will need to check and tidy the display several times a day.

Copymasters 6 and **7** give the children a chance to convert arrays of 10s and 1s into 'numbers' and do the reverse operation.

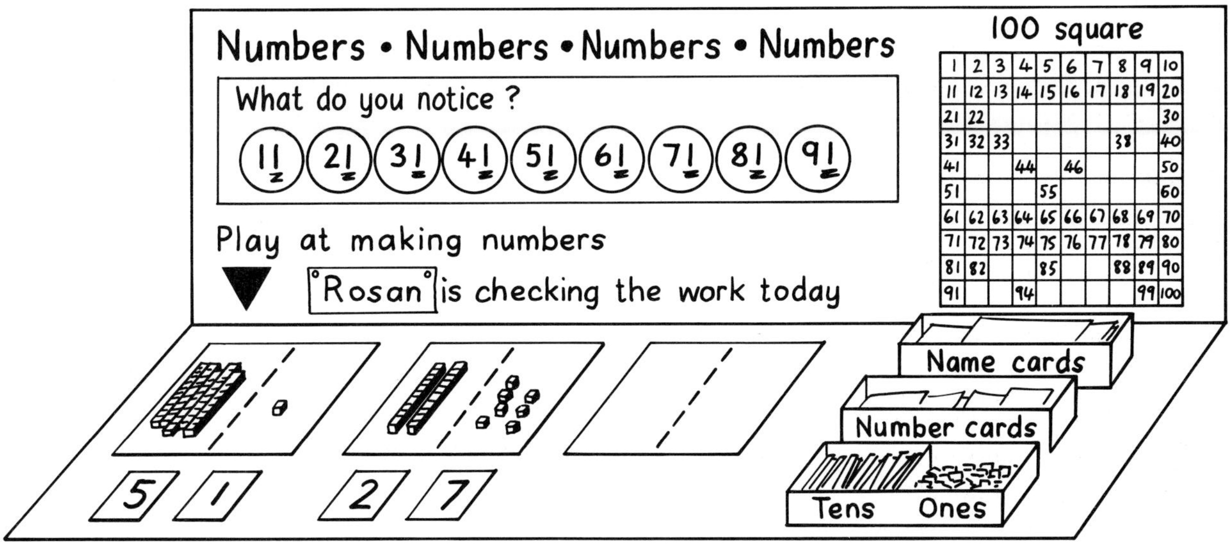

Area of study 2 | P of S 2a | LD 3

NUMBERS TO 1000 AND PLACE VALUE

RC1,2 C8–11

Commentary
At Level 2 the children will have worked on how we write numbers, and how the placing of a digit affects what we read. Revise this using ones and tens (Cuisenaire© or Colour Factor©), or spent matches and elastic bands, to make bundles of ten. Then try some consolidation and extension Activities.

Activity 1: Ordering numbers
Discuss with the children the idea that in 18, for example, the '1' means 1 ten. See if the children can then report, for example, what the '2' in 279 means, or the '5' in 5071. Clear up any simple misunderstandings that may exist, and then let the children place in order some jumbled numbers, ranking the lowest first.

Copymaster 8 offers some suggested numbers for ordering.

Activity 2: 100s and 1000s
Let the children each fill in the numerals on some 100 squares. Each square can then become a count of 100 little squares. Let them play at laying these out to make some really big numbers of squares; for example, 9 sets of 100 little squares gives us 900 little squares.

Resource copymaster 1 is a 10 × 10 grid suitable for a 100 square. **Resource copymaster 2** has two 100 squares on it with numerals added.

Activity 3: Place value match game
Make a large number of play discs or cards with a digit on each, along with the word 'hundreds', 'tens' or 'units'. Put these into a bag. Make a number of base boards, with a picture on each and a range of numbers, all of which can be matched by digits in the bag. Thus if a base board has 127 on it, somewhere in the bag there should be play discs with the digits '1 hundred', '2 tens' and '7 units' on them. Players take turns at taking a play disc from the bag and trying to match it with one of the digits in the numbers on their base board. If they can match the disc they lay it on top of the appropriate digit. A player who cannot use a digit, places it back in the bag. The first to complete his or her board wins.

Copymasters 9 and **10** each have two suggested base boards for the game and **copymaster 11** is a sheet of digit cards, on which there are some blanks for digits you may wish to add to match home-made base boards.

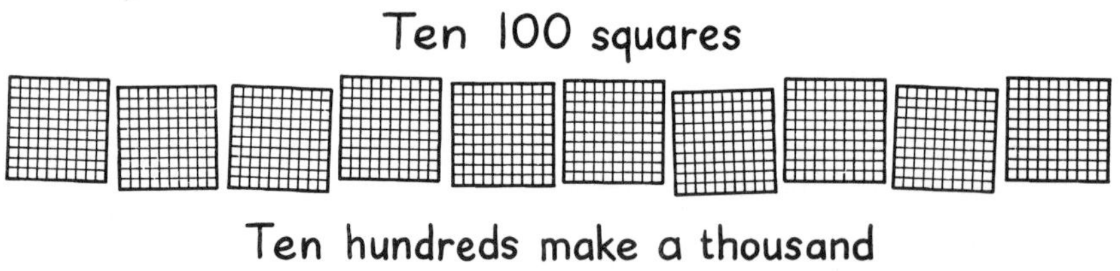

Area of study 3 | P of S 2a | LD 4

WHOLE NUMBERS

Commentary
Whole numbers are usually termed *natural numbers*. This means that the numbers involved are readily associated with natural objects in terms of how many? or how much?

There are excellent opportunities in any consideration of whole numbers to link the work to history and how numbers were depicted in the past.

Activity 1: Big numbers
Engage the whole class in the production of a big number resource bank. Through reference books, letters to companies and newspaper searches collect and display information on the numbers you uncover. Examples that could be included are:

- the distance from the North to South pole;
- the numbers of spectators at football matches;
- the numbers of passengers carried by rail on your nearest main line or in your region (write to British Rail);
- the numbers of beds in the local hospital and patients treated in a year;
- how many children in your school? in your area? (Use local networks of Heads and also contact the LEA.)

Activity 2: What's in a name
Through discussion compile a list of numbers that have special names. For example, century, thousand, dozen, gross, million, billion and trillion. Search for the meaning of these words. In the process the children will probably come up with suffixes that they find in other aspects of their mathematics work, such as penta-, hex- and oct-. You can extend this collection by investigating how other civilisations have depicted numbers. Use, for example, Egyptian symbols and Roman numerals.

Activity 3: Biggest and smallest
Provide children with ten squares of card on each of which is written a single digit (one of each of the digits 0 to 9). Get individual children to select any four and arrange them to make the biggest number they can, the smallest one and the nearest one they can get to half way between. Extend the Activity by increasing the number of digits that can be used. Vary the Activity by letting the children shuffle the deck of digit cards and use only the first four or so off the top of the pack.

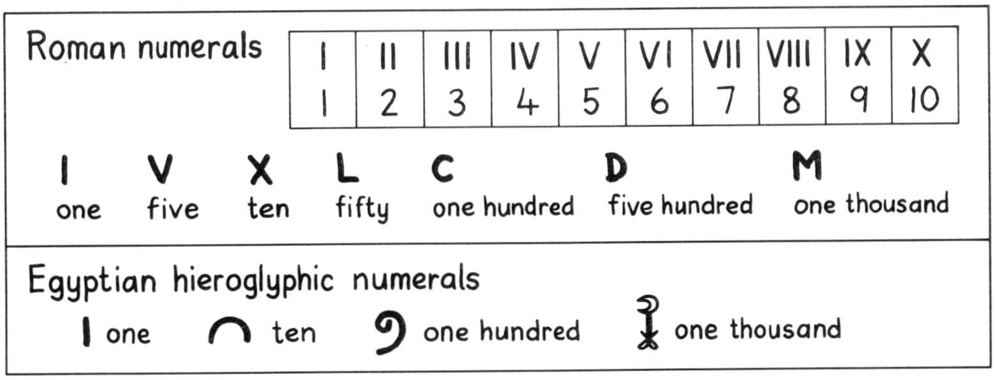

Area of study 4 | P of S 2a | LD 4

MULTIPLYING BY 10 AND 100

C12

Commentary
Base 10 is the base upon which our mathematics is founded. Other bases have been used at different times and in different parts of the world. Whatever the base it is essential that children understand multiplication and division by the base number. They need to be able to do this to get to grips with the concepts of long multiplication and division.

When working with multiplication and division by the base it is imperative that you do not use statements like 'when you multiply by 10 add a 0 on'. This is both inaccurate (adding zero does not change anything!) and dangerously misleading in terms of the child's appreciation of the processes involved. Rather, it is better to work with counting aids to get children to appreciate what is actually happening. Use of a multiplication graph for the base also helps.

Children need to understand the *Associative Law* of multiplication, for example:

$$\begin{aligned} & 40 \times 216 \\ = & (4 \times 10) \times 216 \\ = & 4 \times (10 \times 216), \end{aligned}$$

in order to fully understand long multiplication.

Activity 1: What we already know
Find out what the children already know about multiplication by 10 and by 100. The best context for this is likely to be money. So, do they know that:

100 2 pences is £2,
10 10 pences is £1,
2 10 pences is 20 pence,
10 5 pences is 50 pence, and
5 10 pences is also 50 pence?

Use what is known to explore what might be happening. Reinforce this with the use of the abacus, counting blocks and a graph of the ten-times table.

Activity 2: Some × or ÷ 10 and 100 machines
Draw some function machines. Designate them ×10, ×100, ÷10 and ÷100, machines. Let the children write the numbers 'IN' and numbers 'OUT'.

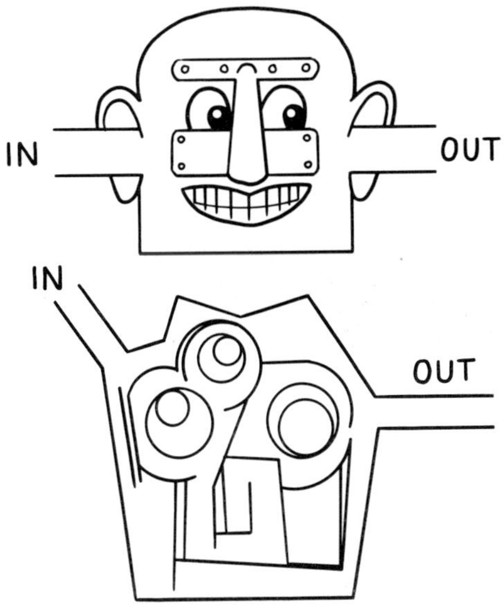

Copymaster 12 has some starter machines on it.

Area of study 5 | P of S 2a | LD 4

PLACE VALUE

C13, 14

Commentary
The use of *place value* was crucial in advancing the development of mathematics. Without the development of a limited set of symbols (in our case zero and one to nine) and the use of position to define what the symbol represents we would not have developed as a society in the way that we have.

This work builds upon place value at Level 3. Children should now be able to describe the effects of our place value system and use their knowledge to investigate different number bases that operate within place value systems.

Activity 1: What I know about place value
Create a 'self-appraisal' sheet for the children to complete. It may say things like 'In the number 5673, I know there are ... thousands ... hundreds ... tens and ... units because ....

Activity 2: Number bases in other cultures
In order to establish the understanding that the children have gained you may extend this work into a consideration of different number bases. Here are some examples from other cultures and communities:

- From an aboriginal dialect in Australia –

one	mal	four	bularr-bularr
two	bularr	five	bularr-guliba
three	guliba	six	guliba-guliba

(This consists of discrete number words for one, two, three; then two-two, two-three, three-three.)

- From Toba tribesmen of Paraguay –

one	natheda
two	cacayni or nivoca
three	cacaynilia
four	nalotapegat
five	nivoca-cacaynilia
six	cacayni-cacaynilia
seven	nathedac-cacayni-cacaynilia
eight	nivoca-nalotapegat
nine	nivoca-nalotapegat-nathedac
ten	cacayni-nivoca-nalotapegat

(This consists of discrete number words up to four, then a mix of addition and multiplication; two-three, two threes, one (and) two threes, two fours, two fours (and) one, two (and) two fours.)

- Finger counting from some South American Indians:

one	hand-one	two-hands-one . . .
two	hand-two	and so on.
three	hand-three	
four	hand-four	
hand	two-hands	

Copymaster 13 has these examples of number systems on it. They could form a starting point for an investigation into number systems and different number bases in use in different cultures.

Activity 3: Base two
The roots of computer development is base two. The children might like to try writing out base two numbers. Doing so is helpful with basic number bond work. Here are the numbers 19 and 12 set out in base two:

16	8	4	2	1	
1	0	0	1	1	19 set out in base two
	1	1	0	0	12 set out in base two

Copymaster 14 has some columns on it for the children to write in numbers using base two.

Activity 4: Using bases other than ten and two
Invent some aliens with a number base other than ten or two. For example, imagine Venusians are asymmetrical and have 15 fingers. Ask the children to draw a Venusian and create symbols for 10, 11, 12, 13 and 14 that the Venusians might use. Then try writing some Venusian 'sums' – and solving them!

Area of study 6 | P of S 2a | LD 5

MENTAL COMPUTATION WITH POWERS OF 10

Commentary
Mental computation with the base number requires an understanding of place value as well as a recall of all of the times tables. This sort of mental computation is a necessary skill for the appropriate use of estimation and approximation.

The requirement at this stage is to use only single-digit numbers of powers of 10 and whole number answers. This means that the children should only be manipulating one 10, two 10s and so on to nine 10s, and one to nine 100s, one to nine 1000s, etc.

Activity 1: Multiply challenges
Make a set of large flash cards with the single-digit multiples of 10, 100 and 1000 on them. Make sets of small cards for the single-digit multiples of 10. Give each child a multiple of 10 card. Choose any of the large flash cards and ask the children to multiply it,

mentally, by the number on the card they hold. Repeat the exercise with as many of the large flash cards as you can in 5 minutes; the children each time having to multiply by the number on their card. For example, if you hold up a card with 500 on it, a child who has a card with 6 written on it should give an answer of 3000.

Activity 2: Getting ready for divide challenges
In order to undertake division the children need to understand that the factors of a number are important if they are to get whole number answers. Get the children to draw up the factors, up to 10, of all those numbers that fit the pattern 100 105 110 115 120 . . . 900, using calculators. Discuss their findings and let the children display them. For example, for the number 230 the factors are 2, 5 and 10.

Activity 3: Divide challenges
Use the work done in Activity 2 above to help solve these divide challenges. Using teacher flash cards with multiples of 10 from 100–900 and children's cards with 10 or 20 or 30 . . . up to 90 on them, challenge the children to say whether their number will divide into the teacher flashcard number producing a whole number answer, and if so what it is. This can be extended using cards with larger numbers on them. For example, if you hold up a card with 850 on it, a child with 30 on their card should say 'No 850 is not divisible by 30'; another child with 50 on their card should say 'Yes and the answer is 17' (because they know 5 is a factor of 85).

Area of study 7 | P of S 2a | LD 5

DECIMALS AND PLACE VALUE

Commentary
Level 5 work should mean a joyous exploration of mathematical ideas. Now is the time to extend and elaborate the number line in both a positive and negative direction.

Activity 1: It's a record
Make a display which is made up of a line labelled from ten millions down to ten millionths. You can use this line to categorise many little-known and interesting facts that you and the children can unearth. Some examples, based on the kilometre, are given here to start you off:

1 000 000 km is about the diameter of the Sun from its top to its bottom;
100 000 km is about $2\frac{1}{2}$ times around the Earth;
10 000 km is about the distance from the UK to Hong Kong;
1000 km is about the distance from Aberdeen to Plymouth;
100 km is about the distance from London to Brighton;
10 km is about the depth of the deepest parts of the Pacific Ocean;
1 km is about the height of the Angel Falls in Venezuela;
0.1 km is about the length of a football pitch;
0.01 km is about the height of the highboard in diving competitions;
0.001 km is about the stride of a grown human;
0.0001 km is about the diameter of the hole on a golf green;
0.000 01 km is about the width of a fingernail;
0.000 001 km is about the thickness of a fine fibretip pen.

Programme of study: Number

Pupils should be taught to:

2. Developing an understanding of place value and extending the number system

b extend their understanding of the number system to negative numbers in context, and decimals with no more than two decimal places in the context of measurement and money;

Area of study	P of S	LD
8	2b	3

ZERO AND NEGATIVE NUMBERS

Commentary
An understanding of the meaning of *zero* is one of the most important things for children to acquire in mathematics. With the introduction, very many years ago, of place value, a symbol for an empty category (zero) became essential.

To appreciate negative numbers the children have to be able to handle abstractions away from the 'real' world of counting objects.

Activity 1: Zero
Use 'zero' in the children's computation and counting. Let them record all the numbers in the pattern of 10s to 1000 and write beside each what the zeros signify. The pattern should begin thus:

Zeros in the pattern of 10s
0 zero
10 zero units
20 zero units . . . and so on until
100 zero tens, zero units . . . .

Discuss the circumstances in which we use zero in everyday life; for example, we talk about the temperature being zero and some dials on household appliances have a zero.

Activity 2: It's cold outside!
One of the few ways negative numbers are important in everyday life is in measuring temperature. Collect some pictures of weather maps or snippets of video of the TV weather forecast, showing minus temperatures. Explain to the children that these temperatures are below freezing and that negative numbers are written with a '–'.

If you have access to one, hang a maximum and minimum thermometer outside and leave it out on a frosty night to see how low the temperature falls.

Activity 3: Inside the freezer
Show the children a freezer thermometer, the kinds of readings obtainable and if the school cook is willing and there is a freezer in the school kitchen, take the children to look at the readings.

Area of study 9 | P of S 2b | LD 3

DECIMAL MONEY

C15

Commentary
Decimalisation makes money 'problems' easier to solve. In the imperial system we were required to use base 12 and 20; now only base 10 is needed. The only added difficulty is a possible confusion in the presentation of money in the same way as decimal fractions. For example 5.21 looks similar to five pounds twenty-one pence, £5.21.

Activity 1: Equivalence
Let the children examine closely, using magnifiers, current coins and notes. Do some matching and exchanging games to ensure that they have mastered the idea of equivalence. For example, using play replica coins (your purse may not contain enough!) let the children see how many ways they can lay out 10p, 20p and 50p. Then lay out two sets of coins of near equal value and ask the children which they would rather have.

Activity 2: Class shop
There can be no better way to find out what happens when shopping than by doing it. Create a class shop selling items for a few pence, gradually increasing the value of the items sold and the prices asked for them. Introduce shopping lists and change. When the children are proficient at these sums, try reducing everything to half price and making special offers and reductions on multiple purchases. For example, the starter 'pence only' class shop could sell the greeting cards, gift tags, wrapping paper etc. A shop where bigger prices can be charged might sell groceries (empty but inviting cartons and packs) or books and toys.

If space is at a premium in the classroom and a table cannot be given up to the shop for some time, or there are few people working at this Level, create shoebox shops like the one discussed in Area of study 50.

Activity 3: Using the decimal point
Let the children plan a shopping trip, using catalogues to price the items and recording and summing them using the decimal point. Remind the children that when writing, for example, five pence, they must write .05 and not .5.

Old till receipts and household bills will serve to show children how we record money. Display some for them to see. Alternatively, use the shop window on **copymaster 15** to which the children can attach pictures from old catalogues or their own drawings, with decimal prices added. They can then work out the costs of various combinations of items.

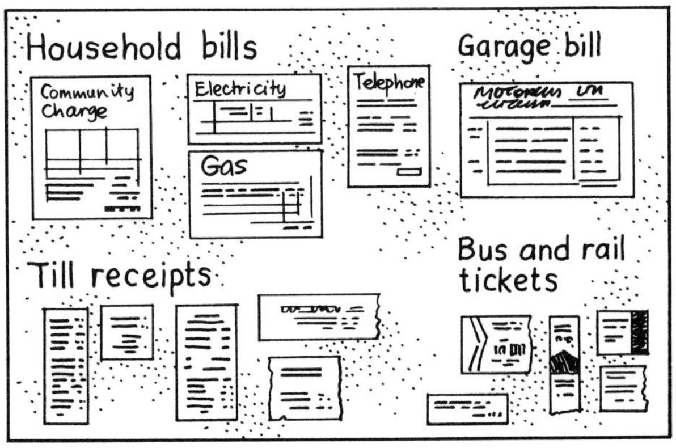

Area of study 10 | P of S 2b | LD 4

UP TO TWO DECIMAL PLACES

RC1,2 C16–17

Commentary
This work builds on what the children already know about fractions and the number line. It may be worth revising this knowledge and their understanding of place value as a first step in offering Activities.

The work here should be done in tandem with calculator work below, although it is important for the children to be able to work with pencil and paper as well as to use estimation and approximation appropriately.

Activity 1: Parts of a square
Using a 100 square discuss with the children the concept of the whole square being divided into 100 equal units each of which is $\frac{1}{100}$ of the whole. This can be written in another form, i.e. 0.01. 10 of these cells can be written both as $\frac{10}{100}$ ($\frac{1}{10}$) or 0.1. Get the children to practise their understanding of this sort of symbolism by shading in numbers of cells and labelling them. Tell the children what $\frac{2}{100}$ might be written as in a decimal form and then develop their ideas of addition of simple decimals.

Resource copymaster 1 is a 10 × 10 square and **resource copymaster 2** has two 100 squares with numerals filled in.

Activity 2: Money
Collect a pile of supermarket receipts. Mount these on card so that they can be used a number of times. Mask the bottom total and enter it on a master answer sheet. Use the items as a start for creating money sums. For example, a child could add the first two items, then the next two and so on, and then add all the sub-totals to see if they match the total on the master answer sheet.

Let the children create a present list for the family, using items from a catalogue and their accompanying prices. They can work out how much the children's, men's and women's presents will cost.

Activity 3: Planning an expedition
Engage the class in a project to plan an expedition. The work can be linked to geography and history, and the expedition can be acted out in drama and using music. To undertake the expedition you need to equip everyone with the right gear and manage the availability of supplies. You could include things like:

- tents, sleeping bags, cooking stoves, gas supplies;
- water bottles, cooking and eating equipment;
- compasses, torches, first aid.

You would need a definitive list of equipment, which includes plenty of choice, plus the cost of items. Different groups in the class could pretend they are going to different locations. Thus, for example, some may need clothing for hot, dry conditions and others quality waterproofs or cold weather gear. Alternatively, all the groups could be planning the same trip, but on different budgets.

Copymaster 16 and **17** show kit lists to which prices can be added along with some ideas of special prices and offers available for children to work on.

Area of study 11 | P of S 2b | LD 4

MEASUREMENT TO TWO DECIMAL PLACES

Commentary
To measure to two decimal places children need to understand the nature of the number line and the fact that we can get smaller and smaller divisions of that line. They also need to be able to relate this work to what they know about place value.

Measuring to two decimal places supports you in further discussions with the children about the concept of 'accuracy'. There is an opportunity here, not to be missed, of looking at the notion of a standard measure. Questions concerning how rulers are made and why a metre or yard have been adopted as measures can be fruitfully explored.

The children will already have experience of the measurement of length using rulers and tapes as well as trundle (click) wheels. Build on this to extend their understanding of the notion that we choose and use units and measuring instruments to match the task at hand.

Activity 1: Measure this and that
Offer the children a whole range of measuring opportunities. These should include large lengths, such as the school hall or the classroom, and medium lengths, such as the dimensions of desks, tables, cupboards and doors. For small lengths use books, pencil lines drawn by the children, pens and pencils, erasers and pencil-sharpeners. The aim is to get in lots of practice at several orders of magnitude. Get the children to work in groups on this Activity and use the results they come up with as a discussion opportunity (adding your own results to this discussion). This approach will give a genuine opportunity for diagnostic appraisal of the understanding and measurement skills of the children.

Activity 2: Extending measurement skills
Build on Activity 1 by developing the theme of accurate measurement. Write, as a class, to the surveying department of the local authority asking for information about the ways in which, for example, they measure the lengths of roads that are to be re-surfaced. If any of the children's parents are bricklayers, architects or home extension suppliers, see if they would come and explain their measuring and estimating skills to the children.

Area of study 12 | P of S 2b | LD 5

NEGATIVE NUMBERS IN CONTEXT

Commentary
In using negative numbers we are working entirely with numbers that do not exist in the real world. Negative numbers are abstractions. This often causes problems. In one sense negative numbers are simply inventions. If we cannot solve the sum $6 - 8$ using natural numbers we can, as mathematicians, invent an answer (in this case negative 2).

The use of the minus (–) sign for negative numbers is unfortunate as this is also the sign for subtraction.

Ideally, negative numbers should be labelled in another way, but history and tradition have dictated otherwise.

Negative numbers do not have a real, practically observable manifestation so it is necessary for children to learn the rules that mathematicians have laid down for handling negative numbers. These rules are amenable to investigation using a number line, for addition and subtraction, but are not so easily applied for multiplication and division. Graphs which have positive and negative axes in two dimensions can help the children to visualise what is happening, but there is no real way of avoiding having to memorise some of the rules. Below is a graph which explains this statement.

You will see that for a sum such as $(+2) \times (-2) = (-4)$ we can visualise 2 lots of 2 expressed in a negative direction on the graph. Similarly $(+4) \times (-1) = (-4)$ can be seen as 1 negative set of 4.

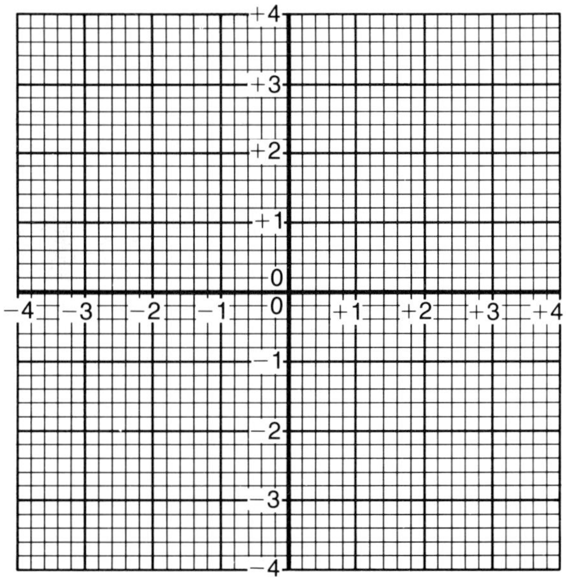

For multiplication (and division) these rules are:

×	+	−
+	+	−
−	−	+

Activity 1: Number lines

Using number lines revise what the children know about moving forwards and backwards on these lines, and what the spaces between whole numbers or fractions of whole numbers represent. Introduce them to the idea of calculations which have a result which is not a natural number, i.e. that is 'below' zero. Use weather reports to help the discussion. With the children make up additions and subtractions which need everyone to be aware of negative numbers.

Activity 2: Graphs

Get the children to plot a graph of degrees Fahrenheit against degrees Celsius (unless they have already done this in earlier Activities). They will observe that the line crosses one axis before it reaches the other one. Use this graph to discuss the idea of there being numbers less than zero.

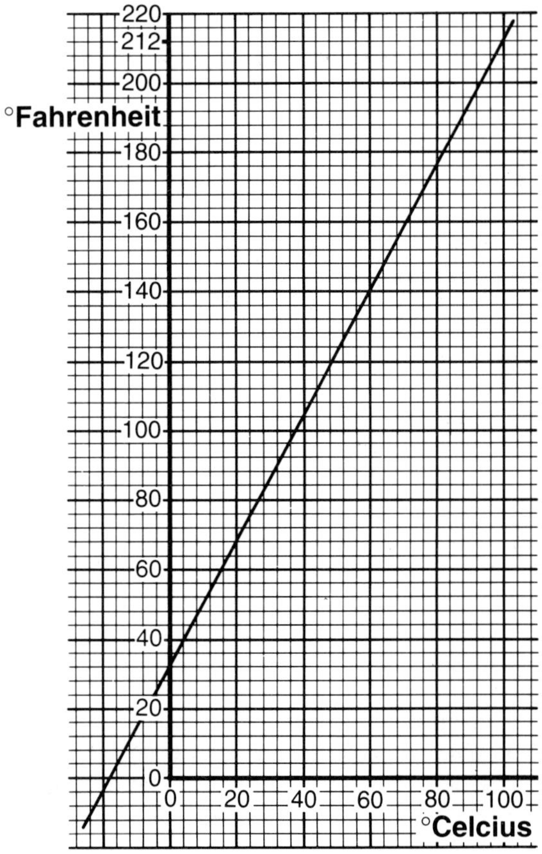

Programme of study: Number

Pupils should be taught to:

■ 2. Developing an understanding of place value and extending the number system

c understand and use, in context, fractions and percentages to estimate, describe and compare proportions of a whole.

Area of study 13 | P of S 2c | LD 2

HALF AND A QUARTER

C18, 19

Commentary
This is the first experience children have of fractions, so make it good! It is on these beginnings that an understanding of the usage of, for example, the decimal point, pie charts and eventually irrational numbers, will depend.

At first, help children to see fractions as part of a whole and then in relation to quantities. Thus half a pint of milk and a quarter of a chocolate bar come before fractions as ratios (as in use in, for example, work on scale and cogs and gears).

Activity 1: Half
List the ways we meet and use 'half' in everyday life. We say, for example, half an hour, half-time, half each, half brother, half-way, half-eaten, half-open, half-term. The children may be familiar with more. Prepare some real items that have two halves, for example:

- a domino;
- a twin bar of chocolate;
- a flan or pie (use an empty package where the food is depicted full-size on the box; cut the box in two).

Let the children handle these and then set them to work drawing and cutting in half pictures and shapes.

Make a little quiz display where the children have to identify the pictures that depicts half.

Copymaster 18 presents some pictures where halves can be labelled and coloured.

Activity 2: Quarter
Quarters are not as common in everyday life as halves. Look for ways in which we use 'quarter', for example:

- quarter of an hour;
- quarter-final;
- quarterly.

As in Activity 1 above, assemble some items that can be divided into quarters, including, for example, a model hot cross bun, an apple and a cube made from eight multilink cubes.

Do drawing and cutting to produce quarter pictures. Display some of the children's work.

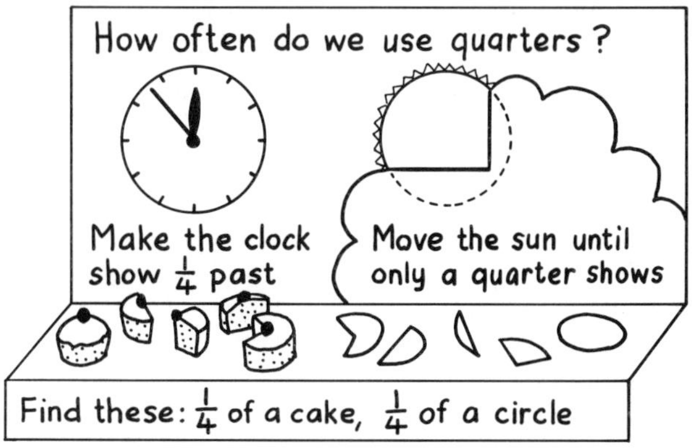

Copymaster 19 is a worksheet to test the children's grasp of a quarter.

Activity 3: Signs for half and quarter
Show the children how we write '$\frac{1}{2}$' and '$\frac{1}{4}$'. Tell them that this mathematical shorthand shows a whole one (1) shared by (÷) either two (2) or four (4).

Activity 4: Fractions to eat
Make some biscuits using geometric and gingerbread-man-shaped cutters. Let the children cut them into halves and quarters before eating them. This can be seen as preparing the children for division at Level 3.

Activity 5: Finding half/quarter of a number
When children know about finding half of a 'whole one', let them find a half and quarter of sets containing small numbers (set up by you to be exactly divisible by two or four). The sets could be of, for example, marbles or pencils. Then ask the children to find half or quarter using just a numeral.

Area of study 14 | P of S 2c | LD 4

SIMPLE FRACTIONS

C20

Commentary
With the advent of cheap calculators the 'fraction' and its manipulation has become of much less everyday importance. However, children do still need to know and understand the underlying principles involved in discussing the parts of a whole.

We use only a few fractions in everyday life so you can limit the children's work to a small range of fractions.

Give the children the chance to demonstrate some understanding of the equivalence of fractions, i.e. that $\frac{2}{4} = \frac{1}{2}$ and $\frac{1}{3} = \frac{2}{6}$. Although equivalence of fractions is pursued at Level 5 do not discourage these connections at this time for they will help children to refine their understanding of simple fractions.

Activity 1: What fraction is this?
Make a collection of objects of regular shape. These include a broom-handle, a brick, strips of card or paper of different sizes, a pencil and a skipping rope. Get the children, in small groups, to agree to mark these objects in given fractions, such as $\frac{1}{3}$ of the broom-handle, $\frac{1}{4}$ of the pencil, $\frac{1}{2}$ of the skipping rope and so on. Check the accuracy of their responses with them and use this as an opportunity for discussion.

Activity 2: Comparisons around school
Developing from Activity 1, try estimating with larger dimensions around the school. For example, what fraction of the length of the playground is the length of the hall? What fraction of the front wall of the school is the side wall? Some of the children might like to try variations at home too. Challenge the children to come up with ways of establishing these fractions within agreed levels of accuracy.

Activity 3: Equivalent fraction families
Look with the children at a range of common fractions and point out those that are equivalent to one another. Quiz them, by, for example, giving them an array of fractions and asking them to say which are equivalent. Include $\frac{1}{2}, \frac{1}{4}, \frac{1}{3}, \frac{2}{3}, \frac{3}{4}$. If the sample fraction is $\frac{1}{3}$, from an array of $\frac{4}{5}, \frac{2}{3}, \frac{2}{6}, \frac{1}{2}$ and $\frac{3}{11}$, the children should point out that only $\frac{2}{6}$ is equivalent.

Copymaster 20 gives the children a chance to record some fractions as equivalent.

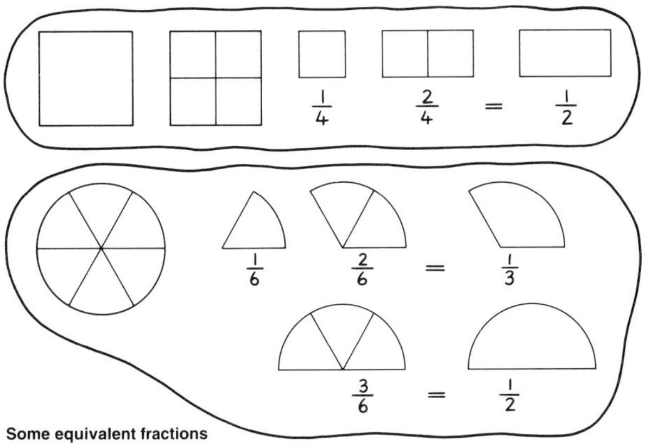

Some equivalent fractions

Activity 4: Paper folding
Get the children to carefully fold a number of regular shapes into three, four, six or eight sections. If, for example, a square piece of paper is folded into four, the children can show that $\frac{2}{4}$ is equivalent to $\frac{1}{2}$. If a circular shape is folded into six, $\frac{2}{6}$ can be shown to be the equivalent of $\frac{1}{3}$.

Area of study 15 | P of S 2c | LD 4

SIMPLE PERCENTAGES

Commentary
The use of percentages allows comparisons to be readily made. Even when different observations of related events are made the fact that you can describe each one as a percentage (being out of 100) means that 'at a glance' comparisons are available.

Percentages are often used in presentations in the media. However, it is important to look at the actual numbers in any survey as these are important in making judgements about the worth of any claims being made. For example, to claim that your brand of goldfish food is preferred by 90 per cent of goldfish has more credence if you have tested it with 1000 goldfish rather than just 10! Children need to recognise that whilst percentages are very useful in comparisons they can hide things if the numbers in the sample are very small.

There are clear connections between work in percentages and the need for the children to be able to work confidently with fractions.

Activity 1: Surveys
In order to get a real sense of the value of percentages it is essential that you and the children collect real data which can then be used for comparative purposes. Percentages can be derived by the use of graphs. Below is a graph from which can be read off the percentages of children present each day from a whole class number of 34.

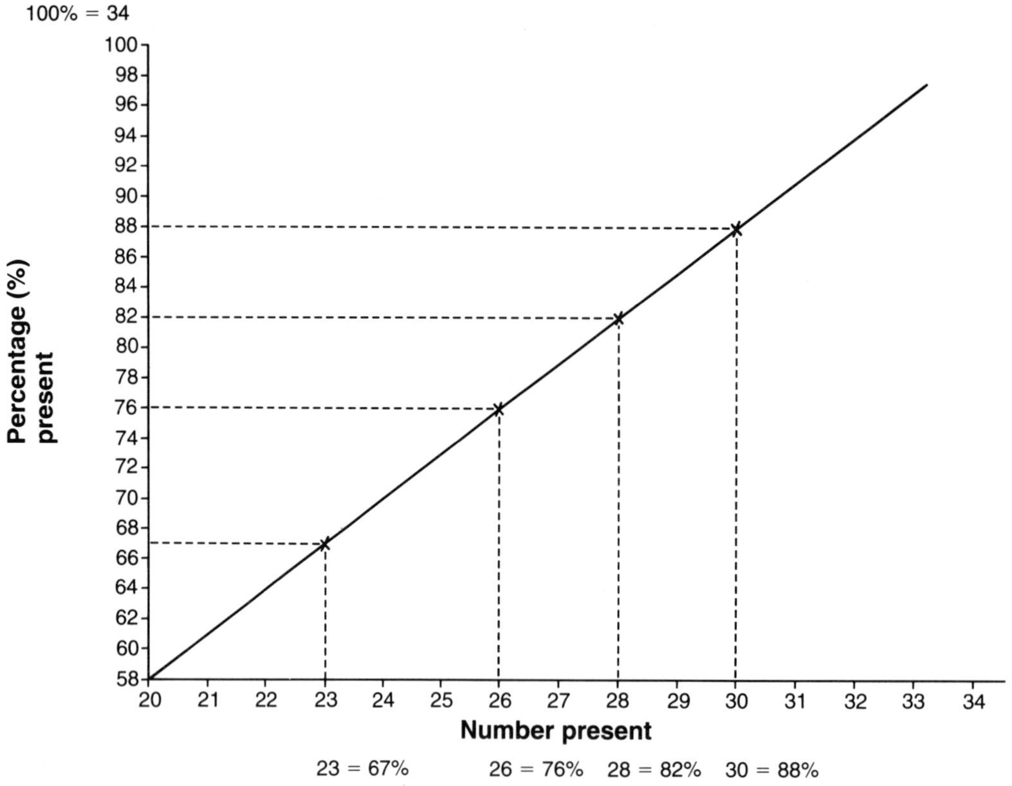

Examples of an appropriate survey

- Collect a record of which term of the school year each child in the class started school. Use this to work out the percentages for the Autumn, Spring and Summer terms. You can expand this by doing a school survey, but this time by the months in which children's birthdays fall.
- Do a traffic survey on two different roads or on the same road at different times of the day. Results can be charted in different ways, for example, to attempt to locate peak traffic times or the proportions of private cars compared with commercial vehicles using the road throughout the day.
- Within a road safety campaign see if you can survey the numbers of people who use official crossings and those who do not.
- Use a weather survey to look at, for example, the percentage of fine days, wet days, windy days and so on.

Link the data collected here to the use of calculators. Children need to be able to convert fractions to decimals, using the calculator. The results can then be used to promote a discussion of place value as well as percentage.

Area of study 16 | P of S 2c | LD 5

FRACTIONS AND PERCENTAGES

Commentary

The use of fractions and percentages gives us a lot of information which allows us to make comparisons.

There are important links to be made between fractions, percentages, decimals and ratios.

Fractions had to be invented to help fill in the gaps between whole, natural numbers on the number line. They are part of the system which we call *rational numbers*.

Activity 1: Egyptian fractions

Owing to their lack of a place value system the Egyptians could only handle fractions of the 1/something variety. Get the children to draw a 6 by 4 rectangle on squared paper so that there are 24 small squares inside it. Colour $\frac{1}{2}$ of them (12 squares), then $\frac{1}{4}$ of them (6 squares), then $\frac{1}{6}$ of them (4 squares) and finally $\frac{1}{12}$ of them (the last two squares). Let the children find out whether there are other rectangles that you can do this with. Ask the children to work out how many ways there are to make 1 using only 1/fractions without using any fraction more than once, and say what percentages of the rectangles are being shaded each time.

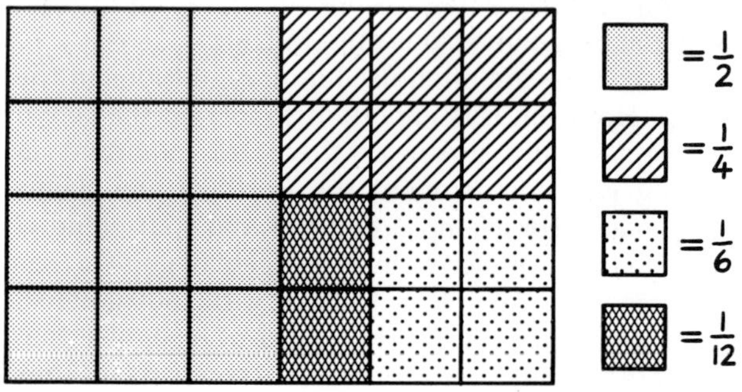

See if you can, in discussion with the children, explain why lack of place value means that only some fractions are possible, and how the Egyptians managed to build some fantastic structures, despite using a system which had no concept of place value.

Activity 2: Making comparisons
Using a wide range of topics get the children to make lots of different comparisons in terms of fractions and percentages.

Some examples include:

Music
How many votes go to popular groups? What fraction of the class is this vote? What percentage of the class is for each type of music or for each singer?

Reading
What is the class readership of magazines, newspapers and comics (both head counts and percentages) and how does this compare with circulation figures or readership throughout the school?

Attendance
How many children are in class today? How many are in on each day of a week? Specifically on Fridays? In the whole school? Why might there be fluctuations? What percentage of absences are explained by illnesses or holidays?

Animals and plants
Collect the vital size statistics of a range of animals and plants. Let the children compare their own heights with, for example, that of a giraffe and a Californian Redwood tree. What fraction is the giraffe's height of that of a Californian Redwood tree? What fraction is a mouse's length, nose to tail, of your height? What about a mouse and an elephant? What is the average height of people in the class? What fraction of the class have heights within 10 per cent, 15 per cent or 20 per cent of that average figure?

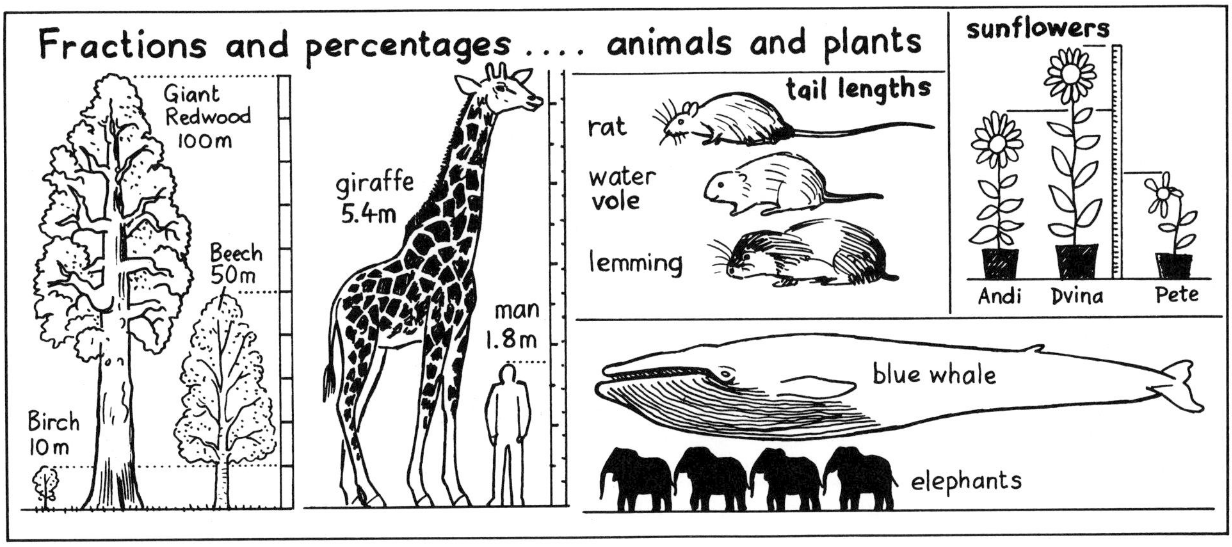

Area of study 17	P of S 2c	LD 5	EQUIVALENT FRACTIONS	C21

Commentary
The children, whilst being familiar with the computation of fractions of whole numbers, may not yet have appreciated that fractions can be written in equivalence form, for example:

$\frac{1}{2} = \frac{2}{4} = \frac{3}{6} = \frac{4}{8}$ and so on.

Activity 1: Patterns
This work should be seen as part of the extension of fractions work in Area of study 14. Get the children to explore a series of equivalent fractions in order to determine how they are linked.

Copymaster 21 provides the starter fractions for 'equivalent fraction strings' that the children can generate.

Area of study 18 | P of S 2c | LD 5

FRACTIONS AND RATIOS

RC3 C22,23

Commentary
Fractions need to be seen as part of a whole or as ratios between quantities. For example, $\frac{1}{3}$ can be seen as part of a whole item or as perhaps 1 cm depicting 3 cm in a scale drawing.

Children need to be able to explain a given fraction in relation to a set of equivalent fractions. For example:

$\frac{1}{2} = \frac{2}{4} = \frac{3}{6} = \frac{4}{8} \ldots$

In searching for patterns in equivalent fractions the intention is that the children should eventually come to see that:

- an equivalent fraction can be obtained by multiplying the numerator and denominator by the same number; and
- the inverse of this process will reduce the fraction to its simplest form.

Activity 1: Equivalent fractions: paper folding
We have included this Activity in AT2 at Level 4. If the children have not tried it, let them do it now and work on a wider range of shapes, perhaps producing $\frac{1}{8}$ths and $\frac{1}{12}$ths.

Get the children to fold carefully a number of regular shapes into 3, 4, 6 or 8 sections. If, for example, a square piece of paper is folded into 4, the children can show that $\frac{2}{4}$ is equivalent to $\frac{1}{2}$. If a circular shape is folded into 6, $\frac{2}{6}$ can be shown to be the equivalent of $\frac{1}{3}$.

Activity 2: Fractions and ratios: mathematics apparatus
Set out some Cuisenaire© apparatus and challenge the children to demonstrate the ratio of one piece to another, and the fraction one piece is of another.

Activity 3: Equivalent fraction and ratio families
Look with the children at a range of common fractions and ratios and identify those that are equivalent to one another.

The children should observe that × and ÷ are used in determining equivalence. For example:

$\frac{1}{3} (\times 2) = \frac{2}{6} (\times 2) = \frac{4}{12}$ and $\frac{4}{12}$ is equivalent to $\frac{1}{3}$.

Activity 4: Life-like problems
Set up a number of problems which give children practice in inspecting and demonstrating their understanding of equivalence. Here are some examples:

Fractions

- If 250 g flour makes 12 gingerbread men, how much flour is needed to make 10?
- What proportions are used in mixing paint?
- How many gallons of water are required to do the washing?
- How many packets of sweets or biscuits are needed to give equal shares?
- Look at the area of study 'Up to two decimal places', Activity 3: Planning an expedition, at Level 4. Using a similar expedition list, invite the children to work out, for example, what fraction of total costs will be food, and the cost for 40 children to go away, given a total costing for 15 children.

Ratios

- Get the children to bring in models of cars and of people. Measure the models. Do they have similar proportions to the real thing? Decide which models could 'go' together. Create some ratios and discuss which would fit together, for example, models that are 1:12, 1:6, 3:6.

Activity 5: Using ratios – enlarging and reducing
Use the work done in AT Shape, space and measures with regard to two- and three-dimensional space to assist in projects involving enlarging and reducing. Here are some examples:

- Offer the children challenges to build cuboids to a given degree of accuracy.
- Using a toy dolls' house or garage, invite children to work in a group to produce a replica with a specified ratio. Then discuss the order of ratio between the toy and the real thing, and work out the ratio of the children's models to the real thing.
- Using squared paper with squares of different sizes, invite the children to draw a picture on one sheet and copy the same picture onto another with squares of a different size; then compare the results.

Copymaster 22 gives children the chance to do a scale drawing of themselves using a specified ratio. **Resource copymasters 3** and **4** offer squares of different sizes.

Activity 6: Ratio work on the computer
Use a desk-top publishing software package to produce a class newsletter or magazine. The children will have to make decisions about how to fit headlines and text (with pictures if possible) and use scale, font size and so on.

Copymaster 23 is a reporter's pad.

Activity 7: Ratios in model-making
Invite someone from the local railway modellers' society to talk to the children about the ways in which they measure things, and the ratios in common use among modellers.

Area of study 19 | P of S 2c | LD 5

FRACTIONAL, DECIMAL AND PERCENTAGE CHANGES AND CONVERSIONS

RC3,4

Commentary
In everyday life there is a whole range of potentially confusing messages about fractions and percentages. For example, banks, building societies and car retailers publish information about a variety of interest rates, and shops advertise $\frac{1}{3}$ off or 25 per cent reductions in prices. Children therefore need to know how to operate fractions and percentages in order to make economic decisions; that is whether to invest, borrow or buy.

The use of fractions at other times and in other cultures would make an interesting investigation.

Use calculators to look at fractional, decimal and percentage links. This facility will give children access to additional information (for example, that in newspapers).

Activity 1: All change!
Collect a variety of samples of data related to fractions and percentages. Here are some examples:

- What are the percentages of children in the school who have school dinners? Are absent on a particular Friday? Are absent on an average Friday?
- Teacher absence, and the percentage due to illness, courses or family reasons.
- Survey data gleaned by asking, say 100 children, one of these questions:
- What is your favourite kind of music?
- Who is your favourite painter?
- Which 'green' issue do you feel most strongly about?
- What do you consider you are really good at?
- What qualities in people do you most admire?
- What are your ambitions?
- What are your views on the monarchy?

Present the data to the children and let them discuss and find out a variety of fractions and percentages. Help them to decide whether a fraction or percentage is of more use in a given context.

Activity 2: Conversion charts
Use data like that available for Activity 1 and let the children produce conversion tables, with the help of calculators, presenting sets of data as fractions or percentages. Conversion tables may look something like these:

$\frac{1}{5} \rightarrow 0.2 \rightarrow 20\%$

$\frac{2}{5} \rightarrow 0.4 \rightarrow 40\%$.

Resource copymasters 3 and **4** are graph paper sheets.

Activity 3: Making economic decisions
Let the children go and look for some data which offers situations in which they can discuss economic decisions. Here are some suitable kinds of data:

- special offers in the supermarket, with for example, 25 per cent off, buy two packs and save 10p, or 15 per cent more for your money;
- bank exchange rates — by what percentage would we be better off changing one currency for another;
- building society interest rates - which kind of account offers the best return.

Activity 4: Public data
Let the children collect the results from studies reported in the newspapers, and rewrite the news items, putting to use fractions, decimals or percentages each time. They can then judge which piece of writing seems to make most sense and discuss the ways the media use figures to give bias to a story. You may find it useful to look for local data in, for example, local council reports, the local paper, the local weather record, and national data from the Meteorological Office or *Social Trends*.

Programme of study: Number

Pupils should be taught to:

3. Understanding relationships between numbers and developing methods of computation

a explore number sequences, *eg counting in different sizes of step, doubling and halving, using a multiplication square,* explaining patterns and using simple relationships; progress to interpreting, generalising and using simple mappings, *eg C = 15n for the cost of n articles at 15p,* relating to numerical, spatial or practical situations, expressed initially in words and then using letters as symbols;

Area of study 20 | P of S 3a | LD 2

PATTERNS IN ADDITION AND SUBTRACTION TO 10

C24

Commentary
The detection of pattern is an essential component in the development of algebraic ideas. Algebra is centrally concerned with offering us a tool through which we can make generalisable statements. To do this we need to be able to predict on the basis of observed patterns.

Do the work in this Section alongside Level 2 Number. Number and Algebra are inextricably linked.

Activity 1: Addition
Let the children set out the patterns in addition bonds to ten, using Multilink©, Unifix© or other similar-coloured counting apparatus. Make a display of twos, threes and so on, showing all the patterns the children can make. Let them make the patterns in print, sticky shapes and numerals.

Activity 2: Subtraction
Let the children experiment with counting aids to produce all the subtraction patterns that they can with numbers up to ten. The children can record these for wallcharts or their own strip books. For example, if one child completes a series of number patterns, 5 − 1, 6 − 2, 7 − 3, 8 − 4, 9 − 5, each on a separate strip, they all make 4. Staple the strips together with a cover sheet with a large numeral 4 on it. This can be used as a group resource or kept by the child.

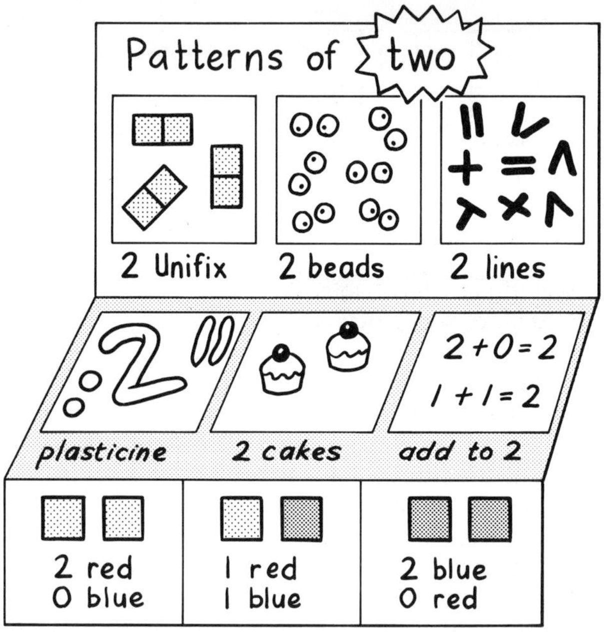

Copymaster 24 presents some strip sums for completion.

Area of study 21 | P of S 3a | LD 2

ODDS AND EVENS

C25

Commentary
Being *odd* or *even* is an attribute commonly used to describe natural numbers. Recognition of this attribute is very useful in making decisions later on about the factors of a number.

There are lots of superstitions which are focused on odd numbers and there are many folk tales and nursery rhymes in which odd numbers figure significantly.

Activity 1: Stairs and zigzags
Let the children write in the numbers to 20 (or more if you have room) on a 'staircase' so that the odd numbers are on the risers and the evens on the treads. Tell the children which is which. The children can also write all the numerals on a zigzag which sets the odds and evens apart.

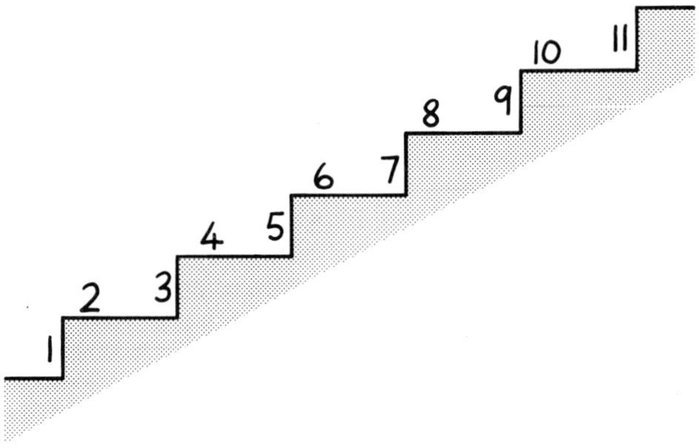

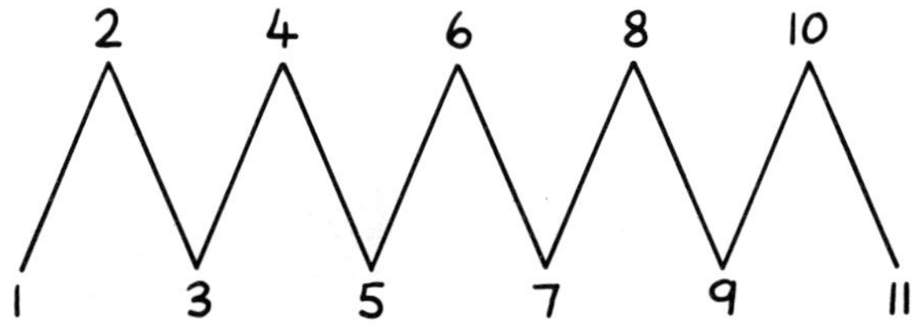

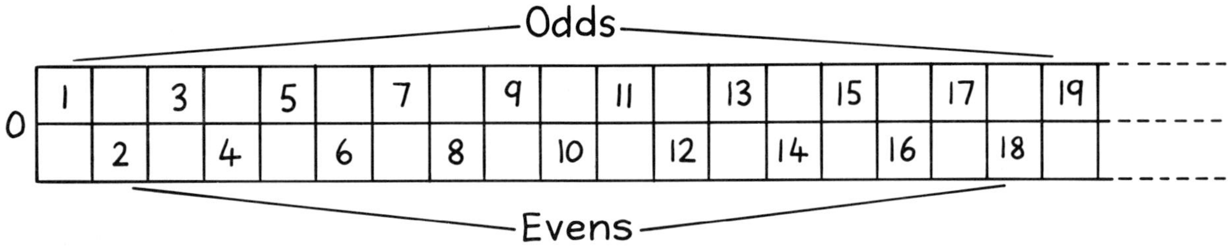

Activity 2: Counting in odds and evens
On a display strip of paper, marked with two rows of large squares, write all the numerals to 100, so that the odds appear along one row and the evens along the other.

Take the children out to a local street where the numbers are odds on one side and evens on the other. Let the children draw and number the houses and label the sides odds and evens. Then let the children draw and embellish the number of their own house on a piece of card. On the back they can write whether the number is odd or even. These cards can be laid out on a display for the children to handle and test themselves on odds and evens.

On **copymaster 25** are some odds and evens quizzes.

Area of study 22 | P of S 3a | LD 4

STRATEGIES FOR CALCULATING

Commentary
A number of strategies in the exploration of number patterns have, over many centuries, been found to be consistently useful. These include doubling, halving, squaring and finding square roots. It is at this Level that children should start to refine their problem-solving approaches in relation to such strategic moves. The development of formal strategies are part of the foundation for more advanced problem-solving later in a child's mathematical career.

In manipulating numbers using a variety of strategies you are supporting the child in gaining confidence over their control of numbers. It is too easy for children to feel that they are being controlled by numbers rather than, as it should be, the other way around.

Activity 1: Doubling and halving
Let the children use a calculator to produce a chart of the results of doubling a number, for example, 6, then its product and so on. Create a wall display of the patterns the children find. See if they can recall these patterns to assist mental calculation.

Now do a similar exercise with some really big numbers, producing a list of numbers occurring when the original number is halved again and again. Let the children establish where odd numbers appear in the chart.

Area of study 23 | P of S 3a | LD 5

SEQUENCES

Commentary
A *sequence* is a series of items which are connected by some general rule or law. The children will have to be able to recognise repetition in order to detect the rule for a sequence.

Activity 1: What we already know
Children will be aware of some sequences and that these can be used to rehearse the idea of sequence. Examples range from counting and nursery rhymes, through organising children by height, to multiplication tables.

Remind the children that they have already gained a lot of experience in the generation of number sequences and the detection of pattern, for example, when doing work on function machines at Levels 3 and 4, and addition and multiplication squares at Level 4.

Activity 2: Fibonacci
The sequence:

1, 1, 2, 3, 5, 8, 13, 21, 34 . . .

is developed by adding two consecutive numbers together to obtain the next number in the sequence; that is:

$1 + 1 = 2$
$1 + 2 = 3$
$2 + 3 = 5$
and so on.

This series of numbers is known as the *Fibonacci series*.

The sequence has many connections to the natural as well as man-made world. For example, the spirals on ram's horns and those created by the seed covers on pine cones conform to the Fibonacci series. Greek architects and painters were much concerned with the *golden section* or *ratio* in their design and structures. The ratio is about 1:1.62 and if you take pairs of Fibonacci numbers they are, as they get larger, nearer and nearer to this ratio. This means that, adopting a Greek view of what is beautifully in proportion, a sheet of drawing paper measuring 21 inches by 34 inches (two of the Fibonacci series) will be ideal in the ratio of length to breadth. This use of dimensions has been used for room sizes and in building facades.

Develop the Fibonacci series with the children and use it to explore ideas about ratio as well as a vehicle for creating a class book on the series in art, architecture and nature. Try creating new series where you follow the same rules but start with, for example, 1, 3, 4, 7, 11, . . . (known as the *Lucas sequence*). Draw a spiral based upon the Fibonacci series. Below is one way of doing this.

Activity 3: Puzzles: what comes next?
Look at 'Explaining and predicting number patterns' at Level 3, in which the children may have already had considerable experience. Get them to produce a series which follows a rule that they invent and then keep secret. The challenge is to work out the rule and state what comes next. Some examples are:

- 5, 10, 15, . . . (+5 or the 5× table);
- 4, 9, 16, . . . (square numbers);
- 1, 3, 7, 15, 31, . . . (created by ×2 and then +1).

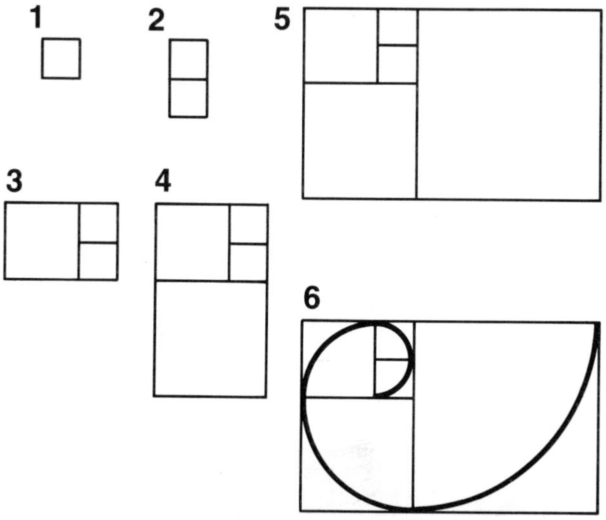

Area of study 24	P of S 3a	LD 5	RC6, 7

NUMBER PATTERNS

Commentary
There are three main two-dimensional shapes which are important in exploring number patterns through spatial arrangements. These are the triangle, the square and the hexagon. Of these the children should certainly become familiar, at an everyday working level, with triangular and square numbers. The children can also explore the arrangements of numbers within shapes through such items as arrays, including magic squares.

The terms *square number* and *triangular number* come down to us from the Greeks who saw all of their mathematics in terms of geometry.

In exploring number patterns through shapes it is important that the children use a variety of resources. These should include counters, square templates, geoboards and dotty paper. (**Resource copymasters 6** and **7** are dotty paper.)

Activity 1: Square numbers
Remind the children of what a square number is. They might like to re-examine earlier multiplication squares worked on at Level 4, where they will see the square numbers lying on the main diagonal. Using squared paper, get the children to lay out the first few square numbers as squares, shading the additional squares needed to be added each time to make the next square numbers, as shown below.

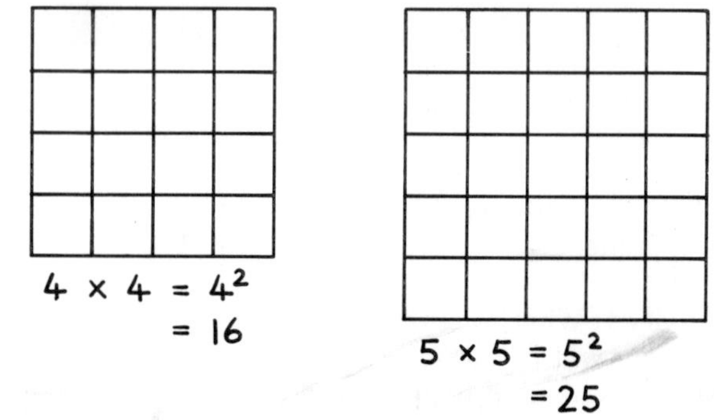

With your support the children should come to see that each new square number can be made by adding consecutive odd numbers so:

$1 + 3 = 4$
$4 + 5 = 9$
$9 + 7 = 16$ and so on.

Try to progress the children so that they see the following pattern:

$$\begin{aligned} 1 &= 1 = 1 \times 1 = 1^2 \\ 1+3 &= 4 = 2 \times 2 = 2^2 \\ 1+3+5 &= 9 = 3 \times 3 = 3^2 \\ 1+3+5+7 &= 16 = 4 \times 4 = 4^2 \end{aligned}$$

and so on.

Some children may come to see that there is a relationship between the odd number at the end of the string and the square number that results. Thus, 1, 3, 5 and 7 added together make 16 (4^2); 7, the last number in the string, is the *fourth* odd number and the sum of the string is the square of *4*.

Activity 2: Triangle numbers
Use triangular dotty paper to allow the children to draw increasing sizes of triangle. They can count the dots in order to work out the series of triangular numbers:

1, 3, 6, 10, 15 and so on.

This Activity can be reinforced by using counters. The rule is that each counter must be in contact with at least two others. Using different coloured counters the children should record how many counters are added each time and make a chart of these.

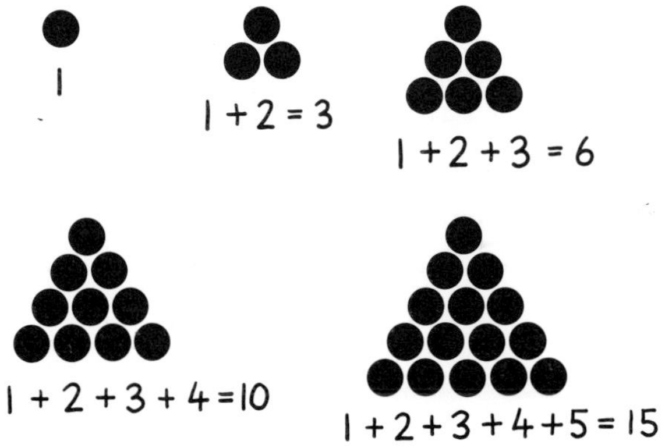

The children should see that each triangular number is the sum of consecutive numbers starting with 1:

$$\begin{aligned} 1 &= 1 \\ 1+2 &= 3 \\ 1+2+3 &= 6 \\ 1+2+3+4 &= 10 \\ 1+2+3+4+5 &= 15 \end{aligned}$$

They can extend this table of connections.

You can then ask the children if they can think of a general rule to find, say, the 20th triangular number? or the 100th?

The children may also notice that the sum of consecutive triangular numbers is always a square number. For example:

1st and 2nd triangular numbers $1 + 3 = 4 = 2^2$;
4th and 5th triangular numbers $10 + 15 = 25 = 5^2$.

Activity 3: Other shapes
Similar work can be done with other shapes. Particularly profitable is the hexagon, but the children might also try three-dimensional shapes, such as cubes.

Activity 4: Magic squares
The first nine consecutive whole numbers can be arranged in a 3×3 array so that the totals of the columns, rows and diagonals is the same:

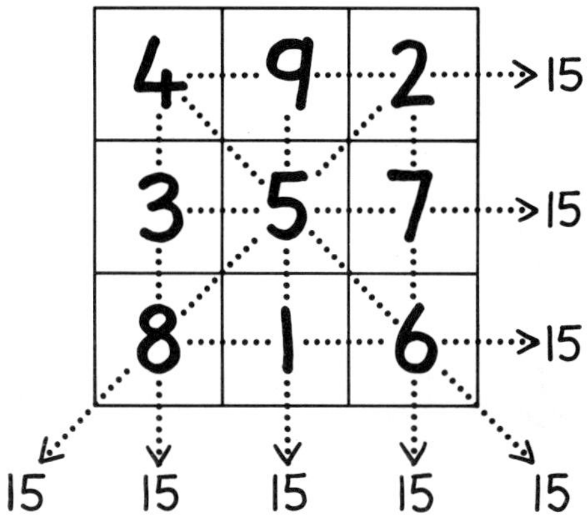

Get the children to see if there are different ways of organising a 3×3 magic square. What happens if you add the same number to each member of the square? What about taking away? or multiplying and dividing?

Try 4×4 and 5×5 squares. Do even-numbered squares have the same rules as odd-numbered squares?

The earliest example of a magic square is the Chinese *lo-shu*. Ask the children to find out about this and any other historical evidence of the magic square.

Activity 5: Revision and consolidation
Challenge the children to develop a number of sequences in which they can use only given rules and operations. Link this work to earlier work, for example, on function machines. Can they take these ideas further?

Invite the children to create a puzzle book for other children in the school (and parents?) which they can publish and circulate.

Area of study 25 | P of S 3a | LD 5

SIMPLE FUNCTIONS

C26

Commentary
This work builds upon the experiences that the children should already have had with simple function machines. It may be worth reminding them of such machines.

Function is a mathematical term which, when used in Algebra, means that a solution to a problem can be arrived at from a given equation by substituting values for symbols. For example:

if $x = 2y$ then
$x = 2$ if $y = 1, x = 4$ if $y = 2, x = 6$ if $y = 3$ and so on.

This area of mathematics should be related to work on co-ordinates and mapping. It may be that you choose to use such areas as the main way of developing ideas to do with simple functions.

Activity 1: Some exercises
Create a setting in which children can use data to explore simple functions. A class shop, data base or fact sheet is appropriate. For example, if an apple in the tuck shop costs 9p children can work out what 6 apples cost and then the formula for the cost of N apples.

Copymaster 26 has some function problems for the children to try.

Programme of study: Number

Pupils should be taught to:

■ 3. Understanding relationships between numbers and developing methods of computation

b recognise the number relationship between co-ordinates in the first quadrant of related points on a line or in a shape, *eg the vertices of a rectangle, a graph of the multiples of 3*;

Area of study 26 | P of S 3b | LD 4

CO-ORDINATES

Commentary
In a two-dimensional arrangement of points on a graph there are four possible areas in which the points can lie:

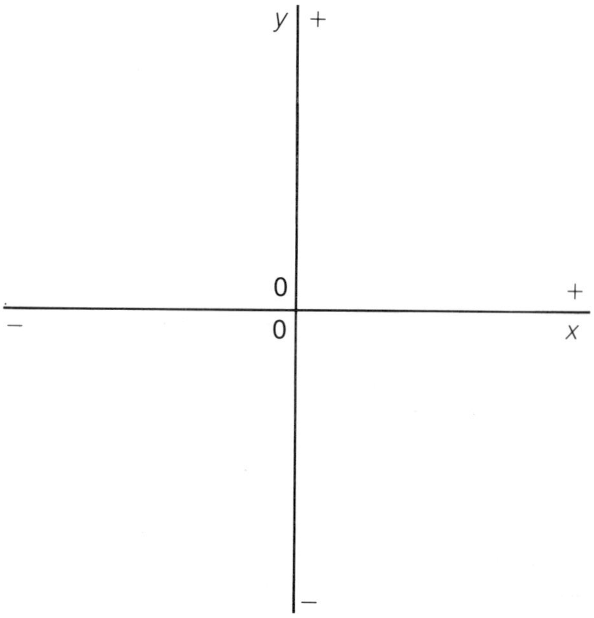

The first quadrant is the quarter of the graph in which all points are described by positive integers.

Convention dictates that we always name the horizontal (the x axis) position first. The vertical axis is labelled the y axis. The use of x and y can come later for the children, but it is important that they work in the correct order from the beginning of their work with co-ordinates. They should begin by working in the first quadrant.

Activity 1: Communication
Using squared paper with marked horizontal and vertical axes get the children to draw a simple shape using a pencil and ruler. Working in pairs or with the whole class the children must describe their shape just by telling others the co-ordinates. The other children must attempt to draw the shape using the given co-ordinates.

Activity 2: Across the curriculum
Using work in Shape, space and measures and Handling data, as well as in geography, ensure that the children get lots of practice in describing positions and points through co-ordinates listed in the correct order.

Activity 3: Computer software
There is a range of computer software, including LOGO, which uses co-ordinates for searching, mapping, drawing and so on. Expose the children to as broad a range of such software as is available to you.

Area of study 27 | P of S 3b | LD 5

CO-ORDINATES

Commentary
At this Level all four quadrants of the two-dimensional graph can be used (see 'Co-ordinates' at Level 4).

In using all four quadrants the children are making use of what they already know about negative numbers as well as categorisation within data-handling.

The children should be helped to understand that a figure can be described using negative or positive co-ordinates, or a combination of both, as shown below.

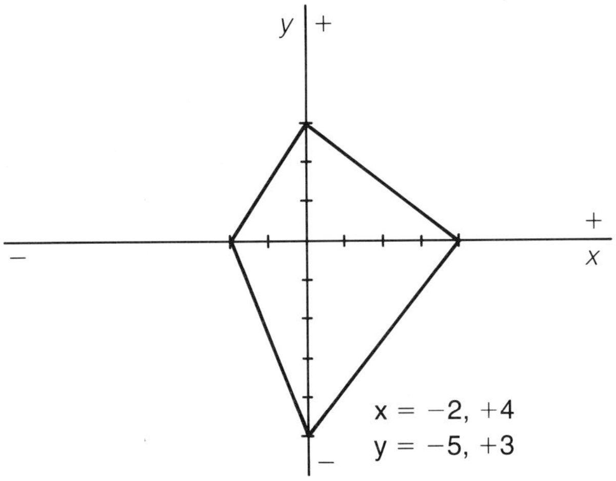

They should also start to see that a straight-line graph can continue into negative areas:

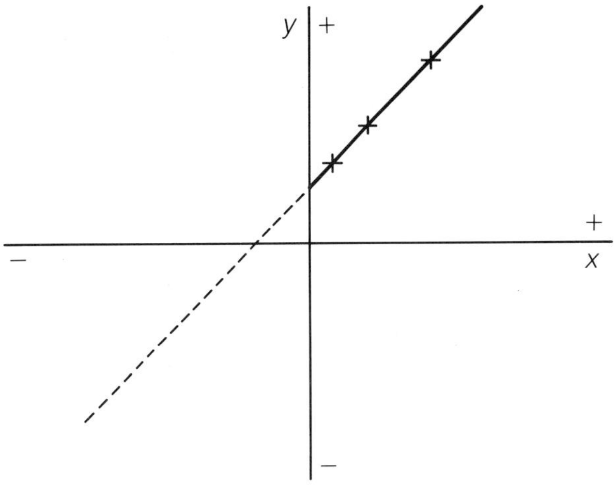

Activity 1: Communicating shapes
As with the work in 'Co-ordinates' at Level 4 the children can communicate shapes that they make on squared paper by use of their co-ordinate descriptions. These should include negative numbers in this case.

Activity 2: Graphs
Whilst the use of mappings appear at Level 6 it is possible, here, to attempt the plotting of some graphs which will use negative as well as positive co-ordinates. An example is a temperature conversion graph (°F and °C).

Area of study 28 | P of S 3b | LD 5

MAPPINGS

Commentary
Simple mappings are functions where there is a one-to-one correspondence between points. For example, in translating the cross shown below each point has a unique relationship to its translation.

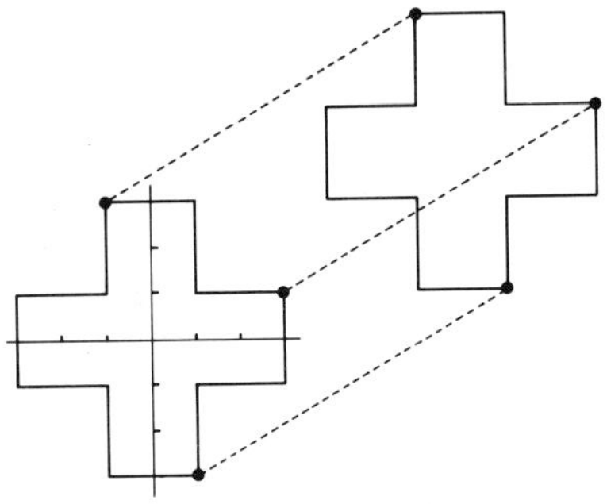

Descartes (1596–1650), the French mathematician and philosopher, was the first to combine algebraic and geometric ideas and it is after him that Cartesian co-ordinates are named. The *Cartesian co-ordinates* system is one in which a point is identified by its distance from the axes of a graph.

Activity 1: Links to geography
The children should be able to read co-ordinates to a good degree of accuracy at this stage. Use their experience in geography to polish their understanding of the description and ordering of co-ordinates.

Activity 2: Graphs
If you gain access to some graphics calculators use these to plot a range of mappings. They speed things up and allow the children quickly to see the effects of, say, adding a constant to an equation such as $y = x$ and $y = x + 5$. If these are not available then the children will have to plot by hand (and in any event some physical plotting is a good idea as it allows the children to get a real feel for what is happening). You could get different children to plot different but related mappings which can then be shared for the purposes of discussion.

Programme of study: Number

Pupils should be taught to:

■ 3. Understanding relationships between numbers and developing methods of computation

c consolidate knowledge of addition and subtraction facts to 20; know the multiplication facts to 10 × 10; develop a range of mental methods for finding quickly from known facts those that they cannot recall; use some properties of numbers, including multiples, factors and squares, extending to primes, cubes and square roots;

Area of study 29 | P of S 3c | LD 2

ADD AND SUBTRACT TO 10

C27, 28

Commentary
Mathematics is about patterns. Much of the fun to be got from mathematics is in the patterns that occur, and the ones we can make with numbers. Many adults who feel they are no good at mathematics are people who have never been shown that the patterns in mathematics are as beautiful as patterns in language and art. We believe it is important to say this because our liking or disliking for mathematics as adults may be dependent on our teachers' attitudes when we were young. It is very important that children and their parents begin to see that mathematics is not just sums, and sometimes has little to do with sums.

Let the children use concrete objects and counting aids for as long as necessary. Many children seem to experience difficulties in learning when they are pressed into abstraction too soon. How many adults do you know, and they may include yourself, who need to see the actual items they have bought before being sure what shopping they still have to get; and how many of us solve number problems by using aids as well as pencil and paper? Our first aim as teachers of mathematics must be understanding, not speed. The child who understands an operation, even with the use of aids, is ahead of the one who gets either the right or the wrong answer by guesswork or the replication of a method that is not understood.

Most teachers seem to work on addition first. There is a case for approaching subtraction first, for young children are all too familiar with the idea of things being taken away from them. However, once children reach junior age, whatever their past experience of mathematics, whether in school or at home, they should be able to add to a set as well as take away from it — so addition first it is.

Numbers to ten are manageable so the aim of the sums must be to make children confident enough to do them in their heads.

Activity 1: Addition bonds to ten
Show the children the patterns in addition to ten. Display them in a class book or on the wall. Play oral addition games, by asking, for example, 'What do I need to make 10? . . . 1 and what? . . . 4 and what?' Look for all the patterns there are. 1 + 1 + 1 + 1 + 1 + 1 + 1 + 3 is a pattern too!

Let the children have counting aids, and do sums with a variety of presentations. Here are some examples:

3 and 2 make

4 and 1 make ....

six and three make ....

2 add 2 equals ....

2 + 5 = ...

Copymaster 27 presents some examples of layouts for the children to try.

Activity 2: Subtraction bonds to ten
Show the children the patterns in subtraction to ten. Offer the children a variety of layouts and give them oral subtraction sums to do; for example, '10 birds on a wall, 2 flew away, how many left?' and 'If Susie starts with 8 sweets and finishes with 5, how many has she eaten?' Keep playing oral subtraction sums whenever there are a spare few minutes, until all the children are confident about number bonds to ten.

Copymaster 28 presents some examples of layouts for the children to try.

Area of study 30 | P of S 3c | LD 3

ADDITION AND SUBTRACTION FACTS TO 20

C29, 30

Commentary
The children should have mastered all the addition and subtraction facts to ten at Level 2. Now they need to extend that knowledge to 20. Through rehearsal of computation, using counting aids, and recording their efforts, they should be able to commit important number bonds to memory. This is not rote learning, *if* they fully understand what is happening to the numbers.

Activity 1: 'Eager beaver' games
Make a number strip out of stiff card, large enough for a large group or the whole class to see. Divide the strip into 20 equal parts. Make it two-sided, and leave the divisions blank one side and marked from 1 to 20 on the other. Hold the strip before the class and ask a group or individual child to call out what must be added to, for example, 13, to make 20. On the blank side of the strip, count along 13 and show that the 7 required to make 20 is in fact the remainder of the strip. Use a child to be the 'pointer' on the number line while the children do some more sums orally. Now try some calculations using the numbered side of the card. After a few 5 or 10-minute sessions doing this process many of the children will no longer need the number line to do the necessary addition or subtraction in their heads.

You can make number strips for other numbers up to 20 and reinforce those number bonds in a similar fashion.

Make some bingo base cards with, for example, 16 numbers on each. (All the numbers should be between 1 and 19.) Have a 'caller' say any number between 1 and 19 and the children, working in pairs, have to cover the number which added to the number called, makes 20.

Keep a record of the numbers called and a child can check the work of the pairs who call 'Bingo' first, using the caller's record of the numbers called.

Copymaster 29 shows four Bingo base boards.

Activity 2: Interactive display
Set up a display where children can use a variety of ways to set out the number bonds to 20. Here are some sample ideas:

- an oral number quiz sheet;
- a chance to print or replicate shapes to give a line of 20;
- a day for each number, for example a 14 day, on which a couple of children set up all the ways they can of making 14 and another couple add any new ones, and so on. At the end of the day draw the children's attention to the work on show. The following day leave the display for all the children to see and invite those who set it up to write up the bonds they found with their comments. (They may say, for example, 'We found x ways of making 14 and used patterns of numbers going up and down in our work.') Add all the children's efforts to a class book.

Activity 3: Calculations to check
Marking does not seem as arduous as actually doing sums, so give the children sheets of completed addition and subtraction sums with numbers to 20, and invite them to 'mark' them by ticking those they believe are correct.

Copymaster 30 is a sheet of completed calculations for marking. There are only two incorrect ones. While we do not believe children should be presented with calculations that are incorrect, it is important that we do not 'cheat' by asking them persistently to check calculations we know to be 100 per cent correct. Do make sure the children detect which sums are wrong though, and set them right.

Area of study	P of S	LD
31	3c	3

2, 5, 10 TIMES TABLES AND ALL THERE ARE TO 5×5

C31

Commentary
Multiplication and division are generally regarded as being much more difficult operations for children to understand than addition and subtraction. The links that we can see between, for example, multiplication and repeated addition, are not obvious to children and lots of varied work will be needed to forge such links.

Multiplication and division are inextricably linked. However, because we think it is easier to tackle one kind of operation at a time, we have chosen to introduce them to children separately. It is important to make links, when the children understand both operations.

It is a moot point as to whether the teaching of multiplication should precede the teaching of division. 'Sharing' is often the more common experience of children. It is worth considering using some 'sharing' talk alongside your early work in multiplication.

Activity 1: Staging posts
Give the children some really long strips of squared paper. If you wish they can colour them, but number only the squares which are multiples. Set the task as 2s, 5s or 10s and display the children's efforts.

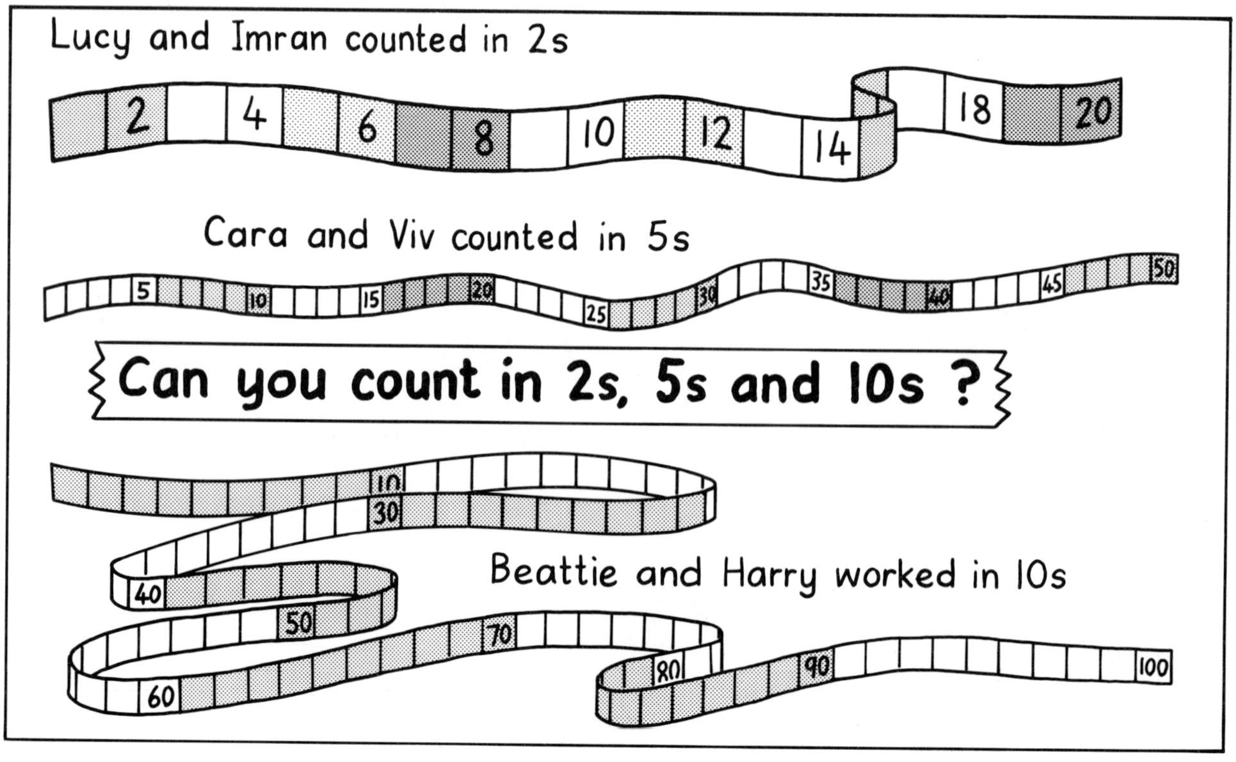

Activity 2: Cartoon charts
To give repeated addition some appeal, ask the children to create a comic strip version of the 2s, 5s or 10s, using, for example, things like:

- hairy legs in 2s;
- ferocious fingers in 5s;
- terrible toes or alien antennae in 10s.

Each child could produce one of these pictures, then use all the efforts to produce a chart of 2s, 5s, 10s.

Activity 3: The language and sign for multiplication
Make sure the children understand 'times', 'multiply' and the '×' sign.

Check their knowledge of the +, − and × signs by giving them some sums that are complete, apart from the sign, and ask them to enter in the appropriate sign.

Activity 4: Fathom the facts
Give the children some 'answers' to multiples of numbers to 5 × 5, and those for the 2, 5, and 10 times tables, and ask them to write possible 'sums' alongside.

Copymaster 31 has some starter answers with one done for the children to follow.

Be a real mathematician!
Instead of saying 'lots of' say

multiply or **times**

You could say:

5 lots of 4 is 20

but we mathematicians say:

5 times 4 equals 20

or

5 multiplied by 4 equals 20

and we write:

5 × 4 = 20

Activity 5: The multiply game
Make a set of cards, where half the cards carry a series of multiplication sums and the other half the answers. The full set could comprise all multiples up to 5 × 5 and all others in the 2, 5 and 10 times tables. Subdivide this complete set so that games with the cards are manageable in a few minutes and let the children play the following in pairs:

- Turn over all the cards and take turns at looking at two cards in the hope of finding a match of sum and answer. The winner is the player with the greater number of pairs (checked by the teacher).
- Shuffle the cards and then take turns to time each other at setting out the complete set of matching sums and answers (checked by the teacher).

Area of study 32 | P of S 3c | LD 4

MULTIPLICATION FACTS TO 10×10

Commentary
There is a continuing debate for many teachers about the place of rote learning in the business of getting children to 'catch' their times-tables. There are those who insist that chanting is the effective way of memorising these important number facts. Others claim that understanding the concept of multiplication is the most important element. Most, of course, take a position between these two extremes. Our experience is that 'chanting' can be fun (just as number nursery rhymes, songs and playground chants can be enjoyable). But knowing the tune and singing the words is in itself not enough, it is essential that we give children opportunities to develop further their understanding of number bonds and relationships.

Activity 1: Graphing times-tables
Plot graphs of the results of the times-tables from 2 to 10. Plot the points with the digit being multiplied on the horizontal axis and the answer for the multiplication on the vertical axis. All the graphs will be straight lines, but with different slopes. Discuss with the children which is the steepest and why.

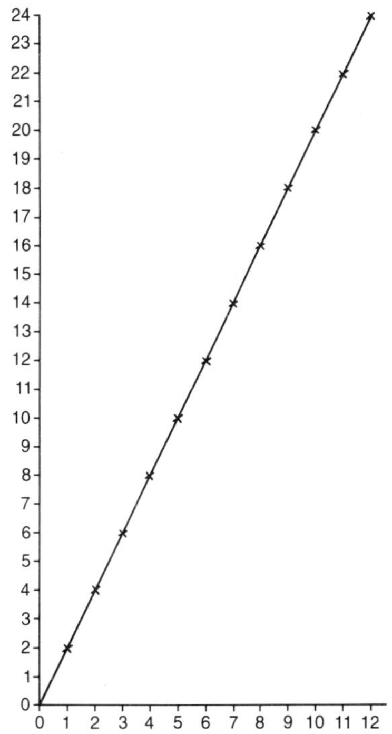

A graph of the 2× table

Activity 2: Using multiplication facts in problem-solving
Try and give regular opportunities which allow the children to practise their multiplication facts. Such opportunities can be made in the context of everyday school life. Here are some examples:

- How many plants do we need to buy/grow for the school window boxes?
- How many days to half-term? How many of those are school days?
- How many weeks to the harvest festival? How many school days? If we practise our contribution twice a week how many times will we rehearse? Is this enough? Too much?
- We have six jobs to do. How many children in a group to share these out?

Area of study 33 | P of S 3c | LD 4

POWERS OF WHOLE NUMBERS

Commentary
In this age of science and technology the use of very large quantities, such as the speed of light, has reinforced the need for mathematicians to have simple notation to represent these huge numbers. *Index notation*, to express powers of whole numbers, is an elegant way of doing this.

You can relate the work done here to that included in the Section on the conversion of metric units above.

The children will already be familiar with the square numbers. It is now that you can introduce them to simplified ways of representing such numbers, for example, $4 = 2^2$ or $25 = 5^2$. It is an important step from there to get the children to see that, for example, $10 \times 10 = 10^2$, $10 \times 10 \times 10 = 10^3$ and so on.

A calculator which will accept the series of key presses: N(number) × = = =, etc., to keep producing the result of multiplying orders of the number is most useful: this is *iteration*. Other features are mentioned in the commentary to Area of study 49: Using calculators.

Activity 1: Play and record
Give the children the necessary information about the simplified way in which mathematicians (and scientists) record powers of whole numbers. Using calculators, let the children explore the rapid growth in answer that arises when you multiply a number by itself and itself, and so on. Limit the starting number to no more than ten. Record the findings of this Activity. Of special interest might be the starting numbers two and ten.

Activity 2: Place value and number bases
Use Activity 1 to revise all that the children now know about place value and number bases. They will notice that in base ten we could write the places as 10^2 instead of 100 and in base two the column of 16s could be written as 2^4. Discuss what ten could be written as, and one, and negative 100.

Area of study 34 | P of S 3c | LD 4

MATHEMATICAL TERMS

RC1, 2

Commentary
Mathematics has its own specialist vocabulary as well as its symbols. The acquisition of this vocabulary is essential for the continued mathematical development of the children. The difficulty is often linked to the fact that some of the words also have a looser use in everyday language. It is important, therefore, that you give special attention to honing the children's use of the appropriate words for precise meaning.

The Greeks explored geometry by drawing in the sand and they attempted to solve all mathematical problems through geometrical drawings. In contrast, we have the computer. This allows us to see the effect of a set of statements very rapidly. Whilst computer programming is seen as the domain of specialists, in our experience it supports children's understanding if they are allowed to write short programs. The programs could compute, for example, square and triangular numbers. However, do not forget the Greeks and it is worth exploring LOGO as well as *Basic*.

	2	3		5		7			
11		13				17		19	
		23						29	
31						37			
41		43				47			
		53						59	
61						67			
71		73						79	
		83						89	
						97			

Activity 1: Prime numbers
The Greek mathematician Eratosthenes is credited with the development of a method for finding prime numbers. His sieve consists of a number square (a 100 square is quite convenient) from which the multiples of 2, 3, etc. are removed (but note that 2 and 3 remain). The numbers remaining are the prime numbers. We do not usually include 1 as it is a number with unusual qualities.

Resource copymasters 1 and **2** have 100 squares on them to be used by the children to find prime numbers to 100 employing this sieve method.

Activity 2: Squares, cubes and roots
Using calculators and what the children already know about squares get them to try keying in a number and multiplying it by itself. Let them then try using a series of numbers.

The square root key (√) on the calculator can be explained and used. Discuss with the children how they might find a cube root. This will give the children lots of practice in estimation, number bonds and increasing degrees of accuracy. This work can be linked to Area of study 56: 'Trial and improvement'.

Activity 3: Computer programming
If possible, try to give the children the opportunity to write and use simple computer programs of their own. Here is one which adds 3 to the numbers 1 to 10.

```
10  FOR NUMBER = 1 TO 10
20  PRINT NUMBER + 3
30  NEXT NUMBER
```

and one for the 6× table:

```
10  FOR NUMBER = 1 TO 10
20  PRINT NUMBER × 6
30  NEXT NUMBER
```

The line numbers 10, 20, 30 are necessary for the computer to understand the sequence of instructions (they could be labelled 11, 12, 13 or 100, 200, 300). The FOR and NEXT are telling the computer which numbers to operate on and to continue until all have been used. Line 20 in each case is the 'sum' that you want the computer to do and output.

Activity 4: A mathematical dictionary
This would be a good point at which to allow the children to consolidate their now extensive knowledge of mathematical terms and expressions through the construction of a class dictionary. This could embrace all of the areas of mathematics, not just Algebra, and would be useful to you as part of your evaluation of what the children have understood.

Programme of study: Number

Pupils should be taught to:

■ 3. Understanding relationships between numbers and developing methods of computation

d develop a variety of mental methods of computation with whole numbers up to 100, and explain patterns used; extend mental methods to develop a range of non-calculator methods of computation that involve addition and subtraction of whole numbers, progressing to methods for multiplication and division of up to three-digit by two-digit whole numbers;

Area of study 35 | P of S 3d | LD 2

FIND THE DIFFERENCE

Commentary
If the children have played 'oral number bonds' until they are quick and confident about the answers, the notion of finding the difference between two numbers will come easily to them.

Activity 1: More oral number play
Help the children to compare numbers and say what is the difference between them. Play practical difference sums by setting out two sets of objects and comparing the numbers in each. Then give the children written 'difference' sums, using a variety of layouts.

Area of study 36 | P of S 3d | LD 3

NUMBER PATTERNS TO HELP MENTAL SUMS

Commentary
Pattern sequences need to be committed to memory in order to make mental arithmetic quick and easy to do. Now is the time to rehearse these patterns until the children can recall them without difficulty.

Activity 1: Play with numbers
To awaken (or reawaken) the children's awareness of the power of pattern in number, let them play with numbers by completing some patterns that you have begun. The patterns should present a range of challenges, including all four rules and the idea that a pattern can lead to numbers increasing or decreasing in size. This work does need to be done orally, but you may find it helps the children to internalise the steps in pattern generation if you sometimes act as scribe and stand ready to commit the next number they call to the board or a large sheet of paper.

Activity 2: Managing numbers
Numbers can be made more manageable for computation by breaking them down into their constituents. Thus, adding 68 to 21 is easier to do if we remember that 60 add 20 makes 80, and 8 add 1 makes 9. Give the children some practice at doing this, first on paper for a few short sessions and then in their heads.

Approximation is a skill you can rehearse with the children too. We know that 89, for example, is nearly 90. 89 add 7 may, in our heads, be quicker as 90 add 7 take away 1. Also, if we have the pattern of, for example, counting in fives in our heads, we know that 25 + 5 is 30. We can also develop a mental pattern that includes 24 + 5 is 29, and 26 + 5 is 31. Try these strategies out with the children. Ask them to suggest other ways of handling the numbers.

Children may find it helpful if you work with a group, setting down a sum and looking together at the ways there are of making the sum 'easier'. Write down the ways, talk them through and finally let the children try them out, by doing some similar sums in their heads.

Area of study 37 | P of S 3d | LD 3

EXPLAINING AND PREDICTING PATTERNS

C32

Commentary
Explanation means that the children should become accustomed to offering a spoken as well as written response to their mathematical work. It is necessary to cultivate a climate in which the children come to see that mathematics is a logical subject and that it can be logically explained. Ordering thoughts and justifying assertions is an important step to generalisation – that essential rationale of Algebra.

Prediction, on the basis of an explained pattern, is important not only in Algebra but when the children come to discuss the idea of probability.

Activity 1: Detecting patterns
If the children have had practice at doing the Activities under 'Number patterns to help mental sums' above, they should find this next step easier. Give them some number sequences and ask them to say or record how the pattern is made. You can begin with some straightforward ones like 1, 3, 5, 7, 9 and then make them more complex, perhaps by inserting two operations. Here are some examples:

- 5, 15, 10, 20, 15, 25, 20, 30, 25 . . . (+10, −5)
- 2, 5, 11, 23, 47 . . . (×2, +1)
- 20, 10, 40, 20, 80 . . . (÷ by 2, ×4)

Activity 2: Predicting patterns
If the children can detect a pattern (see Activity 1) then they will be able to predict the numbers that follow. Test them out on this, by getting them to give the next two or three numbers that follow in sample patterns, including some done orally, some on paper and some they set for each other.

You can ask each child to use their free moments to invent a number pattern that can be continued. They can post these into a 'pattern suggestion box', which can be emptied after a few days and everyone can attempt to predict the next numbers in these patterns.

There are some patterns for extension on **copymaster 32.**

Area of study 38 | P of S 3d | LD 4

MENTAL COMPUTATION: TWO- AND THREE-DIGIT NUMBERS

C33–37

Commentary
- Mental computation with two-digit numbers
- Adding a set of single digits mentally
- Add and subtract three-digit numbers without calculators
- Multiply and divide: two-digit by one-digit numbers

The Activities that you can do here with the children should blend into each other and not be separated. It is essential that children see the principles which apply to numbers of whatever order.

There are a variety of ways in which individuals undertake the process of mental computation. For example, if asked to sum the numbers 97 and 93 the process might be:

97 is almost 100 (3 less)
100 + 93 is 193
but I need to take away the 3
so the answer is 190.

Or the process might be:

97 is three less than 100
93 is three more than 90
so 100 + 90 gives the answer, 190.

Or, a child may see the possibility of using multiplication facts and the process might be:

2 × 90 is 180
3 + 7 is 10
the sum of 180 and 10 is 190.

In supporting children in the acquisition of useful strategies for mental computation it is important to take on board these different sorts of approaches and to give the children opportunities to talk about and share different methods.

As with rounding up and down it is essential that children appreciate the value of using strategies which reduce the demand of the mental task. Important in this sort of exercise is the ability of the children to combine numbers in an order which facilitates recall and computation. Commonly, it seems easier to sum numbers by adding smaller to larger, and by adding numbers in an order which allows 'tens' to be assembled readily. In order to do this the children need to know that addition is *commutative*. That is, for example, that $8 + 2 = 2 + 8$ and that $6 + 4 = 4 + 6$. Both of these examples are also number bonds which the children should know sum to 10.

Offer standard algorithms to the children. An *algorithm* is a routine method for obtaining a solution to a given sort of problem. Whilst algorithms have been developed in order to simplify the approach to a given problem it is the case that, for some children, they can become the solution in themselves. To remember the method becomes the goal rather than the solution of the problem. We are all aware of those occasions when we find children setting out 'sums', which they really do not understand, in the approved physical fashion. It is vital, therefore, that we do not inflict algorithms on children as though they were magic spells or the only (correct) method.

Activity 1: How could we do this?
At the start of this work spend some time finding out the ways the children might already have for solving computation problems. For example, how do they approach the problem of finding out how many children are in school today if they know the total for the infants and the total for the juniors? How would they share out several hundred sweets? What tactics are good for establishing how many biscuits are on a supermarket shelf? Use the skills they have practised with smaller numbers and help them suggest ways of simplifying or arranging the problem.

Activity 2: Rounding up and down
Try lots of 'what is the nearest multiple of 10' challenges. Make flash cards, hold them up and ask for the nearest multiple of 10. Use numbers like: 87, 3, 96, 33, 95, etc.

Giving numbers which end in 5 is meant to open a discussion with the children about what we mean by the nearest. Do we mean the easiest to handle in a computation?

Activity 3: Dice and other games
Support the children in generating their own 'sums' through the use of blank dice on which you have entered numbers, conventional dice, single-digit number cards and 'number straws'. On blank dice you can write a range of two-digit numbers which the children have to sum.

Using conventional (1–6 numbered) dice the children can roll them four times and make up a set of addition and subtraction sums. Similarly, sums can be created with cards which have single digits printed upon them.

Make 'number straws' by taping little number flags to plastic drinking straws which can be upended in a small pot, so that the flags are not visible. A lucky dip selection of two straws would make a sum. Signs could be placed on tagged straws, so that for each pair of straws one of these is taken too. (You will need to check that the selection of straws creates the kinds of sums you wish the children to do.)

Get the children to work in pairs and challenge each other. The challenger must be able to provide the answer, as well as the one challenged!

Activity 4: Using data
Provide groups of children with a range of situations from which data can be assembled. For example:

- Collect the class numbers, for morning and afternoon sessions, for a week.
- Collect a range of objects for weighing. These objects must weigh at least 10 g but not more than 100 g.
- Research a range of products, such as comics, sweets and badges, which cost at least 10p but no more than £1, and chart these giving prices in pence.

Use these examples, and others that you and the children generate to provide you with data which can be used to challenge the children. Here are some sample questions:

- How many children were in classes 3 and 4 on Monday morning?
- How much more/less in grams is the ball of Plasticine© than . . . ?
- What will a comic and a tube of chocolate buttons cost in pence?

Activity 5: Making ten
Remind the children that they know their number bonds to 10. Give the children lots of practice in making the total 10 from as many combinations of single-digit numbers as they can. See what is the greatest number of digits that they can use to make 10. Use their offerings as a way of identifying those that are the 'same'. Extend the Activity so that they combine single digits to make favourite numbers (21 is a common one).

Activity 6: Track sums
Devise some number tracks which are, to some extent, self-correcting. The 'sum so far' is entered up at key points. These can be used for all four rules and are playable by one child or two who could compare their tracks at the end.

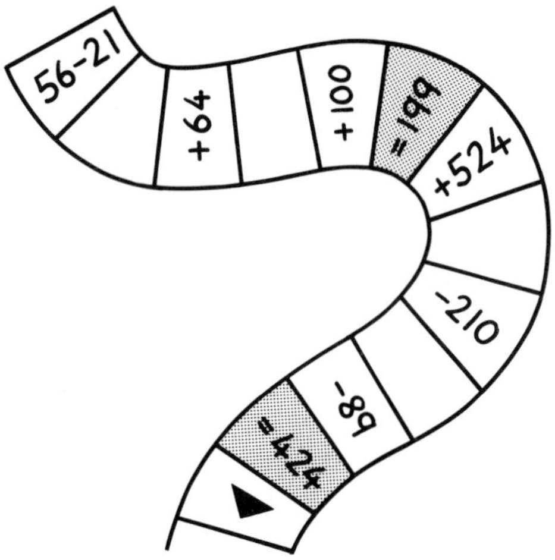

Activity 7: Maze calculations
Devise some maze games where the player is required to solve a calculation at each junction.

Copymasters 33 and **34** set out a maze game which can be played by a single child or in pairs.

Activity 8: Mental arithmetic quiz
Make a series of small cards each with a calculation and its correct answer on it. Let a group of children play, with one child being the caller, taking the cards in the order they come and giving each of the players a go in turn. If a player gets it wrong the caller can pass it to the next one for a bonus. Each correct answer scores 10 points, and the winner is the first to reach 100 or 1000, depending on how long you consider the children should play for. Alternatively, you can use the few minutes at the end of a session, to call out these calculations to each group in the class at a time.

There are starter calculation cards on **copymaster 35**. Add to these and store them in the box which can be made up from **copymaster 36**.

Activity 9: Invent a puzzle or game
Invite the children to work in pairs to compile puzzles involving computation of large numbers and illustrate them. Place the best pages of puzzles in a class book which can be worked through by the children, either in rotation to ensure everyone does them or in odd moments they have to spare. Remember to get the inventors to find the correct answers to their puzzles and place these in a separate 'puzzle answer book'.

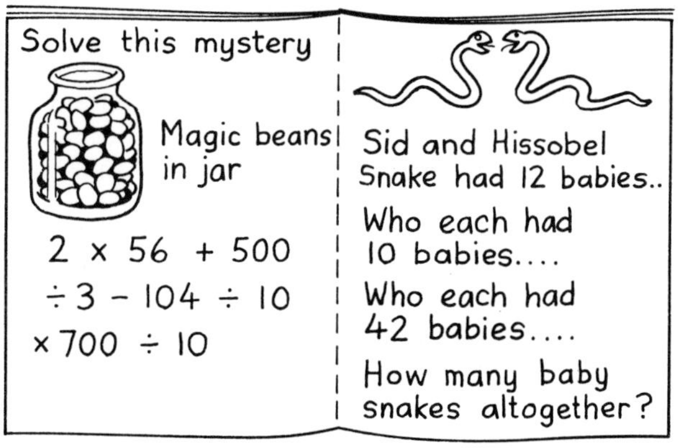

Ask the children to invent a game involving computation. Once they have a draft and all the rules worked out, supply resources like coloured card and felt tips so that an inviting fair copy can be made. Add these to the classroom resources and let the children have a 'games' session as often as possible, where, in addition to traditional games like dominoes and draughts, their own home-made games can be played.

Copymaster 37 is a sample puzzle layout for children to complete and can be used as a model for pages the children invent themselves.

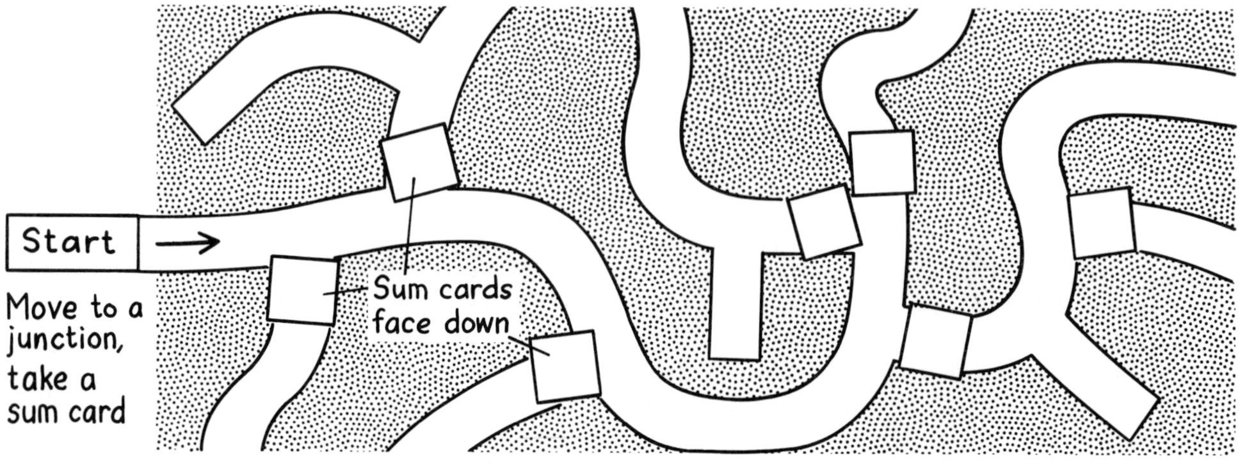

Part of a maze

Area of study 39 | P of S 3d | LD 5

GENERALISING

C38–40

Commentary
Generalising is central to mathematics. Indeed it is essential to human beings in every aspect of their lives as it is through the generalisation of characteristics that we come to be able to classify animals, plants and the common objects around us, and 'make sense of', control and manipulate our environment.

Generalising is about rules, both making them and understanding those made by others. In order to understand rules it is necessary to be able to recognise patterns. At this Level children should be able to begin prediction on the basis of detected patterns. Do impress upon the children that it is far too easy to jump to conclusions and that it is necessary to see early predictions as being conjecture rather than certainty.

In working on generalising start with real data. Avoid the use of general statements at the outset and let the children progressively refine their work.

In the Activities try to continue the development of the children's mathematical vocabulary so that they use words such as multiple, factor and square appropriately and, increasingly, automatically.

Activity 1: Addition and multiplication squares
Link the work in this Activity to addition and multiplication in Number. Try a variety of addition and multiplication squares. Here is an example of an addition square:

+	2	4	6
1	3	5	7
3	5	7	9
5	7	9	11

Get the children to create some more. You can use **copymaster 38** to start them off. You should be looking to promote observations which include looking at the diagonals, finding patterns of numbers which are the same and ideas about line symmetry.

Here is an example of a multiplication square:

×	5	7	9
4	20	28	36
6	30	42	54
8	40	56	72

Copymaster 39 has some multiplication squares for the children to explore. Again you should be encouraging the children to explore all of the possible patterns that they can detect. Get them to invent some of their own squares.

Activity 2: Calendars
Take a calendar and use the array of dates for a set of investigations. Get the children to choose any square of four numbers on any month of the calendar and to explore these for any patterns. Do the patterns they discover work for other squares of four numbers? Try with squares of nine numbers. Does it matter which month you have?

A typical calendar sheet is given on **copymaster 40**.

Activity 3: Some interesting times tables
Set out the 9× and 11× tables. Look at all the products and see if the children can generate a rule for determining the numbers.

Activity 4: Multiple loops
Using the common times tables and starting with the number 1 it is possible to produce loops using the last digit of an answer. For example, here is a loop produced using multiples of six:

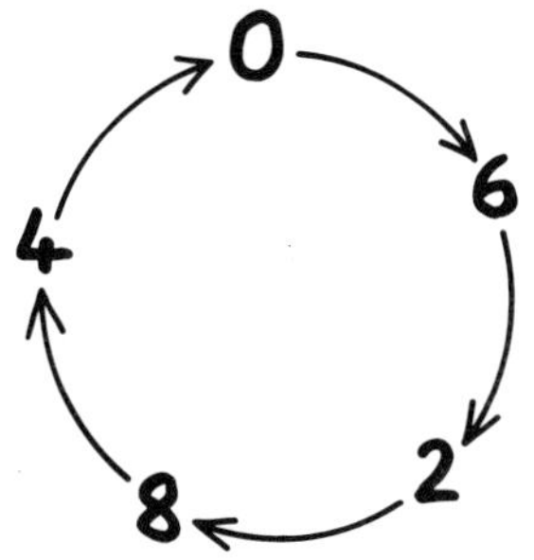

Activity 5: Ancient number systems
Use the work in AT2 Number, Level 4 on number bases to support an investigation into patterns. Expand the examples given there into a whole class or group-based enquiry into place value, or lack of place value, in a number of ancient civilisations. These could include the Babylonians, Egyptians and Romans. Use reproductions of paintings in which mathematical symbols are depicted, and Victorian artifacts and books which were intended to support Number work. This Activity could be linked to work in History.

Area of study 40 | P of S 3d | LD 5

MULTIPLICATION AND DIVISION

Commentary
Children at this Level should be reasonably confident about the processes of multiplication and division. However, they may not yet have appreciated that, for example, $N \times 4 = 12$ is also the same statement as $N = 12 \div 4$.

In exploring the relationship between multiplication and division it is useful to make use of calculators as these allow the children to try out lots of 'sums' in a short enough time for the relationship to become readily observable.

Activity 1: Think of a number
The children will be familiar with puzzles like 'think of a number'. These can be used to illustrate how a process might be seen in forward as well as reverse ways. For example, a simple puzzle is:

think of a number between 0 and 10;
add 4;
double the answer;
divide by 2;
take away the number you first thought of;
the answer is 4.

Using this sort of example get the children to make up some of their own puzzles and try them out with others. Use calculators to generate complex ones.

Activity 2: Calculators
Use calculators to allow the children to see that entering any number they choose and multiplying it by any number they choose, and then dividing the result by the same number as they used for multiplication will output the same answer. The reverse is true too; that is divide and then multiply. In some cases a discrepancy may arise if the calculator automatically truncates or rounds up as a result. Get the children to write out the results of some of their investigations in the form:

A (first number) $\times B$ (second number) $= R$ (result)
$R \div B = A$.

Activity 3: Checking sums
With the children, generate a series of sums, some multiplication and some division. Using the algorithms that they are used to they should solve each sum and check their results by carrying out the inverse of the first operation. So, for example, they might set out their answers like this:

$$\begin{array}{r} 254\times \\ \underline{42} \\ 10668 \end{array} \qquad \begin{array}{r} 254 \\ 42\overline{)10668} \end{array}$$

Area of study 41 | P of S 3d | LD 5

THREE-DIGIT × TWO-DIGIT MULTIPLICATION AND DIVISION

C41

Commentary
There are a number of standard approaches (algorithms) in use for the multiplication and division of three-digit by two-digit numbers. You will have one that you probably favour yourself. Others will appear in different schemes that you may have used. Whilst algorithms have been invented as a means of attacking numerical problems logically and consistently there can be dangers in teaching standard algorithms to children. It is of the utmost importance that children do not come to see the algorithm as being more important than the purposes of the computation.

There is no one standard algorithm that has universal approval. This is recognised in the statutory orders, for no particular method is prescribed.

Multiplication and division are inverse operations. That is if number (N) is equal to number A multiplied by number B, then number B is obtained by dividing N by A.

Symbolically, if $N = A \times B$
then $B = N \div A$

This relationship is profound when the children come to manipulate generalisable mathematics (algebra).

There are a number of approaches to multiplication and division. All have their roots in the past. If children are allowed to sample various approaches they will resist the idea that there *is* a standard way of doing things!

Activity 1: Schemes and supplements
With the children's help make a collection of as many different algorithms for multiplication and division as you can find. Use scheme books and reference books, and get the children to bring in methods used by parents and grandparents. See if the children can group the methods you discover. Let them try out all of the methods for a given collection of problems. Which do they find are most straightforward for them? Why? Are some methods apparently better to use for certain types of problem than others?

Copymaster 41 is a reply sheet for parents to record the ways they have for doing sample sums. These can then be compared and discussed by the children.

Activity 2: Everyday problems
Using real examples gathered from the running of the school generate a set of problems for the children to solve. Typical examples are:

- the likely cost of the school telephone bill if you know the cost for one week (bearing in mind the number of weeks in the year the school is open);
- the cost per person for a school trip or party;
- the number of exercise books to be ordered for the children in the class, a set of classes or the whole school.

Because the data you use here is real and therefore of personal interest to the children, a concertina book containing the investigations and other problems for solution could be displayed.

Activity 3: Egyptian arithmetic

In ancient Egypt multiplication was done by doubling. For example, this is how the Egyptians would have multiplied 36 by 13:

Multiples of 36	
× 1	36 <
× 2	72
× 4	144 <
× 8	288 <

The multiples marked < are × 1, × 4 and × 8 which, added together, make 13 (1 + 4 + 8). Thus the answer to 36 × 13 is 36 + 144 + 288 = 468.

Explain this method to the children and then, with their help, generate a number of sums to solve in Egyptian fashion. Discuss why this method works.

Activity 4: Napier's rods

John Napier (1550–1617) developed 'rods' which were mainly used for multiplication. Make copies of the rods like those shown here, using lolly sticks or card strips, and explain how they work. Invite the children to make up challenges for their classmates to solve using the rods.

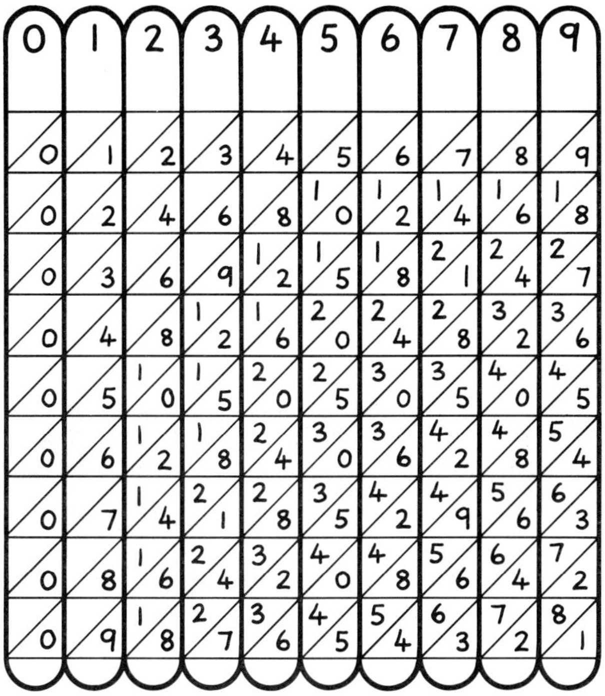

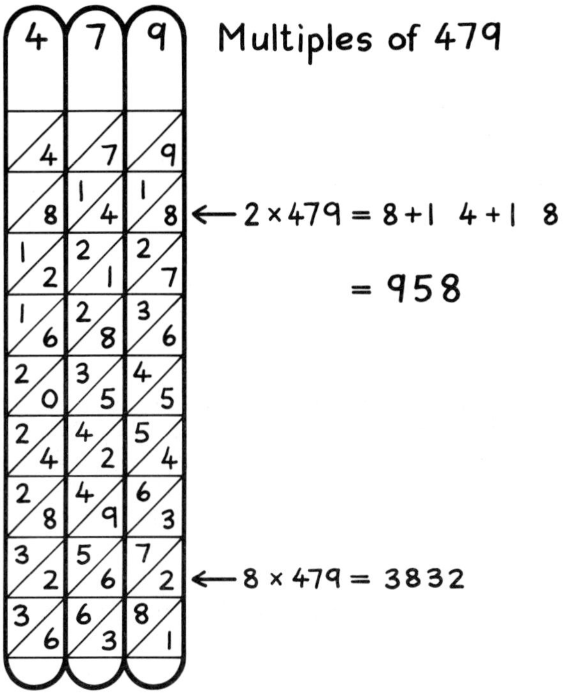

Programme of study: Number

Pupils should be taught to:

■ 3. Understanding relationships between numbers and developing methods of computation

e understand multiplication as repeated addition, and division as sharing and repeated subtraction; use associated language and recognise situations to which the operations apply;

Area of study	P of S	LD
42	2e	3

NUMBERS DIVISIBLE BY 2, 5 AND 10

RC2 C42

Commentary

This work should be linked to AT2 Number in relation to the 2×, 5× and 10× tables as well as to the work done in Algebra Level 2 on odd and even numbers.

Activity 1: Can I divide it by 2?

The 'solution' that the children need to arrive at here is that even numbers can be divided exactly by 2. If you get them to colour the even numbers on a 100 square, and then ring the pattern of 'counting in twos' up to 100, they will quickly realise that the patterns coincide exactly. Reinforce this learning by giving them quick fire numbers, which they can say 'Yes, I can divide by 2 exactly' or 'No, I cannot.'

There are 100 squares on **resource copymaster 2** and a sheet of numbers, some of which can be divided by 2 on **copymaster 42**.

Activity 2: Can I divide it by 5?

Practise calling out the pattern of fives to 100 with the children. Do this until the class, the groups and individuals can do it without faltering. Then vary the exercise by calling a number in the pattern and asking the children to tell you what comes next or what comes before it.

Write up the pattern of numbers divisible by 5 on the blackboard or ask the children to mark them on a 100 square. If they look at the last (units) digit in the numbers they will see that they end in 0 or 5. Let the children see whether all numbers divisible exactly by 5 end in a 0 or a 5.

Resource copymaster 2 has 100 squares on it and **copymaster 42** is a worksheet allowing children to ring the numbers they know can be divided by 5.

Activity 3: Can I divide by 10?

The children should know the pattern of numbers counting in tens to 100. Ask them, using a 100 square, to look for all the numbers that can be exactly divided by 10 and they will have found the rule.

Resource copymaster 2 has 100 squares on it and **copymaster 42** is a worksheet allowing children to ring the numbers they know can be divided by 5.

Activity 4: Detecting big numbers divisible by 2, 5 and 10

If the children have done Activities 1, 2 and 3 they will be able to detect those numbers, no matter how many digits they have, that can be divided exactly by 2, 5 or 10. Pin up a few enormous numbers each day for a couple of weeks, giving the children all day to think and confer about whether they are exactly divisible by these single-digit numbers. At the end of the day give them the 'solutions'.

Which numbers are divisible by 2, 5, 10 ?

1,000,000	77,770
6,525	444
15,010	9350

Area of study	P of S	LD
43	3e	3

DIVISION

Commentary

Even before they are formally introduced to division, the children will have a concept of what it means in real life. The challenge is to give them the ways for recording and signalling what 'sharing out' does to numbers, without divorcing division from the idea of sharing toys with their siblings or cheese sandwiches with their dads. No matter how competent children are as mathematicians, do not be tempted to leave out the practical work. Only links with real situations will convince many children that mathematics is relevant to them.

At Level 2, the children have met a half and a quarter. You may want to remind them of this work and of their recent work on multiplication. When it is appropriate, mention the links between multiplication and division. If the children have been given the confidence to play with numbers, some of them will find and point out the links themselves.

Activity 1: Sharing

Discuss the principle of sharing with others. List the kinds of things we share in school and at home, and display the results.

This discussion could be the springboard for drama or an assembly. Let the children show you how they would share marbles, sweets, toys or books between a group of their friends. Let them act out this sharing to

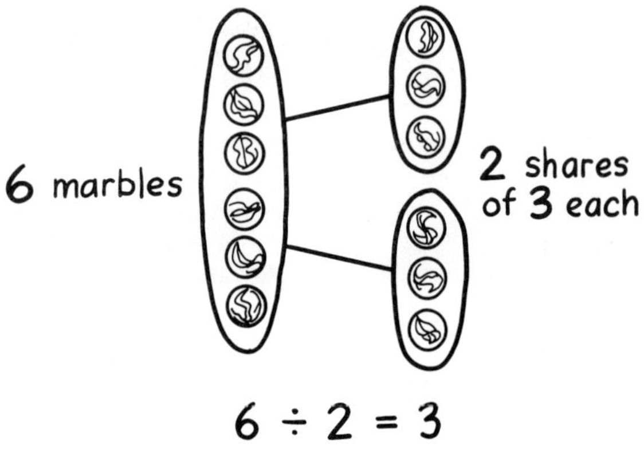

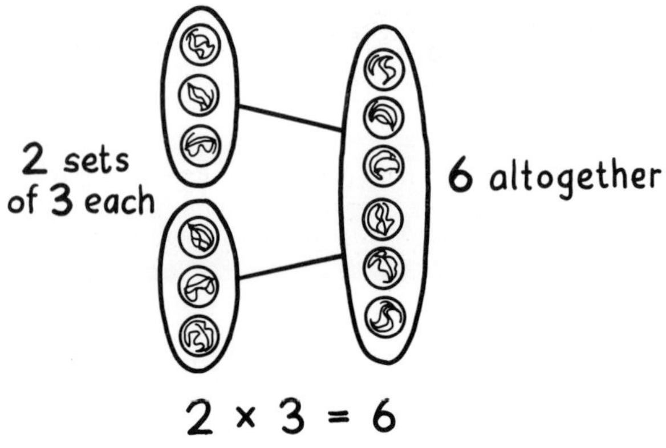

be sure that they understand the principles involved. Ask the children to record some of the activities they have done.

Activity 2: Language and sign for division
Show the children the sign for division and tell them the terms mathematicians use, like 'divide by'. Remind the children of the appearance of common fractions, like $\frac{1}{2}$, and why they are written in this way.

Activity 3: The divide game
Using answer cards prepared in the same way as for the multiply game in Area of study 31, Activity 5, create calculation cards to match, including all the appropriate division sums. Thus, for the answer card 6, you can create 12 ÷ 2. Let the children play games similar to those set out in Area of study 31.

Activity 4: Linking multiplication and division
The fact that multiplication and division are linked may escape some children's notice at this stage, unless you point it out. Draw the process of division and multiplication on a blackboard or large sheet of paper, so that they can see the 'reversibility' of the operation.

Area of study 44 | P of S 3e | LD 3

REMAINDERS

Commentary
It is when they begin to handle remainders that we can see whether children have really understood the principle of division, because remainders preclude 'fair shares'.

Division embraces both 'sharing' and 'grouping'. We either know the number of shares or the size of the groups; for example, we can divide 12 between 3 (sharing) or find how many 4s are in 12 (grouping). Had the starting number been 13, there would be a partly-filled group (a remainder).

Activity 1: Counting groups
Using the number bond facts that the children already know, get them to make equal-sized groups which make up a given number. Make a set of cards, each with a number which has several factors in it; examples include 20, 18, 15 and 12. Thus with the card '20' children may say '2 groups of 10', '10 groups of 2', '4 groups of 5', '5 groups of 4'. Then ask them to add 1, 2, 3, 4 and then 5 to the number on their cards and say what happens to the groups.

Activity 2: A dice game
Give the children three dice marked 7–12 and one marked 2–7. Let them throw the three similar dice and add the numbers together. Then throw the one die and say whether their three-dice total can be divided exactly by the single number. If not, the children can determine the remainder.

Programme of study: Number

Pupils should be taught to:

■ 3. Understanding relationships between numbers and developing methods of computation

f understand and use the relationships between the four operations, including inverses;

Area of study 45 | P of S 3f | LD 2 | C43

MYSTERY NUMBERS

Commentary
If this bit of mathematics is set up like a treasure hunt, Algebra will not seem quite so fearsome as it has to children in the past (and to some of us teachers!).

The key to finding treasure is to assemble all the clues and lay them out in a way that allows deduction; just so in Algebra. Let the children become sleuths armed with organisation skills and they will solve them all!

Activity 1: What's missing from the picture?
As an introduction to Algebra, try looking at some pictures with the children. For example, a quick cartoon showing that a profile, nose, mouth, ear, hair and ? makes a complete face, will allow the children to spot that the eye is missing.

Let the children create some of these 'mysteries' for their friends to attempt. Discuss with the children the strategies they use for solving these. They may talk about 'adding on' or 'taking away' and these are just the ideas they need in order to do the calculations in the next Activity.

$6 + \square = 6$ $\quad 2 + \square = 6$

$5 + \square = 6$ $\quad 1 + \square = 6$

$4 + \square = 6$ $\quad 0 + \square = 6$

$3 + \square = 6$

Activity 2: Find the number
Using the number patterns the children are now familiar with, set out the calculations so that one of the numbers is replaced by a box. With a number array in front of them the children should be able to detect the pattern and race through.

Now give the children some calculations where the product is the same but the pattern is jumbled.

$3 + \square = 6$

$\square + 5 = 6$

$0 + \square = 6$

Finally, give the children some 'real' mysteries to solve. For example, if Lady Lucinda has had all the family jewels stolen, and of the 9 necklaces, 2 bracelets and 5 rings, only 1 necklace, 1 bracelet and 2 rings have been recovered, how many pieces is Inspector Mac still looking for?

Copymaster 43 gives the children some example mystery sums to attempt.

Area of study 46 | P of S 3f | LD 3

FUNCTION MACHINES

C44–46

Commentary
All of us learn best when we are motivated by the tasks facing us. Function machines are, in our experience, highly motivating. Whilst much of the early work you will do using function machines is clearly linked to the doing of 'sums' it is the case that more sophisticated ideas can be developed at a later stage using function machines providing that the children are familiar with them and the rules under which they operate – and they are still a lot more fun than pages of sums!

You might like to explore the idea of the function machine in other areas of the curriculum. For example, a 'plurals' machine which turns any singular word put in into its plural form.

Activity 1: Input/output play
Create a 'machine' by drawing one on a folded piece of card or on the side of a shoe box.

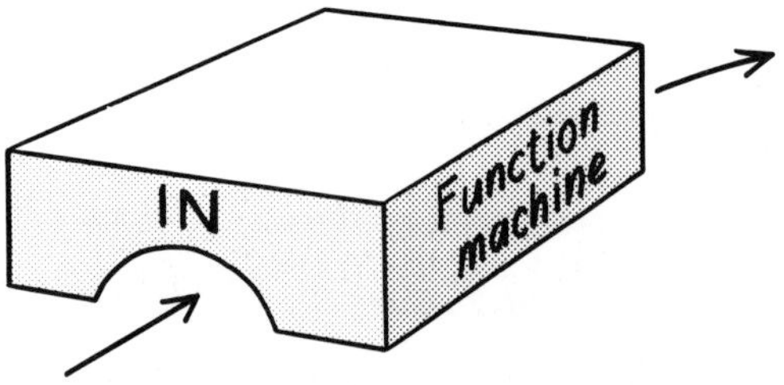

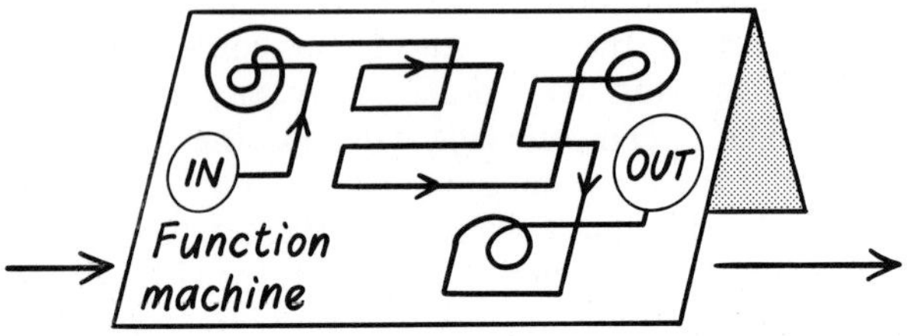

Write some appropriate numerals on squares of card and some operations on function cards. Set up the machine with one numeral on the side you designate IN and the operation card inside the machine. Ask the children what the machine's output will be.

When all the children understand what is required of them, try placing a mystery operation card face down in the machine and setting out given input and output cards. Invite the children to try to deduce what is happening inside the mystery machine. Play this game a number of times.

Finally, set some puzzles where they know the function and the output and have to discover the input.

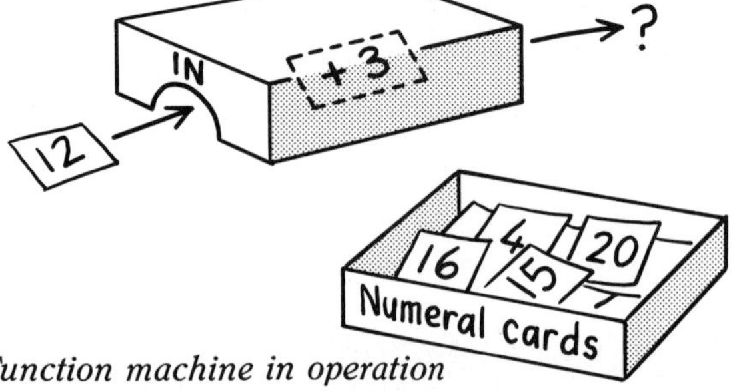

Function machine in operation

Activity 2: Make a function machine
Let the children make their own function machines and card sets, so that they can challenge one another.

Activity 3: Recording function machines
Try letting the children record what is happening in a variety of function machines, using a little machine-like drawing to denote the middle step.

Copymasters C44–46 have function machines on them that the children can complete.

Area of study 47 | P of S 3f | LD 4

FORMULAE AND EQUATIONS: FUNCTION MACHINES

C47, 48

Commentary
Formula is the term used to describe a general rule or law. *Equation* is used to describe two mathematical statements that are equal to each other.

At this Level children need to be encouraged to talk through their interpretation of a problem. This talk should be progressively refined so that the statements made are unambiguous. The use of symbols to describe a problem comes at a later Level and should not be used before the children have gained solid experience in oral description.

The children should be familiar with function machines from Level 3.

Function machines have to be set up with a rule or rules. For example, a '×3' machine will multiply any number put into it by 3 regardless of its size or sign. A '+15 and ×2' machine will always carry out those operations and always in that order. In trying to work out what a function machine is doing children will need more than one piece of information. If, for example, you feed a 6 into a machine and get:

$6 \rightarrow 36$

then the machine might be any one of the following:

a +30;
a ×6;
a times by the number put in;
output a number that added to the input number makes 42.

If you then input a 10 and get:

$10 \rightarrow 100$

then you can narrow the options down to the 'times by the number put in' function, i.e. a squaring machine.

Activity 1: Use and create function machines
Get the children to generate their own function machines. These have to be solved by other children. Ideas for such machines include:

- doubling;
- multiply by 2 and add 1;
- multiply by 5 and take away 4;
- add 3;
- multiply number by itself;
- the sum of the digits of the input number;
- take the number from 100.

Give the children **copymaster 47** on which there are a number of machines with input and output information. Let the children work out some possibilities for what is happening to the machines. If they compare their suggestions they will see that there are a number of ideas about what each machine is doing. Use **copymaster 48** to give them an additional piece of information about each machine. This will enable the children to eliminate some of their suggestions.

Activity 2: Extending the use of function machines
Once the children understand the nature of function machines and the constancy of rules get them to invent machines that have two inputs and one output. Alternatively, link two machines together so that the input of the second is the output of the first.

Activity 3: Working towards symbols
Using the work the children have done on function machines see if they can start to write down, in a consistent way and using whatever symbols and selected words that they choose, a statement about each of the function machines that they have invented. This will support them when they have to work with conventional symbols at Level 5.

Programme of study: Number

Pupils should be taught to:

■ 3. Understanding relationships between numbers and developing methods of computation

g extend methods of computation to include addition and subtraction with negative numbers, all four operations with decimals, and calculating fractions and percentages of quantities, using a calculator where appropriate;

Area of study 48 | P of S 3g | LD 5

COMPUTATION SKILLS

C49–50

Commentary
See Area of study 12; Negative numbers in context, for points to make when showing children how to work with negative numbers. Decimals, fractions and percentages can be worked on when children are solving problems and doing investigations.

Activity 1: Negative numbers in addition and subtraction
Using the number line and graph work give the children the rules for computation where negative numbers are involved. Using two different coloured dice, red for positive and blue for negative, with a yellow tetrahedral dice showing + on two faces and − on two faces, produce calculations to work through. Thus 3 red, yellow − and 4 blue will be written
$+3-(-4)=?$
$+3+4=+7$.

Activity 2: All four operations with decimals
Using a shopping setting ask the children to work on calculations involving all operations. Set prices with two decimal places and ask the children to total shopping lists, find change, price up multiples of one item and work out the cost of one item in a pack carrying many. This will give practice in all four operations.

Activity 3: Fractions and percentages of quantities
Look at some food packs with the children and ask them to work out the number of helpings in a pack, what fraction a helping is of the whole and the percentage of the whole eaten when some helpings have been taken from the pack. Include packs like those for breakfast cereals, biscuits, margarine, juice, dried fruit etc.

Investigate the fractions and percentages of a school day in minutes, spent on a variety of activities.

Invite the children to determine fractions and percentages using pages of a children's newspaper. For example, how much of a line does a word take up? What fraction of the page is devoted to pictures? How much of the page is margin space?

Using the data made available to the children in Activity 2, ask them, for example, to convert the price of one item in a pack to a fraction of the total price. They can also determine, for example, what percentage of the money tendered for goods is returned in change.

Copymasters 49 and **50** offer children practice in finding fractions and percentages in money, length, mass, volume and time.

Programme of study: Number

Pupils should be taught to:

■ 3. Understanding relationships between numbers and developing methods of computation

h understand and use the features of a basic calculator, interpreting the display in the context of the problem, including rounding and remainders.

Area of study 49 | P of S 3h | LD 4

USING CALCULATORS

Commentary
The advent of cheap calculators means that we all have powerful computational power literally at our fingertips. Teachers and children worry that using calculators seems like cheating. However, we are in an electronic age and it would therefore be foolish to exclude the use of calculators in everyday school work. Their use does need to be matched with a concern to ensure that children can do those everyday, mental mathematical operations that human beings are capable of carrying out. As well as doing these and being able to use a calculator children need to have powers of estimation and prediction. These cannot be gleaned by using a calculator but only through practical application.

Calculators vary in their operation. When buying calculators try to ensure that they have, apart from the usual computational features, the following:

- a memory;
- iteration (You can test this by pressing a number, say 2, followed by '+' then '=' repeatedly. This should give a display which increments by two each time.);

- a clear display;
- 'solar' power.

Additional features are not mandatory. However, if children have scientific calculators of their own which have facilities such as automatic use of square roots, you may have to find out how to explain these features to the proud new owner!

The Activities in this section are related to all of the mathematics done at Level 4. Allow the children to make full use of calculators within the context of their need to understand processes and principles. The calculator should not become something to be learned, rather it is a tool for learning.

Activity 1: Construct a challenge
Get the children to use their knowledge of number bonds, place value and other mathematical ideas to produce a calculator puzzle book for younger children in the school. Contents could include:

- a mathematical trail and quiz;
- simple function machines;
- a game to make the biggest/smallest number with different numbers of single digits.

Activity 2: Check your ideas
Use the earlier Activities in this section. Get the children, ideally as they go along, to check their work using a calculator.

Activity 3: Exploring calculators
Playing with calculator displays and the layout of the digits on the keypad of a calculator can offer some interesting number pattern investigations. Try these:

- Enter a number and multiply it by itself (using the iteration procedure described above). Do any of these sums produce palindromic numbers, i.e. those that read the same backwards as well as forwards? Try 11 as your starting number. Do remember to discuss with the children the apparent speed with which the answers grow.
- Try entering rows and columns from the keypad. Do any patterns start to emerge? For example, try the end column 963 and subtract the first column 741. What about the middle column subtracted from the end one and the first from the middle?

Activity 4: Make a machine
Calculators are very useful tools when you are working with function (number and operation) machines. Examples of these can be found in the section entitled 'Multiplying by 10 and 100'. Use the idea of the function machine for the children to produce their own challenges which need calculator support.

Programme of study: Number

■ 4. Solving numerical problems

Pupils should be taught to:

a develop their use of the four operations to solve problems, including those involving money and measures, using a calculator where appropriate;

Area of study 50 | P of S 4a | LD 2

SHOPPING

C51, 15, 52, 53

Commentary
These problems are a good vehicle for getting children working in situations that are close to 'real' problems. Let the children play and practice using coins in the settings discussed under Activity 1 below, and then set them going with picture sums. Using a piece of A4 paper, folded crosswise, the children can create their own shop front book cover, which you can help them fill with sums they have done.

Shopping is familiar to even the youngest of children, but we must not assume that they understand what is happening in a shopping transaction. Plenty of eight and nine-year-olds have never shopped on their own. Thus most children working at this Level will need practical 'play' at simple shopping, before committing anything to paper. A class shop is mandatory.

Copymaster 51 sets out some starter shopping problems, in a format that can form a page in a little booklet.

Activity 1: A class shop
This need not be a big affair; the size you make it should depend on the space available and the use to be made of it. A simple shop which two children can work with at a single desk can be made from a shoebox with a rectangle of attractive material stuck inside the rim of one long side. Roll out the material onto the desk and set small items for sale on it. Use the shoebox lid to display the price of items and the box itself to house the money, and (when not in use) the rolled up material, all the items for sale, and the price lists.

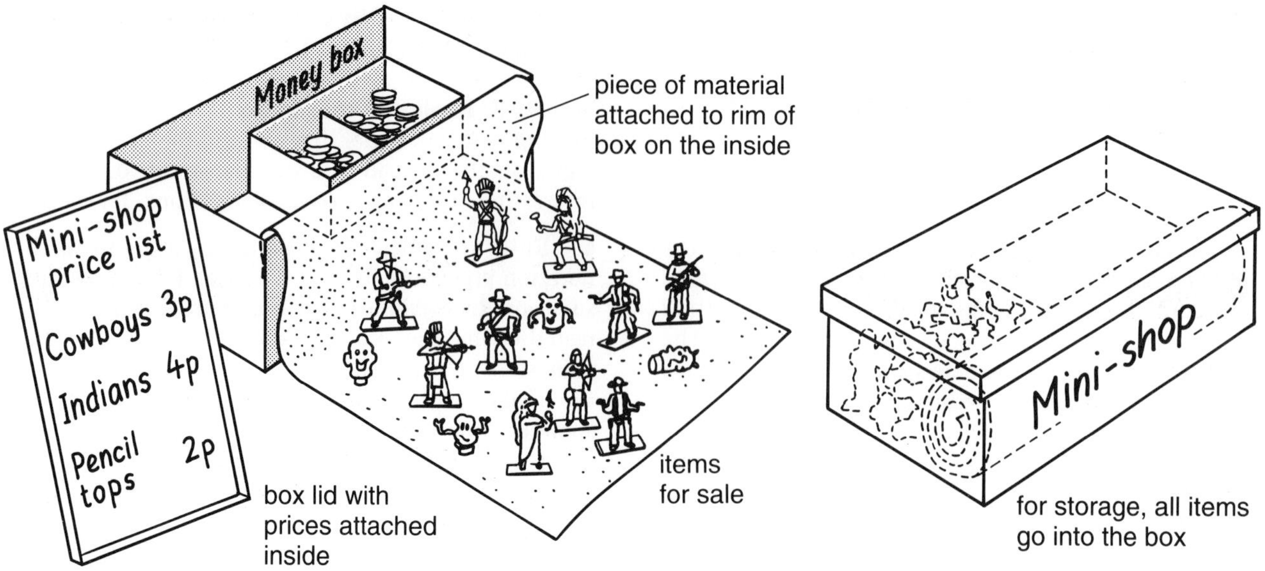

Activity 2: Picture shopping

A next step after playing shops, as in Activity 1 above, is to give children a work card or worksheet with pictures on it. Use your own drawings of small items or pictures of things cut from a catalogue (for example, a stationery or stocking fillers catalogue). Stick these onto card and write out a variety of price labels. Give the children a card with a shop window drawn on it. They can then select a few items for the window, attach prices to these and work through a number of sums, which either they can determine or you can give them on a card. Opposite is one example set out.

Copymaster 15 presents a shop window. **Copymaster 52** has pictures of small items that may be placed in the shop window. They can of course be replicated to provide, for example, a window of small toys or a window of stationery. **Copymaster 53** is a sheet of price tags.

Activity 3: Shopping problems

Using the picture shopping idea (Activity 2) as the principle, create written problems.

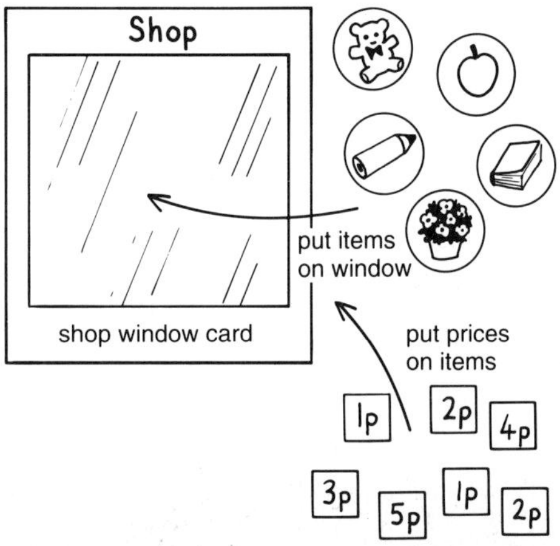

Area of study 51	P of S 4a	LD 3	**PROBLEMS USING MULTIPLICATION AND DIVISION**	C54

Commentary

The word 'problem' is used in everyday life as a catchphrase for all kinds of worries and difficulties, some of which may be soluble by action. The word has often been used in mathematics to denote number work presented through a written description – we can all remember printed exercise books where the sums at the end of a section are called 'problems' and talk about plumbers filling baths or housewives shopping. 'Problem-solving' has now been expanded to an expectation of a situation which can be 'explored'. In such explorations there may be a range of outcomes, dependent on the line of enquiry taken and the persistence of the enquirer.

Activity 1: Sums and stories

Give each child a multiplication and/or division sum to do that they can convert into a 10-second story. For example, given 3×4 divided by 2, they could, in addition to doing the sum say, 'Fido had stored four bones in each of three holes in the garden. When Liam dug the garden all 12 bones were uncovered and he shared them between Fido and his other dog Pinks. They had six each.'

Activity 2: What's the problem?

When the children have done the sums and related their stories in Activity 1 above, they should be ready to extract sums from number stories that you create. There are example stories on **copymaster 54**.

Activity 3: Equipping a work group

Discuss with a group of children how you yourself decide what resources they need for a given Activity. Let the children pretend that they are in a position to make judgements about the quantities of new equipment required for a variety of Activities. Set the children up with a catalogue of items and prices. You can make this like a scrapbook, using pictures from an old educational catalogue.

Then give the children a challenge card, which tells them the work group size they are buying for and the kinds of equipment required. See if they can establish the cost of the number of items they decide are required by six children.

Area of study 52 | P of S 4a | LD 4

PROBLEMS USING MEASURES

C55, 56

Commentary
This is a crucial area in which children can be shown how important maths is in our everyday lives.

Activity 1: Class measures
Respond to 'real' situations arising in the classroom, like the problem of book storage, display space or seating in the classroom, and engage the children in helping to find the measures necessary.

Copymasters 55 and **56** pose problems using a variety of measures for the children to tackle.

Programme of study: Number

Pupils should be taught to:

■ 4. Solving numerical problems

b choose sequences of methods of computation appropriate to a problem, adapt them and apply them accurately;

Area of study 53 | P of S 4b | LD 4

NUMBER PROBLEMS

C57, 58

Commentary
Solving written number problems to 100 is a progression from a mastery of number bonds to 10. However, we must guard against moving children to written arithmetic too quickly. Only the mental agility acquired through practical and oral work will enable children to understand rather than merely learn a 'method' by rote.

Through a wide range of opportunities and approaches do give children the chance of realising that there are lots of ways of writing 'sums'.

Activity 1: Problems requiring addition or subtraction
Devise some oral classroom problems that can be practically solved by the children; for example, 'If a group of children is joined by two more, and the group now requires 10 pencils so that everyone can have one, how many children were in the original group?' If the children get into difficulty with problems of this kind, they can use their classmates and classroom resources to work them through.

When the children are competent problem solvers in practical situations, give them some picture problems to solve, along with the clue as to which operation they will need to use in each case. Some example addition and subtraction problems are set out on **copymaster 57**.

Activity 2: Problems requiring both addition and subtraction
After the children have practised problems of the kind set out in Activity 1, give them number 'stories' where the final outcome depends on both operations. Try not to defeat the children by making the story long-winded!

Copymaster 58 has two number 'stories' on it for the children to try.

Activity 3: How is the problem solved?
Pose the children a variety of problem situations and ask them which operations will be involved in solving the problem.

See Area of study 51: Problems using multiplication and division and Area of study 52: Problems using measures, where there are activities which can prompt discussion.

Programme of study: Number

■ 4. Solving numerical problems

Pupils should be taught to:

c check results by different methods, including repeating the operations in a different order or using inverse operations; gain a sense of the size of a solution, and estimate and approximate solutions to problems.

Area of study	P of S	LD
54	4c	3

PLACE VALUE AND APPROXIMATION

Commentary
A *base number* is the hinge around which other digits in that number system move.

As a total reaches the base number (or a multiple or reciprocal of it) a substitution happens. Thus in our number system which has a base 10, when 1 unit is added to 9 we substitute 1 base ten unit for the 10 individual units.

The children need to know that we write 17 as '17' and not as '10–7' because the digits show their value by their 'place' in the number.

Activity 1: Write the number
Try five-minute sessions where you get the children to write down some numbers which you say aloud, as quickly as possible. Over a number of sessions make the numbers larger and larger, until they can cope with, for example, hundreds, thousands and even millions with confidence.

Activity 2: Describing counts using apparatus
Assemble all the equipment available to help children to work with numbers beyond 10, including, for example, abacuses, Cuisenaire© or Colour Factor©. Ask groups of children to work out how the apparatus is used in setting out and manipulating large numbers. Let the groups tell the rest of the class how the different apparatus works and how well they think each sort helps in doing mathematics.

Activity 3: Give me a number
Play oral approximation by saying a number aloud, to which the children have to give the number to the nearest 10 or 100.

Activity 4: Looking for leftovers
Use practical sharing activities, if necessary, to demonstrate that the shares cannot always be equal and the 'leftovers' are called *remainders*. Show the children that we sometimes 'approximate' answers to real problems by looking at the size of the likely remainder and 'rounding up or down'. For example, a book costing £3.95p costs nearly £4.

Activity 5: Approximate measures
Try approximation with measurement too. See if the children can agree on, for example, approximately how many metres wide the classroom is, or the hall or corridor. Let them approximate the length of a book or pencil, in centimetres. Approximation can be seen to have a real purpose in 'live' situations. Discuss the difference between estimation and approximation. For example, you need to estimate and then measure exactly how much carpet you need for a living room. However, an approximation is appropriate for an amount of wallpaper as you have to buy a number of whole rolls. (In this case you have to round up.)

Area of study 55 | P of S 4c | LD 4

CHECKING YOUR ANSWERS: ESTIMATION AND APPROXIMATION

Commentary
In everyday life we commonly estimate the outcome of 'sums'. For example, when supermarket shopping we often keep a tally of how much we are spending in order to be sure we have sufficient money with us. When making a journey by car we estimate how much petrol we are going to need and approximately how long the journey will take.

Estimation is the act of making a judgement about the validity of a solution. *Approximation* is the act of determining whether the solution is near enough to stand as being the correct solution. In all computation exercises and activities it is essential that the children habitually estimate the order of the answer so as to appreciate whether they have produced a solution which is sensible.

Estimation requires a good basis of knowledge and understanding in number bonds and multiplication facts.

Activity 1: Estimate, approximate, how do we calculate?
Using a variety of challenges, help the children to develop strategies which do not require counting every item. Here are some suggestions for challenges:

- How many leaves on the runner-beans?
- How many words on a page of your reading book?
- How many sheets in a metre pile of writing paper?
- How many eyelashes in the class?

Invent further challenges, using data at hand, for example, bricks in a school wall, planks in the hall floor, coathooks in the whole school and crisps in all the lunch boxes.

Activity 2: Checking addition and subtraction
Using a variety of the 'sums' obtained from the computation work earlier in this section of the book try changing them to 'nearest 10' and 'nearest 100' sums. For example, $367 + 214 = 581$ could be tried as $370 + 210$ and $400 + 200$. Produce a set of answers and then use these for a discussion about accuracy and the order of an answer. Generate a set of sums with the children which they have to solve in 5 minutes using approximation and estimation. Then work out the sums together and see how close you all were.

Area of study 56 | P of S 4c | LD 5

TRIAL AND IMPROVEMENT

Commentary
Throughout their mathematical development the children have been exposed to experiences in estimating and approximating results and outcomes. At this Level they should have a set of strategies, rooted in a wide range of operational skills, for making good estimates of an answer. We need to establish fully that experience at this stage.

Trial and improvement means just what it says. In other words, we have to give the children the opportunity to forecast the answer and then refine this in the light of their experience. This runs somewhat counter to any views that suggest that there must be a clear right answer to every mathematical question.

In Activity 2 you are invited to get the children working with calculators to explore some aspects of powers and roots. It might be that the children take on a sum like the square root of 2. This particular sum does not actually have a solution as it is an irrational number – one that bothered the Greeks greatly!

Activity 1: How many sweets in the jar?
At the local fête children will have seen stalls where one has to guess the weight of the cake, the name of the doll or the number of sweets in the jar. Use this idea to develop some estimation of number games in the classroom. You could use, for example:

- How many sweets in these five tubes of sweets?
- How many teeth on ten combs?
- How many teeth in the class?
- How many leaves on a particular tree?

In attempting these sorts of questions let the

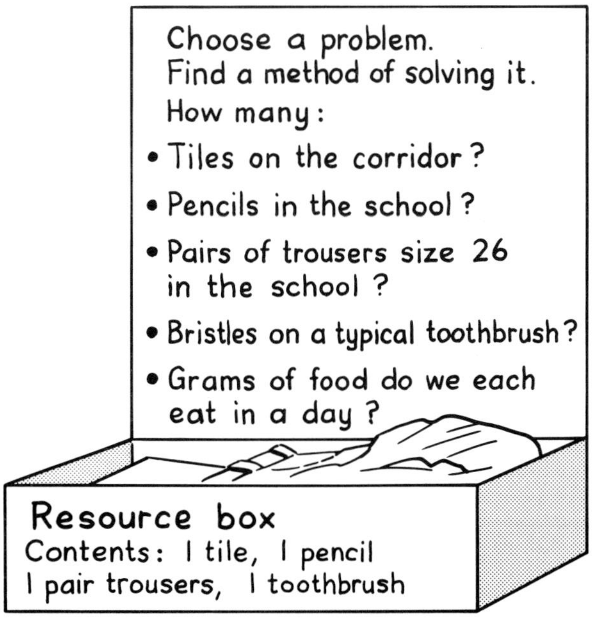

children write down their predictions first. Then they must come up with strategies for improving on their estimates; for example, they might choose to count all of the sweets (but what about counting the contents of one tube and multiplying by five – how close is this to the actual number?).

Activity 2: Number puzzles
This Activity can be done in conjunction with your work on powers of whole numbers. Working in groups, get the children to respond to, and then develop, some puzzles to challenge the other groups. They will need calculators to do this. The puzzles are to do with getting the nearest possible solution.

The first puzzle is to do with square numbers. With all of the children together, remind them of what square numbers are, using the whole numbers 4, 9, 16, 25, 36 and so on. In their groups they first have to try to find the nearest number that they can which when multiplied by itself will give a whole number answer. These are not the easy ones! Here are some examples to try:

19 – (close to 4.36);
35 – (close to 5.92);
70 – (between 8.3 and 8.4);
96 – (between 9.79 and 9.80).

Now the children can choose some whole numbers, calculate the square roots of these, using calculators, and then invite the other groups to get their best estimate of the chosen whole number.

You can then go on to develop this discussion into cube roots. The children, in their groups, multiply a whole number by itself and itself again. They then provide the whole number answer and the other children have to find the original number used. Keep this part of the Activity to whole number answers.

Area of study 57 | P of S 4c | LD 5

SIGNIFICANT FIGURES

C59, 60

Commentary
It is common for us to use numbers that do not go much beyond two decimal places. We approximate $\frac{1}{3}$, for example, as 0.33. In fact it is 0.3 with the 3 recurring for ever. If we give children the idea that two decimal places is all we need to know, they may think that most fractions turn into simple decimals. In fact many fractions are complex and have very interesting recurring patterns. It is important that children are in a position to make a decision about how accurate they want an answer to be. They can choose when to stop and, therefore, what will count as the number of significant figures.

In working with significant figures the children need to know the convention that the final digit may be rounded up if the digit following it is in the range 5–9. So 1.356 would be written as 1.36 to three significant figures or two decimal places, but 1.354 would be written as 1.35.

Activity 1: What is significant?
From their considerable experience of measurement the children will know that there are limits to the accuracy with which we can measure. Use this fact as a starting point for a discussion on the ways in which we can decide how accurately we want our solution to a computation. For example, use the fact that calculators only have space for a certain number of digits. Some calculators will automatically round up at the end of the display; others will simply cut off the hidden digits. Let the children find out why this occurs and the sorts of calculators that have these facilities.

Activity 2: Make a web
The children have by now done a lot of Activities which can be linked to one another. These include *estimation*, *measurement*, *fractions and decimal fractions*, *calculator experiments* and so on. Get the children to draw up webs of connections between these different

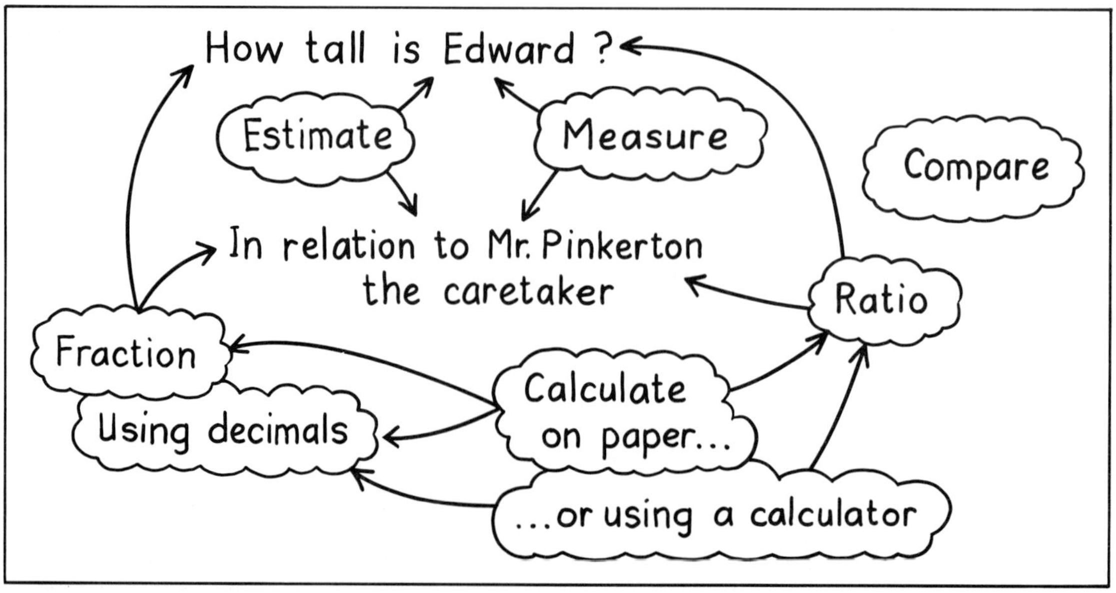

mathematical activities. Discuss these webs and then make a large display which illustrates the connections that you and the children have identified. If necessary, use the web to revise certain aspects of the work that the children have experienced.

Copymaster 59 is a sample web related to the child's height, on which they can record the kinds of Activities they need to engage in to find out data about their own height. **Copymaster 60** is a blank web for each child's own entries.

Area of study 58 | P of S 4c | LD 5

ESTIMATION AND APPROXIMATION IN MULTIPLICATION AND DIVISION

Commentary
This is a revision section and an opportunity for children to demonstrate their now considerable skills in manipulating numbers.

Activity 1: Going mental!
Let the children work in pairs and set each other a page of division and/or multiplication sums. Let them mark each other's work, having first written an approximate answer in the margin. They can discuss together and with you, some of the following:

- the strategies they used to estimate and approximate;
- whether there are other more successful strategies;
- the closeness of the estimated answers.

Area of study 59 | Extension Activities

UNITARY RATIOS AND SCALE

RC3,4 | C61

Commentary
By the phrase *unitary ratios* is meant ratios of 1 to another figure, for example, 1:5 or 1:72.

Ratio, may be a part of the children's experiences from quite early on in their mathematics, though they may not be familiar with the word. In using apparatus such as Cuisenaire© rods the children have been working with materials which depend upon the perception of the ratio of one piece of apparatus to another.

Discussions about ratios can include ideas that children have about fractions. For example, as with fractions, it is quite easy to disguise very large numbers with ratios. A ratio of 1 cm to 1 km is actually, in centimetres, 1 cm to 100 000 cm.

Scaling needs an understanding of ratio, for a scale of 1 cm to 5 cm is the same as the ratio 1:5.

Children are familiar with scale models. All of them will have encountered such things as model cars and aeroplanes, doll's houses and miniatures as souvenirs, but in order to fully understand scale it is essential that children come to see the centrality of ratio. That, for example, in making a scale drawing every line will be in exactly the same ratio to the original as all of the other lines. Having said this there is a degree of freedom adopted by model designers due to both aesthetic considerations and manufacturing feasibility. In drawing scale maps, for example, it is perfectly possible to mix standard units. It is possible to draw a map where 1 cm stands for 10 yds or 1 inch represents 1 km. Although standard units are not commonly mixed like this the children do need to understand the possibilities.

Children need to understand that the scaling in scale maps and scale models operates in both two and three dimensions.

Activity 1: Drawings and ratios
On squared paper, draw horizontal and vertical axes of the same length. With its base on the horizontal axis, close to the top of the scale, draw a vertically standing arrow made from a vertical line with an equilateral triangle as its tip. From the tip of the arrow draw a straight line to the origin (0,0) of the axes.

A vertical line drawn from a point midway between the origin and the vertical line of the arrow will have a

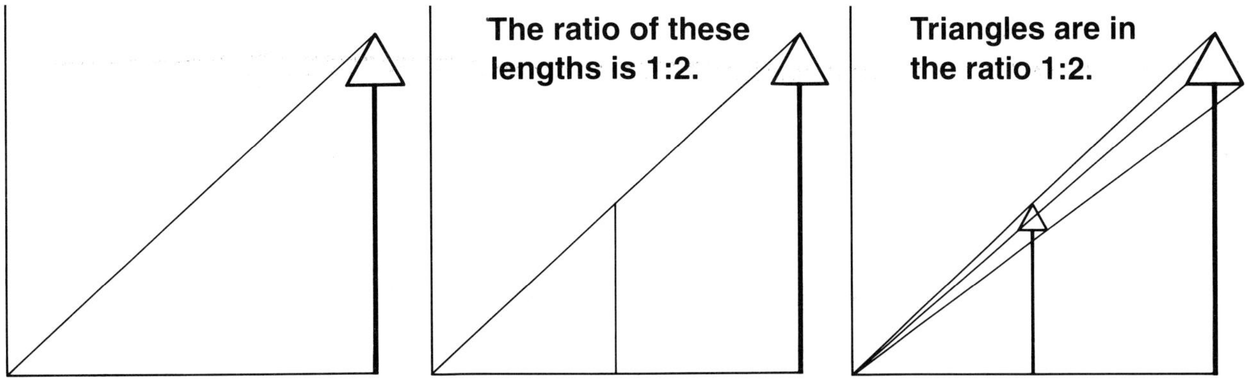

length which is in the ratio of 1:2 in respect of the original. To draw a triangle having this same ratio to the original draw straight lines through the origin from the remaining points of the triangle and draw a line from where the triangle base is cut by the vertical line. These lines will allow you to draw a scaled down equilateral triangle.

Copymaster 61 has a square on it which the children can scale as instructed. Use this to discuss the idea of the ratio. Different ratios can be produced by drawing objects at different places along the horizontal axis. These can be calculated using readings from the vertical axis. **Resource copymasters 3** and **4** are sheets of 2 mm/10 mm/20 mm and 5 mm graph paper for more scale work.

Activity 2: Co-ordinates and drawings in ratio
Extend Activity 1 by using co-ordinates to describe drawings in ratio to each other. If, for example, the co-ordinates of a square are (2,0), (2,4), (6,0) and (6,4) then halving the co-ordinates to (1,0), (1,2), (3,0) and (3,2) will produce a square, the sides of which are in a ratio of 1:2. Let the children try doubling as well.

Activity 3: Ratio drawings around the school
This Activity should be used in conjunction with the development of work on scale.

Using squared paper, rulers, tapes and so on get the children to draw maps of one of the following:

- the hall set out for PE;
- the classroom;
- the playground.

Do this in groups and challenge each group to produce their map at a different ratio from other groups. The ratios will have to be pre-determined by you in the light of available paper and your estimates of overall real dimensions.

Activity 4: Maps and map-making
Link this work with Activity 3 above. Make a collection of maps, ancient and modern, local, national and world-wide. Discuss the collection with the children, emphasising in particular the information available from different scales. Contrast local maps of different scales. This work can be linked to Geography AT1.

Activity 5: Map-makers and model-makers
There are a wide variety of occupations and hobbies in which the use of scale is mandatory. Invite some people who use scale in the course of their job, or collectors or model-makers, into the class to discuss the ways in which they use their scaling knowledge and skills. Examples include:

- kitchens and conservatory consultants;
- museum curators who mount scale models;
- local model club members;
- theatre set designers;
- architects.

Area of study 60

FORMULAE AND EQUATIONS

C62

Commentary
As was pointed out at Level 4 there are clear differences between *formula* and *equation*. Equations are about equalities. There are two forms of equation; one describes situations in which the statements are equal for certain values (*conditional equations*). For example:

$2x + y = 7$ gives only certain possibilities; and
$2x = 8$ gives only one.

The second form of equation is where the equation is true for all numbers (these are called *identities*). For example:

$2(x + y) = 2x + 2y$.

A *formula* is any identity or general rule in mathematics.

In devising and using formulae and equations do make use of practical work in other areas of mathematics. Children should not be memorising formulae that have no real meaning for them. So use, for example, Shape and space or Handling data to support this work.

Activity 1: Perimeters
Do this work in tandem with AT4 Level 5 Shape and space on perimeters and areas.

Using geoboards, square paper or square dotty paper invite the children to draw or make a number of rectangles. They should record the areas, length of sides and perimeters of these rectangles. From the figures obtained, reinforce that *area* = *length* × *breadth*. Use the figures also to get to the formula that allows the perimeter to be calculated using the sum of the length and breadth.

Copymaster 62 has a table of areas for different-size rectangles. In the first part the rectangles are twice as long as they are wide. In the second part they are $2\frac{1}{2}$ times as long as they are wide. The children have to work out the lengths and widths (or breadths) of the rectangles. There is space for them to make up some of their own to whatever ratios they decide.

Area of study 61

COMPUTER FACILITIES

Commentary
A number of spreadsheet packages are available for the common machines found in school. These packages can be used to explore number patterns because of the facility they have for the user to allocate formulae to different cells or groups of cells, in the spreadsheet.

There are now a number of software packages which have been developed which support the investigation of number patterns as well as central algebraic ideas. These include, for example, Association of Teachers of Mathematics (ATM) packages and the *SMILE* packages which should be readily available within your LEA.

Activity 1: Spreadsheets
Spreadsheets allow you to enter formulae into cells so that computation of figures will happen automatically when you have entered information into the spreadsheet. At the simplest level, for example, it is possible to enter a set of numbers (perhaps a list of rainy and sunny days for some weeks or months) and have the package do the overall totals for you. If a number in the list is altered, the total will be automatically altered. The children can use features such as this one to develop a range of spreadsheets, including some involving cash calculations. They will have to be able to work out the necessary formulae for cells as they design the spreadsheet.

Activity 2: Other facilities
There are numbers of packages available which are intended to support the children in their exploration of patterns and sequences. Obtain some of these and allow the children to evaluate them through their exploration of what the packages allow them to do. This evaluation could be made available to colleagues and to LEA representatives.

Area of study 62

SIMPLE EQUATIONS

Commentary
Linear equations are those in which none of the variables is multiplied together or is raised to a power. So, $x + 2y = 7$ is linear, but $x^2 + 2y = 19$ is not and neither is $x + 2xy + y = 0$.

Polynomial equations contain terms which are made up of a constant and a variable (or variables). If you have not met the term before you may recall polynomials from your own school days where they were given names according to their power. So *quadratic* ones involve square numbers:

$$ax^2 + bx + c = 0;$$

and *cubic* ones involve cube numbers:

$$ax^3 + bx^2 + cx + d = 0.$$

At this Level children should be solving (or getting good approximations to) simple versions of linear and polynomial equations such as:

$2x + 3y = 16$ where x and y are whole numbers; and $x^3 = 21$.

Activity 1: Solve this!
Make a collection of all of the formulae and equations that the children already know, such as the area of a rectangle and square, and other numbers. Use these for revision and as a basis for 'inventing' equations.

Get the children to invent a number of equations of the type:

$$4x + 3 = 13 - x.$$

Use these to develop an adventure game in which you need to be able to solve equations in order to be given further clues or information.

Shape, space and measures

INTRODUCTION

Shape and space is one of the two major building blocks of mathematics, the other being Number. It is possible to express an awareness of two- and three-dimensional relationships without a sophisticated number system. Early cave paintings illustrate this point very well, as do early examples of sculpture and carving. Work in Shape and space is different from, although complimentary to, Number work.

In studying Shape and space children, and adults, are opening up their appreciation of a range of relationships to do with the natural and man-made world. Starting from an appreciation of ourselves as having a three-dimensional existence we can move outwards to relationships with others, expressed perhaps in dance or sport. We can locate ourselves, 'our houses in our town', through maps and mapping to our country and our location on the planet Earth. Earth in space, galaxies and the universe all become part of our understanding of spatial relationships. We can take our appreciation of relationships and patterns within ourselves right down to the atoms and molecules of which all matter is made.

Shape and space, then, is not a matter of being able to identify a limited range of named shapes, such as triangles and squares, although the acquisition of this sort of knowledge is important in that it allows an analysis of complex patterns in terms of constituent shapes. Shape and space work should be seen as offering experience from which children can produce increasingly more sophisticated constructions and analysis of two- and three-dimensional structures. Thus it offers a good vehicle for coherent, across-the-curriculum work. The Activities that follow can contribute to, and be enhanced by, work in technology, science, art, PE and geography.

Resourcing Shape and space

In addition to the equipment listed in the resource bank at the front of the book, the following will be useful in work on Shape and space:

- paper, with squares of different sizes and dotty papers;
- constructional materials ranging from paper and plastic straws through to some sets of commercially-produced constructional equipment;
- accurate mathematical shapes, such as Logiblocks© or Poleidoblocs©, and shape templates of different shapes and in different colours, including quadrilaterals (some of which are rectangles and squares), circles and elipses, triangles (some of which are right-angle), pentagons and hexagons;
- plasticised mirrors;
- a collection of natural and man-made objects demonstrating a range of shapes, and posters showing examples of man-made and natural structures (for example, bridges and beehives);
- magnetic compasses, compass designs like those on maps, a weather vane and a globe;
- set-squares with different angles;
- protractors and compasses;
- a collection of maps of different kinds;
- calibrated containers of different shapes and volumes;
- balances, scales and standard 'weights';
- egg timers, interval timers and materials to make sand and water clocks;
- clocks and stop-watches and play clock faces;
- pendulum and rocker devices and timers;
- rules and tapes (both metric and imperial) and trundle wheels;
- a freezer thermometer and a maximum and minimum thermometer;
- biscuit cutters, ingredients and cooking facilities.

Collections of cartons and packaging should include cubes and cuboids (boxes), cylinders (drinking straws, dowels, cylindrical containers) and prisms (chocolate boxes). Add to these a sphere (table tennis balls, marbles, globes), a cone (ice cream ones) and a pyramid (home-made). Work in Shape and space connects with work in science, technology and art, and materials for these areas of the curriculum will also be found to be useful in mathematics.

In addition to all these things the following will help with specific Activities in this Section:

- screws, screwdrivers, screw-top jars, keys, clockwork toys;
- an *Anglepoise* lamp, angle iron, information books about angled decks on aircraft and angular distance;
- LOGO software and turtle;
- books about pattern;
- computer games of the *Dungeons and Dragons* type;
- thick yarn and rope suitable for plaiting and knotting;
- books showing famous paintings and architecture;
- a pantograph;
- books about the work of M C Escher.

Programme of study: Shape, space and measures

■ 1. Pupils should be given opportunities to:

- **a** use geometric properties and relationships in the solution of problems;
- **b** extend their practical experience using a wide range of mawterials;
- **c** use computers to create and transform shapes;
- **d** consider a wide range of patterns, including some drawn from different cultural traditions;
- **e** apply their measuring skills in a range of purposeful contexts.

For this part of the Programme of study we have set down examples drawn from the body of the book.

- **a** Area of study 5
- **b** Area of study 2
- **c** Area of study 17
- **d** Area of study 11
- **e** Area of study 26

Attainment target 3: Shape, space and measures

Level Descriptions

Level 2

Pupils use mathematical names for common 3-D and 2-D shapes and describe their properties, including numbers of sides and corners. They distinguish between straight and turning movements, understand angle as a measurement of turn, and recognise right angles in turns. They have begun to use everyday non-standard and standard units to measure length and mass.

Level 3

Pupils classify 3-D and 2-D shapes in various ways using mathematical properties such as reflective symmetry. They use non-standard units and standard metric units of length, capacity, mass and time, in a range of contexts.

Level 4

Pupils make 3-D mathematical models by linking given faces or edges, draw common 2-D shapes in different orientations on grids, and identify congruent shapes and orders of rotational symmetry. They reflect simple shapes in a mirror line. They choose and use appropriate units and instruments, interpreting, with appropriate accuracy, numbers on a range of measuring instruments. They find perimeters of simple shapes, find areas by counting squares, and find volumes by counting cubes.

Level 5

When constructing models and when drawing or using shapes, pupils measure and draw angles to the nearest degree, and use language associated with angle. They identify all the symmetries of 2-D shapes. They know the rough metric equivalents of Imperial units still in daily use and convert one metric unit to another. They make sensible estimates of a range of measures in relation to everyday situations.

Shape, space and measures

How Areas of study in this book fit the Programme of study and Attainment target 3: Shape, space and measures level descriptions. Points in the Programme of study		Areas of study and 'best fit' with level descriptions			
		Level description 2	Level description 3	Level description 4	Level description 5
■ 2. **Understanding and using properties of shape**	Pupils should be taught to: **a** visualise and describe shapes and movements, developing precision in using related geometrical language;	1, 2, 3	4, 5, 6		7
	b make 2-D and 3-D shapes and patterns with increasing accuracy, recognise their geometrical features and properties, and use these to classify shapes and solve problems;			8, 9	10
	c understand the congruence of simple shapes; recognise reflective symmetries of 2-D and 3-D shapes, and rotational symmetries of 2-D shapes.		11	12, 13, 14	15
■ 3 **Understanding and using properties of position and movement**	**a** transform 2-D shapes by translation, reflection and rotation, and visualise movements and simple transformations to create and describe patterns;			16	17
	b use co-ordinates to specify location, *eg map references, representation of 2-D shapes*;			18	19
	c use right angles, fractions of a turn and, later, degrees, to measure rotation, and use the associated language.	20		21	22
■ 4 **Understanding and using measures**	**a** choose appropriate standard units of length, mass, capacity and time, and make sensible estimates with them in everyday situations; extend their understanding of the relationship between units; convert one metric unit to another; know the rough metric equivalents of Imperial units still in daily use;	23, 24	25, 26, 27	28, 29	30, 31
	b choose and use appropriate measuring instruments; interpret numbers and read scales to an increasing degree of accuracy;		32	33	
	c find perimeters of simple shapes; find practically the circumferences of circles, being introduced to the ratio π; find areas and volumes by counting methods, leading to the use of other practical methods, *eg dissection*.			34, 35, 36	37, 38

Programme of study: Shape, space and measures

Pupils should be taught to:

■ 2. Understanding and using patterns and properties of shape

a visualise and describe shapes and movements, developing precision in using related geometrical language;

Area of study	P of S	LD
1	2a	2

RECOGNISING AND DESCRIBING 2-D SHAPES

C63 –69

Commentary

The children will already know something of the characteristics of two-dimensional (2-D) shapes. They will be aware of the straight and curved boundaries and the completeness of a given shape.

In working with 2-D shapes it is important that the children continue to have lots of experience of handling and drawing shapes. They will have to come to an understanding of the ways in which shapes can fit together later in their mathematics. Having a good grasp of the characteristics of named 2-D shapes will help with this development.

The children need to be starting to use the characteristics of shapes to identify them in the environment. It is important that they see, for example, triangles in a variety of positions and not always with a horizontal base line and that they meet a variety of different triangles.

Mathematics has its own vocabulary and 2-D shapes have a variety of names. The children should be learning to use the appropriate vocabulary for the shapes they are working with.

Activity 1: Squares and rectangles

Assemble a collection of quadrilaterals, including a variety of irregular ones, squares of varying sizes and rectangles of varying sizes. Tell the children that *quadr* means four, and that all the shapes in the collection are called *quadrilaterals*. They should have no trouble in declaring why this is so.

Now select a rectangle from the collection. Ask the children to pick out a shape that is similar. Tell the children that this is a special quadrilateral, called a rectangle. Find and set out all the rectangles from the collection. Ask the children what they can say about rectangles. They may note that the rectangles have two sets of matching sides and four matching corners.

Now do the same with a square. If squares were included in the rectangle set, they may have been eliminated in the discussion of sides. Tell the children a square is a special kind of rectangle and the children will be able to compare the sides of a rectangle with the sides of a square.

The children can build up a cast of characters for a shape identification parade, by drawing round some shapes to make Suky Square and Roddy Rectangle.

Copymaster 63 is a suggested cover for a shape book to which subsequent copymasters (and other work) can be added. Shapes have been drawn on this cover sheet. Suky Square and Roddy Rectangle have been drawn in. The children can, if you wish, add features and names to the remaining shapes. If stapled together on the left the book could form part of a child's work portfolio. **Copymaster 64** has some facts about quadrilaterals and invites children to say where they see them. **Copymaster 65** helps children pick out rectangles and squares.

Activity 2: Circles

Get the children to identify circles from a collection containing circles and ovals. Add Celia Circle to the shape collection.

Copymaster 66 invites the children to look for circles and ovals.

Activity 3: Triangles

Cut out a collection of triangles. Make sure you include not only acute-angled, equilateral, isosceles and right-angled ones, but also some with obtuse angles.

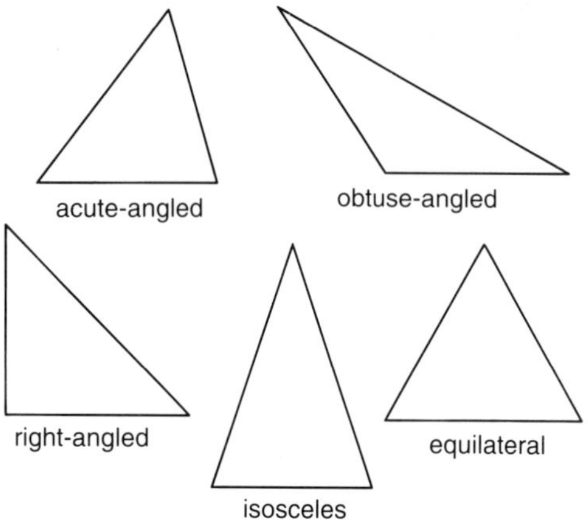

Make up a mixed set of shapes, including some from the previous Activities, and let the children identify the triangles. Discuss the key property (three sides) and the meaning of *tri*. Let the children draw and name their triangle character.

Copymaster 67 has triangle information on it and asks the children to look for triangles around them.

Activity 4: Hexagons and pentagons
Assembling a grand collection of some of all the shapes you have used so far, add some irregular polygons and some hexagons and pentagons. Let the children discuss, name and match the shapes, and tell them why they are so-called.

Add Harry Hexagon and Poppy Pentagon to the shape character list.

Copymaster 68 depicts and discusses hexagons and pentagons. **Copymaster 69** offers the children a chance to answer questions about the characteristics of 2-D shapes.

Activity 5: The concept of right angle
Show the children a square or rectangle template and point out the right-angled corners.

With the children's help, make a little collection of things or pictures of things that can have right angles, for example, arms and legs at elbows and knees, desk lamps, set squares, paper corners and hinges. See what other things the children can add to this list. Set up a little display in the corner of the room (itself a right angle).

Right angles on display

Activity 6: Right angles in 2-D shapes
Using the collection of 2-D shapes once again, let the children find the right angles in the squares, rectangles and right-angled triangles.

Area of study 2 | P of S 2a | LD 2

RECOGNISING AND DESCRIBING 3-D SHAPES

C70, 71

Commentary
Ours is a 3-D world. The children will already know something of the characteristics of these shapes. In working with them it is important that the children continue to have lots of experience of handling and making shapes.

Begin in the classroom, school and its immediate environment and look for shapes, both man-made and natural. Then the children can pore over diagrams and photographs, and finally start to deal with mathematical abstractions.

There are, in fact, only five regular 3-D shapes. By *regular* is meant that the faces of these shapes are all equal regular polygons. We do not intend that you should teach the children these shapes, but it is important to see the direction of some aspects of 3-D work. The regular solids are:

Cube
Six faces, each face being a square. Three faces meet at each corner or vertex.

Tetrahedron
Four faces, each face being an equilateral triangle. Three faces meet at each vertex.

Octahedron
Eight faces, each face being an equilateral triangle. Four faces meet at each vertex. (A regular octahedron can be made by sticking together two identical square-based pyramids which have triangular faces that are equilateral.)

Icosahedron
20 faces, each face being an equilateral triangle. Five faces meet at each vertex.

Dodecahedron
12 faces, each face being a pentagon. Three faces meet at each vertex.

A sphere shares with the regular solids the characteristic that its shape does not change, you just get larger or smaller versions of spheres; but spheres do not have plane faces. When you take a section across a sphere the plane cut is always a circle.

Activity 1: Cubes and cuboids
Find out from the children if they know of anything that is shaped like a cube or cuboid. If they do, you may be able to go straight on to giving the children an assignment to find three cuboids in the junk model box or two cubes on teacher's desk, and write what they are. If the children are uncertain you need to produce a cube and a cuboid and then help them list some things they know conform to these shapes. The lists may run something like this:

- cubes – ice, sugar, stock cube, die;
- cuboids – house, box, suitcase, door, notice board, table top.

Then assemble a collection the children can handle, for example, you could draw out from a large box (itself a cuboid) a number of dice; food boxes, like cereal and chocolate boxes; matchboxes; an empty ice tray (shows the cube shape the ice would be); dominoes; and boxes which once held kitchen foil or greaseproof paper.

Give the children the mathematical vocabulary for the discussion and talk about the shapes, for example, they need 'face', 'edge', 'corner' or 'vertex'. Count how many faces there are on the shapes. Cut up a box so that it lies flat and count the faces again.

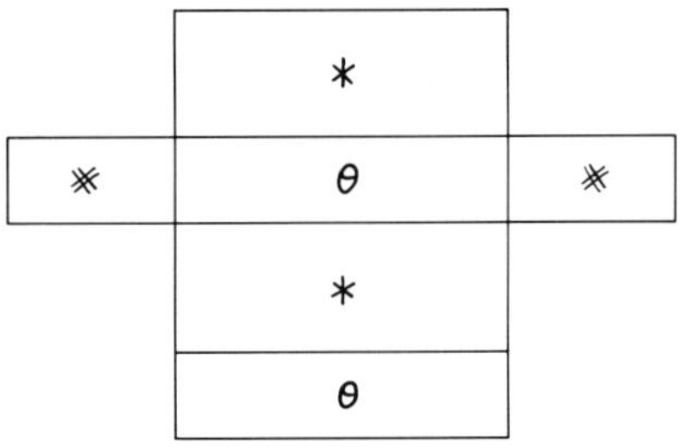

Let the children cut open a box and stick it onto a sheet of paper before counting the faces and noting other characteristics.

Copymaster 70 is a record sheet about cubes and cuboids.

Activity 2: Cylinders
The children can help you list the things that come in a cylindrical shape. Stick their results onto a giant cylinder (or corrugated card Greek column). The list may include the following:

- telescope;
- worm;
- garden hose;
- vacuum cleaner nozzle;
- broom handle;
- kitchen cleaner container;
- coin;
- toilet roll;
- pencil.

(Be careful with chimney pots, most are truncated cones.)

See if the children can identify and name the shapes of the faces of a cylinder. If they are in any doubt, you can cut one open and demonstrate that the faces are two circles and a rectangle.

Copymaster 71 is for the children to record what they know about cylinders and where to find them.

Activity 3: Spheres
For this Activity you need a globe, an orange, a ball, a marble and anything else you have to hand that is spherical. Before you show any of these things to the children, establish what they can name as spherical. (In fact the world is not quite, but almost spherical.) Do not get trapped into trying to identify the properties of a sphere at this stage. It is enough that the children should recognise and name it.

Activity 4: Mathematics apparatus
Allow the children to inspect and experiment with 3-D shape apparatus available in school. You may have, for example, wooden construction blocks, Poleidoblocs©, and Artstraws© and Constructo-straws© for making nets.

Area of study 3 | P of S 2a | LD 2 | RIGHT ANGLES IN 2-D AND 3-D SHAPES | C72

Commentary
Right angles are commonplace in our everyday lives. The right angle is part of a complete rotation. It is a quarter turn and two of them make a straight line. From the early days, in the mathematics of Shape and space right angles and straight lines have been of central significance.

Right angles are important in a variety of settings including our understanding of structures, telling the time, and understanding the vertical height of objects.

Activity 1: Fold and compare
Let the children fold a scrap piece of paper roughly in half to give a straight edge at the fold. If they fold the paper again, this time carefully, they can make a right angle at the corner.

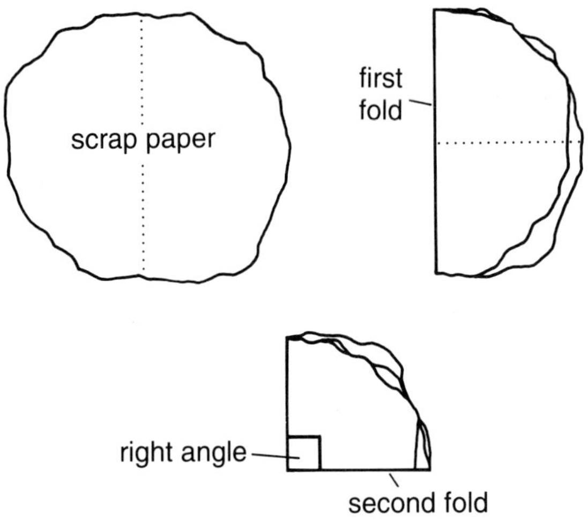

The children can compare this right angle against things around the room and report back to you all the right angles they find.

Activity 2: Corners
If the children have not tried Activity 5 in 'Recognising and describing 2-D shape' this would be a good introduction to right angles. Look with the children at the corners of the 3-D shapes you have used in Activities 1–4 in 'Recognising and describing 3-D shapes', and establish which ones are right angles.

Activity 3: Stick men
Let the children use a set square or a square or rectangle template to draw some right angles. They could turn them into little stick men.

Copymaster 72 has a series of angles on it and the children are required to identify the right angles and make them into stick men.

Area of study 4 | P of S 2a | LD 3

SORTING 2-D SHAPES

C73

Commentary
At this Level the children should be using the knowledge they have about particular characteristics, such as straight lines, right angles, curves and physical measurements, to be able to sort shapes into different categories on the basis of choices which they can explain.

Activity 1: Detecting a sort
With a group of children looking on, and using a collection of irregular polygons and regular shapes, do some sorts and challenge the children to detect the criteria you have used. This will remind them of many of the attributes of shapes which they need to take cognisance of in mathematics.

Let the children make sorts and detect the criteria their classmates have used.

Activity 2: Sorting challenges
Set the children some sorting challenges which they can undertake, either independently or one at a time while others look on. You may include in this bank of challenges tasks such as the following:

- Take a collection of triangles and see how many sorts you can do within triangles (apart from colour). Some children should be able to sort, for example, the equilateral, isosceles, right-angled and obtuse-angled from the rest, in separate sorts.
- Take a collection of quadrilaterals. How many sorts can you do within this set, apart from colour?
- Ring the sets of shapes on a worksheet and tick why they are sets.
- Draw round shape templates to make a set with an 'odd one out'. Challenge a partner to say which it is and why.

Copymaster 73 presents a sorts quiz.

Area of study 5 | P of S 2a | LD 3

IDENTIFYING AND SORTING 3-D SHAPES

Commentary
As with 2-D shapes the children should now be able to sort a range of 3-D shapes on the basis of stated characteristics. Include at this Level prisms and pyramids.

We live in a 3-D world and opportunities should be taken to consider both living and non-living examples of 3-D shapes. This means isolating general 3-D shapes in a group of shapes. For example, a house may be seen as a cuboid with a triangular prism on top.

Activity 1: Prisms and pyramids
Show the children some prisms including those with triangular and hexagonal bases, and a square-based pyramid. Name them, let the children handle them and discuss their characteristics.

Activity 2: Detecting a sort
Using a collection of cartons and containers and/or a collection of commercially-produced mathematical shapes, including cubes, cuboids, cylinders, cones, prisms and pyramids, do some sorts for the children to inspect and comment on.

Let the children do their own sorts and comment on one another's work. This will help them to become confident about the characteristics of 3-D shapes.

Activity 3: Sorting shapes in the built environment
Ask the children to look at all the school buildings and the buildings that can be seen from school and sort all the shapes they can see. They may like to present their findings as a shape 'picture'. It may look something like this.

It may be easier for some children to match the shapes they can see in buildings with those in a box of mathematics apparatus. They can then set the shapes out on a piece of paper which represents the ground beneath the school and neighbouring buildings.

Activity 4: Shapes at home
Show the children two items that belong in the kitchen and have an easily recognised shape. For example, you may show a rolling pin and a container of

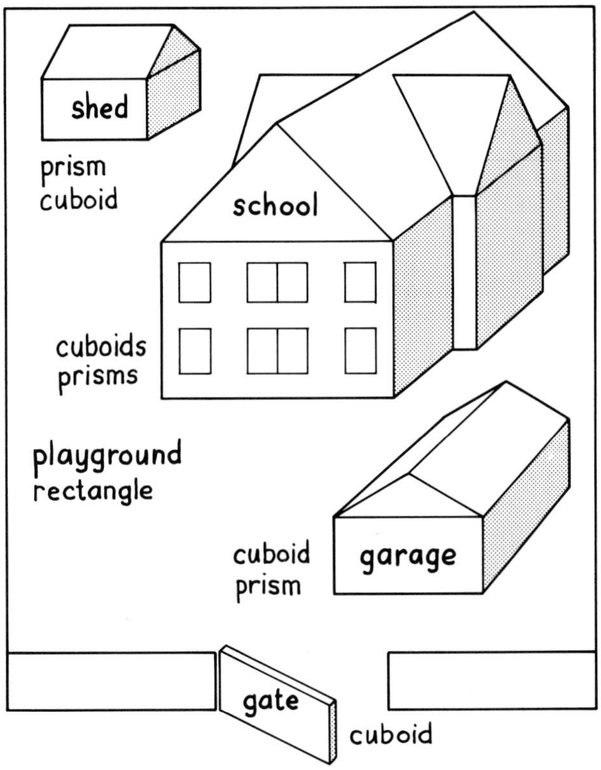

powder cleaner. See if they can identify these as cylinders. Ask them to look at home for more things in the kitchen that have a distinctive shape.

Fill a kitchen-shaped list with these items in shape groups. Then add another room, until the children have identified hosts of items of various shapes from all over the house. Display the lists.

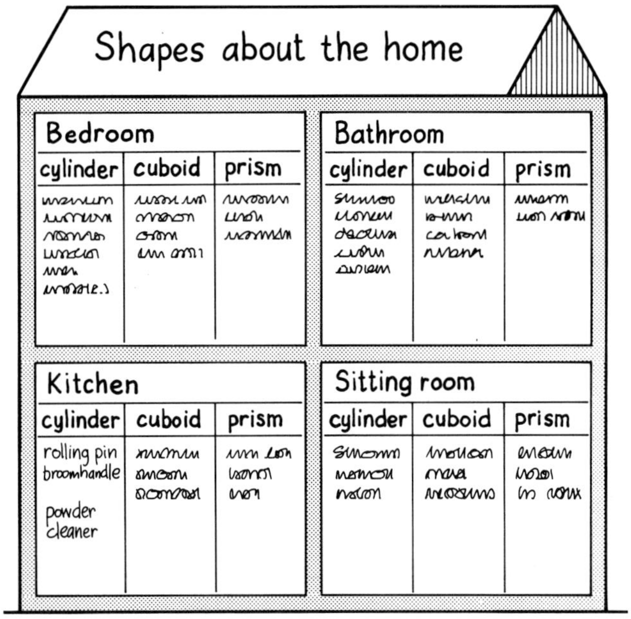

Activity 5: Shape in everyday expressions

Ask the children to help you collect sayings and expressions that use the vocabulary of Shape and space in the wording. Discuss what we mean when we say them. Here are some examples:

- 'It is as broad as it is long.'
- 'Rounding off . . .'
- 'Get to the point.'
- 'Keep to the straight and narrow.'
- 'There is no side to her.'
- 'I'm on edge.'

Area of study 6 | P of S 2a | LD 3

LOGO

Commentary

LOGO is widely and readily available in a number of forms. Your LEA will be able to help if, for any reason, you do not have a version of LOGO already available in school.

LOGO is an environment within which you and the children can readily create a myriad of opportunities and responses, patterns and drawings, problems and solutions. There are programmable robots which use LOGO ideas as well as computer-based LOGO packages.

To use LOGO successfully the children will need to have a notion of angle and know about right angles.

Activity 1: Pre-LOGO

Using groups of children as the first resource, working in the hall, choose a child from each group to be a robot. Let the remaining children give the robot instructions to allow him or her to move across the hall, without touching obstacles like chairs or crossing barriers like skipping ropes that you have set up beforehand.

Activity 2: Introducing LOGO

Using a commercially-produced electronic robot, allow the children to let it trace pathways across the hall. If you have a robot with a pen attachment, it can record the path taken – providing you have paper on the floor!

Activity 3: Computer-based LOGO

Using a software package, or computer chip, attempt to produce a set of regular two-dimensional shapes using a routine. For example, a square can be produced using a routine like this one:

```
TO SQUARE
REPEAT 4 [FD 200 RT 90]
END
```

FD 200 means forward 200 tiny steps and RT 90 means turn right through 90°.

Use the shapes to construct some pictures which can be printed out and displayed.

Area of study 7 | P of S 2a | LD 5

PROPERTIES OF LINES AND SHAPES

C74

Commentary
This is a chance for children to demonstrate their, by now, prodigious knowledge of the properties of shapes. The language of angle can now be married to that knowledge to give children a repertoire of concepts with which to identify, describe, and explain.

Activity 4 on Euler's relation is an opportunity to explore some aspects of 3-D shapes which links to Algebra and Handling data and supports a revision of important characteristics of those 3-D shapes.

Activity 1: Lines and angles
Explore the angles in a variety of shapes and in the juxtaposition of lines.

Let the children demonstrate that the angles of an acute-angled triangle add up to 180° by cutting out a paper triangle, cutting off the corners and sticking the corners together.

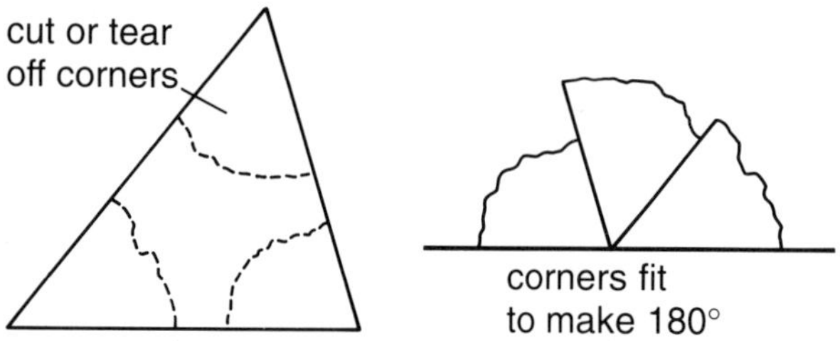

Then let the children do the same experiment with the corners of a quadrilateral, to find they make 360° together.

Get the children to draw pairs of lines which intersect and then get them to measure the opposite angles.

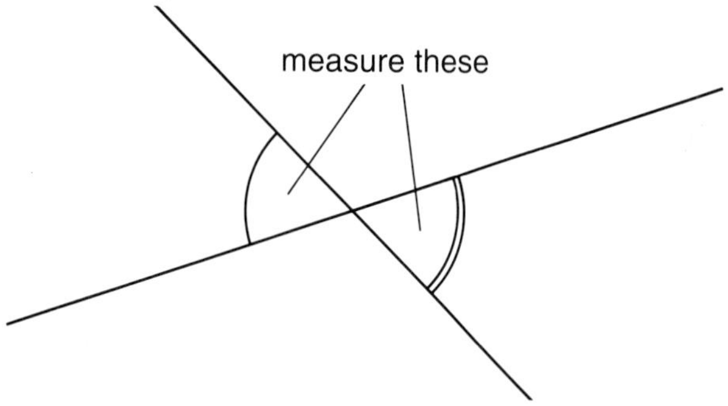

Get the children to construct a parallelogram using only a ruler and a pair of compasses.

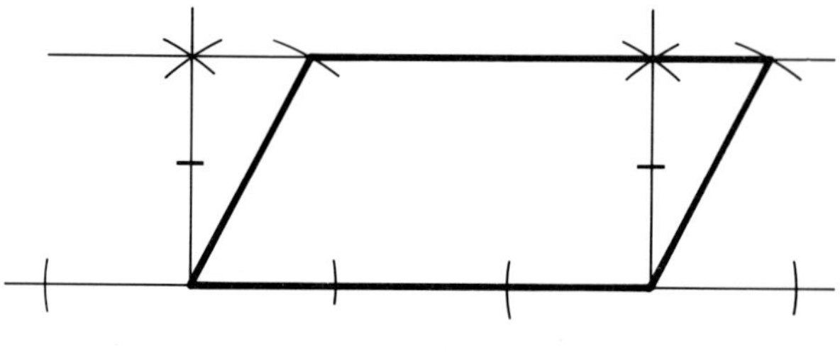

Discuss all of these investigations with the children in groups or as a class. Help the children to develop generalisable statements about what they have observed.

Activity 2: Explain yourself!
Let children do some talking about shapes around them and the shapes and lines in geometric art and design, using the knowledge gleaned in Activity 1 as well as what they know from their work at earlier Levels.

Ask them to set themselves a design challenge and carry it through. For example, they could decide to design and describe a hexagonal badge or do a repeat pattern involving parallel lines and acute angles. Let the children make a verbal presentation about their intentions and the outcomes to the class, before displaying designs and descriptions. Again relate this to your technology work.

Copymaster 74 is a design and record sheet for a challenge.

Activity 3: The pentagram
A number of shapes are intrinsically interesting and their exploration can inform, excite and consolidate children's knowledge and understanding. The pentagram offers such possibilities. Get the children to construct a regular pentagon and then draw in all of its diagonals (how many?) and they will see that there is a smaller pentagon in the centre. The star shape that is formed is knows as a *pentagram* and it was used as the symbol for the society formed by Pythagoras and his followers. Try exploring other shapes, such as the Star of David and the Maltese Cross.

Activity 4: Euler's relation
Get the children to record in tabular form the numbers of faces, vertices and edges of a variety of 3-D shapes. These should include square-based pyramids and prisms as well as the regular solids. By observation, the children should come to see that the number of edges is always greater than the numbers of faces or vertices. Try plotting a graph of faces plus vertices, against edges. This should help towards the discovery of Euler's relation, which is:

$$F + V = E + 2$$

where F is faces, V is vertices and E is edges.

Activity 5: Using a clinometer
Use clinometers to measure the angles of elevation of a number of objects, such as trees and buildings. Doing this and producing diagrams from which to arrive at an estimate of vertical height for the chosen objects is a good vehicle for discussion and the pulling together of a number of areas of Shape and space.

Commercially-produced clinometers are quite suitable, but if you want to use the making of a clinometer as part of your technology work then there are a number of ways of doing this. Get the children to seek out ideas and information from reference books and invite a surveyor into your classroom to talk about the ways in which surveying instruments are used. The children will have to learn about plumb lines and the vertical, how to read off the appropriate angle and the measurement of horizontal distance. They will also have to do work on scale and relate this to location work.

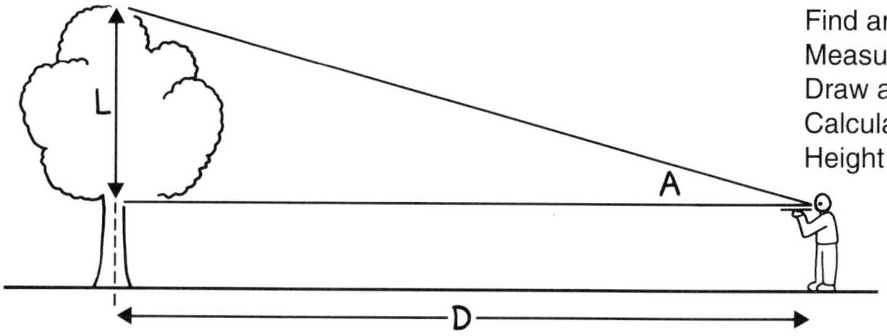

Programme of study: Shape, space and measures

Pupils should be taught to:

■ 2. Understanding and using patterns and properties of shape

b make 2-D and 3-D shapes and patterns with increasing accuracy, recognise their geometrical features and properties, and use these to classify shapes and solve problems;

Area of study 8 | P of S 2b | LD 4

CONSTRUCTING 2-D SHAPES

Commentary

At this Level the children have to learn to construct 2-D shapes using compasses, protractors and set-squares. The most accurate constructions come from the use of compasses.

In order to progress to the construction of accurate 3-D shapes the children will need to master the construction of common 2-D shapes, such as squares, rectangles and equilateral triangles, as well as be able to produce circles.

Activity 1: 2-D shapes using a ruler

Make sure the children have access to a good ruler each (that is one that really does enable them to produce a straight line). Let them inspect it and really look at where the measurements start because many rulers have about 1 cm at the end unmarked and some children may not yet have realised this. To give children practice in producing some straight-sided shapes let them use their rulers on squared, dotty and plain paper. Over a number of sessions, invite them to draw a variety of squares, rectangles and triangles. You may need to discuss the best position to put pressure on the ruler to hold it still and the angle at which to hold a pencil, for success. Discuss also the accuracy with which they can draw specified shapes using only a ruler, including, for example, the children's ideas about why an equilateral triangle poses problems.

Activity 2: 2-D shapes using a protractor

Add a lesson on how to use a protractor to the mastery of the ruler gained in Activity 1. Show the children how the protractor enables more accurate drawing and checking of angles. Move from squared paper to plain in order to help the children see the particular needs and demands of accurate construction.

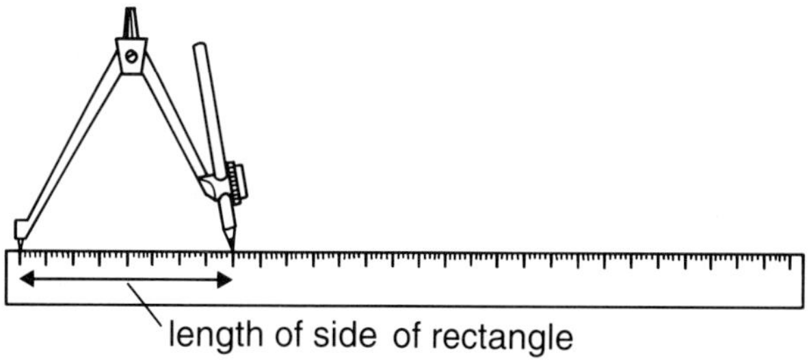

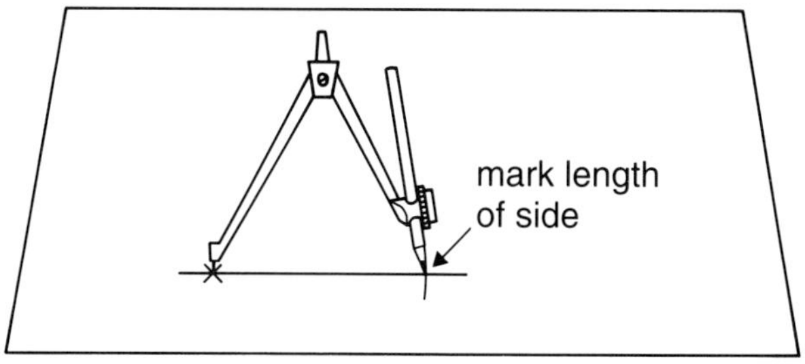

Activity 3: 2-D shapes using compasses

When the children are familiar with rulers and protractors (Activities 1 and 2) show them the skills necessary in using compasses safely. Tell the children that this is the most accurate way we have of drawing circles and other 2-D shapes using pencil and paper. (Some computer drawing packages can be used to produce very accurate drawings.) Show the children how to, for example, extend their compasses to the length of a side of a rectangle or triangle using a ruler, and then transfer this to their drawing.

Activity 4: 'Line' vocabulary
In mathematics and in art sessions use and demonstrate the labels we apply to lines. Show the children horizontal, vertical, parallel and perpendicular.

Test their understanding in a dance session by using this vocabulary in getting them to take up positions.

Area of study 9 | P of S 2b | LD 4

CONSTRUCTING 3-D SHAPES

Commentary
There are three processes which the children will have to be able to engage in, in order to construct accurately a named 3-D shape. These are addressed again at Level 5 when the children should be able to construct angles accurately. The processes are the construction of appropriate 2-D shapes, the physical construction of the 3-D shape, and the translation of a 3-D shape into its 2-D net (and vice versa). A *net* is a diagram showing all the faces of a 3-D shape. A folded net makes the corresponding 3-D shape.

The regular 3-D shapes that the children will need to make are cubes, square-based pyramids and prisms.

Activity 1: Cubes
If the children have not had the opportunity to handle solid cubes and make nets of them rectify this now. Make available dice, boxes, sugar cubes, stock cubes, wooden or plastic construction blocks and other examples the children bring in. Open out and flatten some boxes to see how they are made.

Let the children use drinking straws and Plasticine, card strips, craft straws, and pipecleaners to make nets of cubes.

Activity 2: Wrap it up!
Using regular shapes, ask the children what the box would look like that accommodated an object of unusual shape. For example, they may say that a hot water bottle may best fit in a shallow cuboid with an elliptical cylinder to accommodate the neck! Here are some more suggested objects:

- a trophy cup;
- a coil of hose;
- a tea pot;
- a suit of armour;
- a dolls' house.

Supply the children with a vast array of supermarket packaging, strong adhesive tape, scissors and glue. Using their skills at drawing shapes they can draw and create boxes of the shapes they have suggested.

Activity 3: Square-based pyramids and prisms
Show the children a pyramid block and some prism blocks from a school set of accurate mathematics apparatus (Poleidoblocs© is one example). Discuss the attributes of these shapes and let the children make nets as in Activity 1.

Activity 4: Polyominoes
These are shapes made from squares. Using from two to six squares you can make the following:

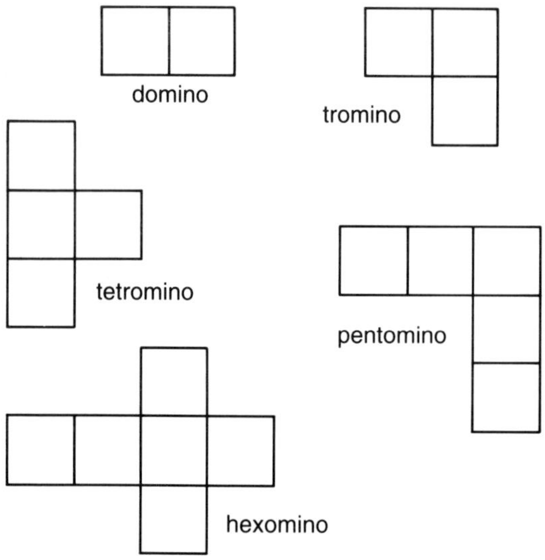

Get the children to work out how many different arrangements of three, four, five and six squares can be made (the domino has only one arrangement). You will have to discuss the rules that we might operate. For example, do we allow mirror images or do they count as only one arrangement? Opposite is the set of 12 pentominoes. The numbers of arrangements for the others are:

- tromino 3
- tetromino 5
- hexomino 35.

Get the children to use their pentominoes for three different investigations to answer the following questions:

- Can you produce some tessellating patterns?
- Which of the pentominoes are a net for an open-topped box?
- Can you make different-sized rectangles using your pentominoes by combining different ones? (Each pentomino to be used once only.) What is the smallest? Largest?

For some children it might be appropriate to go onto hexomino investigations where, for example, some of them are nets for cubes.

Area of study 10 | P of S 2b | LD 5

2-D REPRESENTATIONS OF 3-D SHAPES

RC6–9

Commentary
In making 2-D representations of 3-D shapes we are dealing with an important skill which is to do with perception and our ability to visualise solid objects.

Two-dimensional representations can illustrate some mathematical connections that are not readily seen otherwise. For example, the overall outline of a cube drawn on triangular dotty paper is a hexagon and there are connections between hexagonal numbers and cubes.

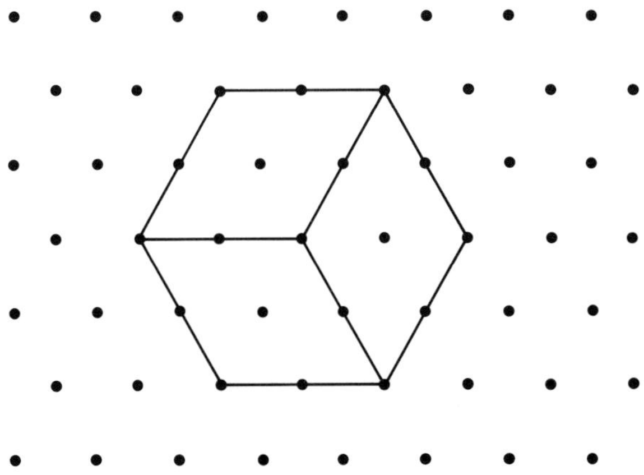

Make use of dotty papers as well as isometric paper with lines.

Activity 1: 'Doodles'
Give the children a variety of dotty and ruled papers and a collection of 3-D shapes, either made by themselves or manufactured. Invite the children to sketch shapes on the papers, using the lines or dots as a guide to depict some of these 3-D shapes. Discuss their efforts and display the attempts so that the children can look at them again and again. Challenge the children to try drawing some really difficult shapes, such as a tetrahedron. Some of the sketches might be appropriate for constructing the depicted 3-D object. Challenge the children to see if this is possible.

Resource copymasters 6–9 present a range of dotty and isometric papers.

Activity 2: Illustrations and blueprints
With the children make a collection of books and magazines in which there are examples of the 2-D representation of 3-D shapes. See if a local engineering or building firm has drawings which you could borrow. Approach the local secondary school design and technology department for any resources they might be able to lend.

Activity 3: Perspective
You can extend this work by looking at the ways in which artists depict 3-D objects using perspective. Make a collection of postcards of paintings which exhibit clear perspective – usually architectural. Discuss these and have a go at producing drawings which start with lines drawn to a vanishing point. Artists also use tones and hues to draw the eye into a picture.

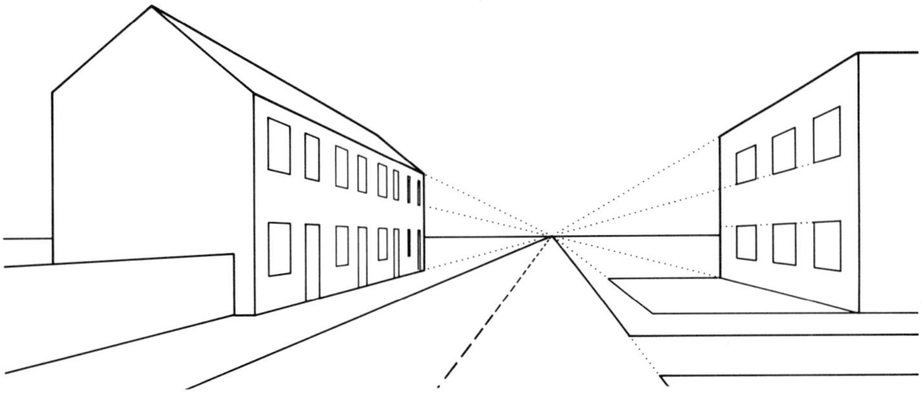

Programme of study: Shape, space and measures

Pupils should be taught to:

■ **2. Understanding and using patterns and properties of shape**

c understand the congruence of simple shapes; recognise reflective symmetries of 2-D and 3-D shapes, and rotational symmetries of 2-D shapes.

Area of study	P of S	LD
11	2c	3

REFLECTIVE SYMMETRY

Commentary

Reflective symmetry is about a balance in which two halves look alike and is sometimes called line symmetry or mirror symmetry.

Reflective symmetry is often used in design and exists, in broad terms, in many natural objects including plants and animals.

In order to fully appreciate and discuss reflective symmetry children have to be able to distinguish left from right. They should be able to do this at this stage, but if they cannot then an exploration of reflective symmetry will help.

Activity 1: Making pictures that 'match'

Make one fold across pieces of paper. Let the children produce pictures with matching halves by using a variety of media, including, for example, water colour paint and washable inks (ink blot 'butterflies'), sticky shapes and cut patterns. Start a display which can be added to with the results of subsequent Activities.

Activity 2: Symmetry in letters

Ask the children to see what happens when a 'safe' plastic mirror is placed on a picture of their own initial. Record which letters have reflective symmetry. A, B, D, E, H, I, K, M, O, T, U, V, W, X, Y all can have at least one axis of symmetry, depending on how they are written and whether the mirror is used vertically or horizontally.

Activity 3: Symmetry in numbers

Repeat Activity 2 using numerals. Numbers with two, four or more digits can be produced using mirror play.

Activity 4: Lines of symmetry in 2-D shapes

Using accurately-produced templates, let the children try to find 2-D shapes that display reflective symmetry.

Activity 5: Planes of symmetry in 3-D shapes

This can prove more difficult to understand than axes of symmetry. Try using construction straws and other aids to produce nets for shapes, so that a sheet of paper can be placed inside the shape to show where the plane of symmetry lies.

Try cutting a matchbox, a cuboid of cheese, an apple, a stock cube, a marshmallow and other shapes into halves so that the children can see the planes of symmetry.

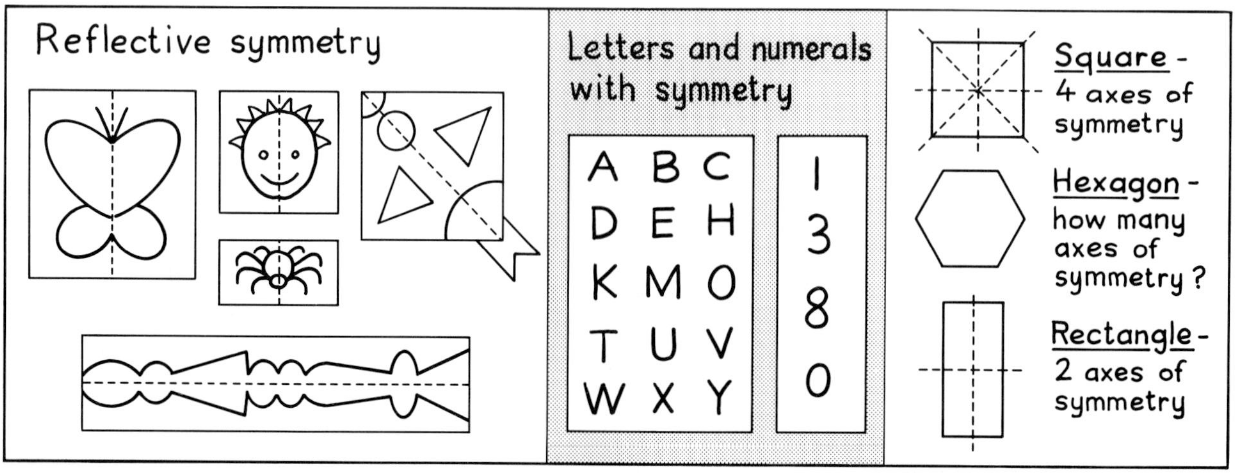

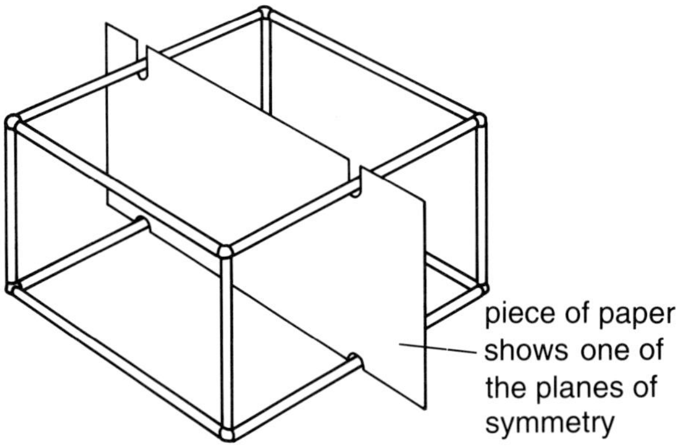

Display the results of your own and the children's efforts in Activities 2–4 alongside those they may have done in Activity 1.

Activity 6: 'Copycat' dances
Let the children work in pairs to produce 'mirror dancing' where one child is the dancer and the other the reflection in a mirror.

Activity 7: Pattern and culture
Investigate the use of patterns which demonstrate reflective symmetry in other cultures. You may have children in the class, who because of their family links or their travels, have books or artefacts that show the kinds of patterns in use in other cultures, either now or in the past. Use these as your first resource. If the school library cannot yield a range of resources, select one set of cultural traditions to investigate and assemble plenty of examples before you begin. Some examples, where children can produce fairly simple near copies of patterns with reflective symmetry, include:

- Islamic patterns;
- North American Indian art.

Area of study 12 | P of S 2c | LD 4

CONGRUENCE

C75

Commentary
Congruence in shapes means shapes are identical except in their location. So, if there are two equilateral triangles on a sheet of paper and by cutting one out you can exactly place it over the other then the triangles are *congruent.*

Some confusions can arise with the fact that shapes can be similar without being congruent. For example, two squares are similar in that they are both squares but they will not be congruent unless the lengths of their sides are the same.

Some shapes are always *similar*. These include squares, equilateral triangles, cubes and circles. But rectangles, isosceles triangles, cuboids and ellipses are not necessarily similar in that their dimensions need not be in the same ratio.

Activity 1: Sorting for similarity/congruence
Set out a collection of 2-D shapes and some 3-D shapes. Allow the children to sort them into sets of 'similar' and then into sets of 'congruent'.

Copymaster 75 is suitable for testing the children's understanding of similarity and congruence.

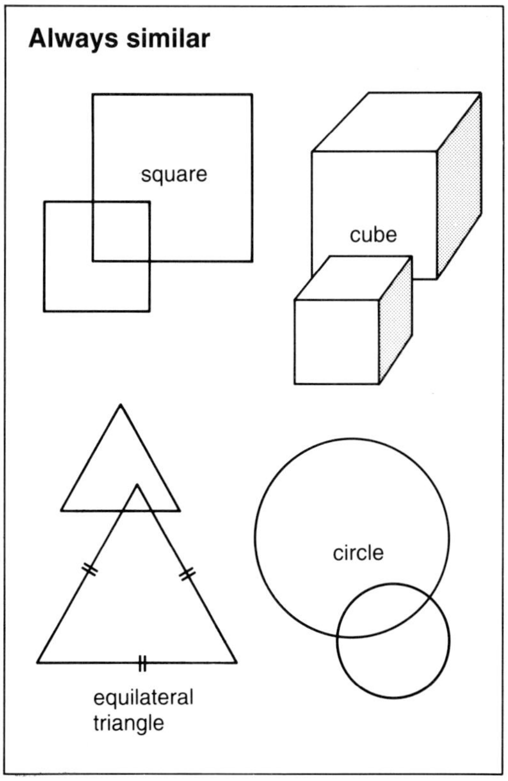

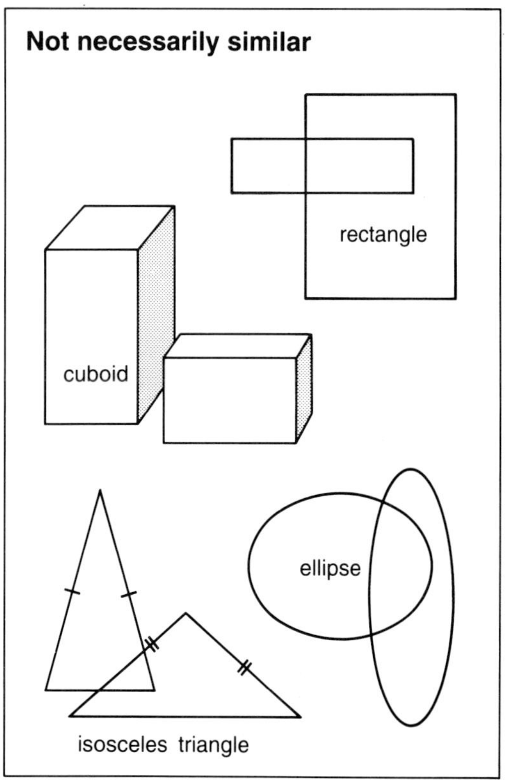

Activity 2: Making shapes
Polyominoes were made using combinations of congruent squares in Area of study 9: Constructing 3-D shapes. Now try making other named shapes using congruent basic shapes. For example, a trapezium can be made from equilateral triangles.

Try making squares, parallelograms and hexagons. Are there shapes that cannot be made in this way? You can link this work to the use of turtle graphics as well as symmetry and tessellations.

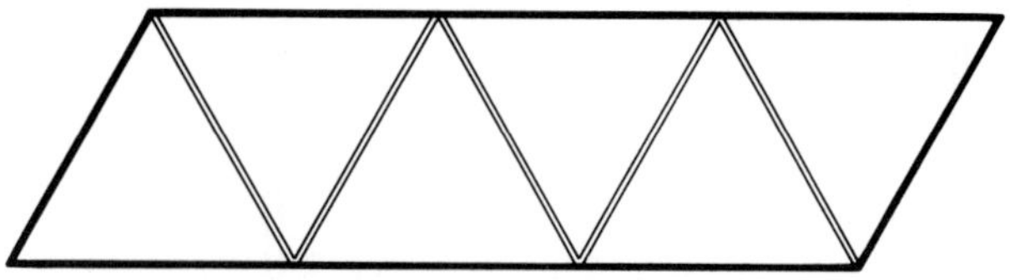

Area of study 13 | P of S 2c | LD 4

LINE SYMMETRY

C76

Commentary
This work builds on the broad experiences of reflective symmetry that the children had at Level 3.

As the children carry out work in this area it may be that they translate lines of symmetry in relation to 2-D shapes into a discussion of planes of symmetry in 3-D shapes.

Activity 1: Mirror play
Let the children play with some safe plastic plane mirrors. Give them challenges. Here are some suggestions:

- What happens when you put a mirror on the nose of a photo of yourself?
- Can you make a full 'man' from a half drawing of a man?
- What can you draw that makes a complete button or pair of trousers when you use a mirror?

Copymaster 76 has some pictures for mirror play.

Activity 2: Badges and emblems
Lots of badges, emblems and flags display line symmetry. Make a collection of these with the children. Then get them to design some of their own badges.

Activity 3: Music making
All composers use scales and arpeggios in their compositions. These have a sort of symmetry about them. Try getting the children to write simple tunes for the recorder and then, using a mirror if necessary, repeat the notes in the reverse order. See how their efforts sound.

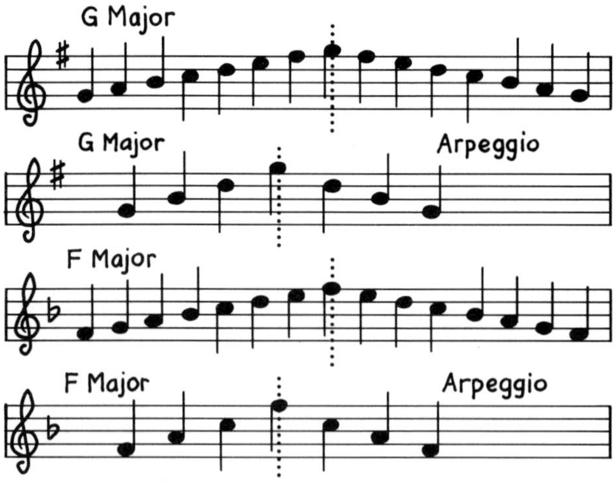

Let the children compose symmetrical tunes like this.

Area of study 4 | P of S 2c | LD 4

ROTATIONAL SYMMETRY

RC1,3 4,6 | C77

Commentary
By now the children should be familiar with the qualities of reflective symmetry and these experiences can be used in a discussion of rotational symmetry.

A shape or pattern shows *rotational symmetry* if it can be rotated, completely or in part, so as to look the same as in the original position.

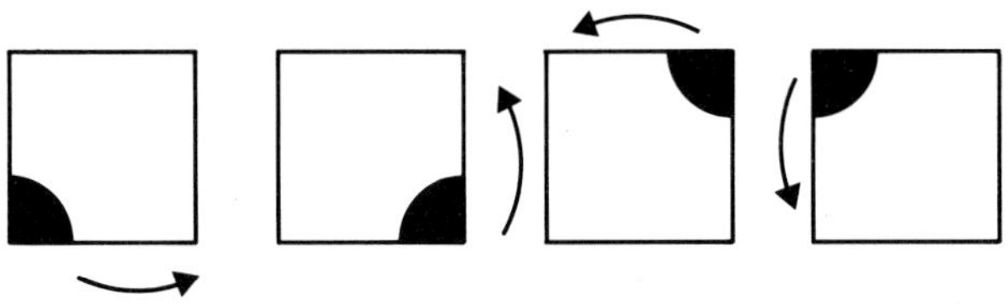

Combinations of both reflective and rotational symmetry can be found in the design of such things as needlepoint, wallpaper, fabrics and architectural decoration. It is worth stressing the aesthetics as well as the mathematics of such patterns.

Activity 1: Looking for rotational symmetry
Tell the children what rotational symmetry is and then let them look around for shapes and objects that demonstrate it. For example, it can be seen in some fruits (cut crosswise), some flowers, the king and queen in a set of playing cards and the letter S. Some shapes have only one rotational match, others six or more.

Copymaster 77 has some shapes on it and children are required to identify where there is rotational symmetry.

Activity 2: Creating rotational symmetry
Let the children fold squares of paper into four and circles into six, make little snips out of the folded paper across the folds and then when opened out the shapes will demonstrate rotational symmetry.

Draw some experimental shapes on squared or dotty paper, repeat them about the paper and see if a pattern showing rotational symmetry can be produced.

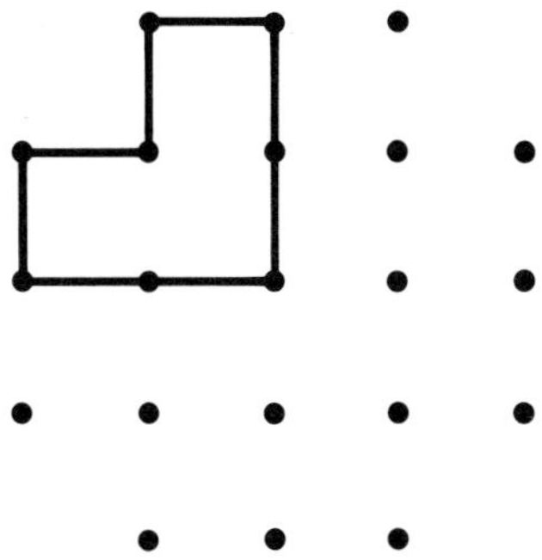

Resource copymasters 1, 3 and **4** are squared paper and **resource copymaster 6** is a sheet of dotty paper.

Area of study	P of S	LD	
15	2c	5	**SYMMETRY** C78

Commentary
Refer to Level 4 Activities too because this Section is about consolidation of symmetry ideas.

Activity 1: A symmetry resource box
With the children's help create a symmetry resource box. It could contain some of the following:

- postcards showing paintings and designs from our own and other cultures (some of them may show reflective, some rotational and some no symmetry);
- regular-shaped templates;
- decorated numerals and letters;
- cut paper patterns and instructions for making them;
- a plastic mirror or take-away meal lid;
- a challenge sheet setting out ideas about where to look for and experiment with symmetry, for example, in composing music and dance routines and pattern making in technology, art and design;
- found objects, such as shells, rock crystals and pebbles;
- dried flowers and leaves, and drawings of sections of fruits;
- other things the children suggest and contribute.

Many of the items can be stored in a folder or file with transparent pockets, or stuck on card under coverfilm. The box could form an invaluable resource for the class or central resourcing. It could be shared with parallel or adjacent classes or the children could make one each to keep.

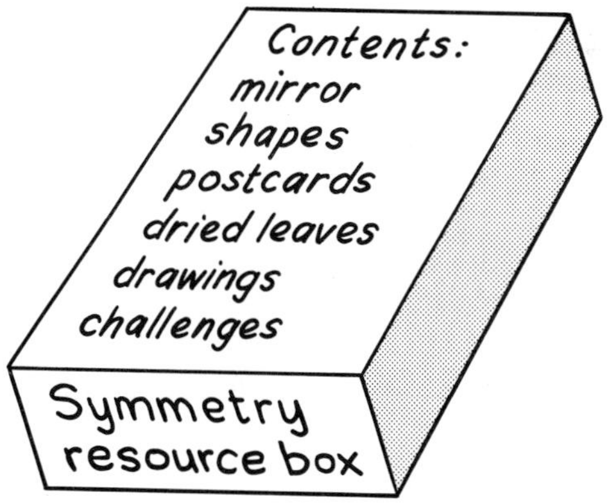

Activity 2: A symmetry trail
Set the children a trail route around the school and other classrooms, and let them list all those things they spot that show symmetry. For example, there may be rectangular notice-boards everywhere so they can count these as one, wherever they spot them. A chart can be created as shown on page 70.

Use the data the children have collected in a variety of ways to match tasks in AT5. They can offer this particular mathematics trail to other classes.

Copymaster 78 presents a collection sheet for this kind of data.

	What seen	Where	Shapes noted	Kind(s) of symmetry	Discussion lines/planes etc.
example entry	Notice board	Hallway	Rectangle	Reflective Rotational	2 axes 2 positions

Programme of study: Shape, space and measures

Pupils should be taught to:

■ **3. Understanding and using properties of position and movement**	**a**	transform 2-D shapes by translation, reflection and rotation, and visualise movements and simple transformations to create and describe patterns;

Area of study 16 | P of S 3a | LD 4

TILE PATTERNS

Commentary

For centuries tiles have been used to decorate, both inside and outside buildings. The design of such tiles has always attracted the mathematician. A simple design on a template tile can be made into an intricate and complex pattern by reflection, rotation and transformation. Link this work to commercially produced mathematical 'MATS'.

Activity 1: Tiles and logos

For this Activity you can build on the work done on badges and emblems in line symmetry. Using a square, get the children to design a symmetrical pattern inside the square which displays rotation. Using the square as a template make a pattern of tiles – this may be done through printing, using turtle graphics, or photocopying. Make a display or a class frieze.

Get the children to use these experiences to create a personal, class or school logo which displays both rotational and reflective symmetry.

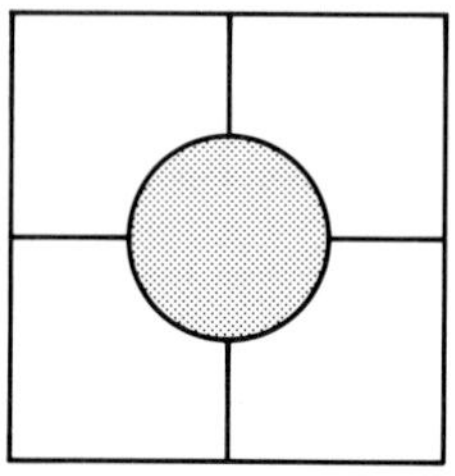

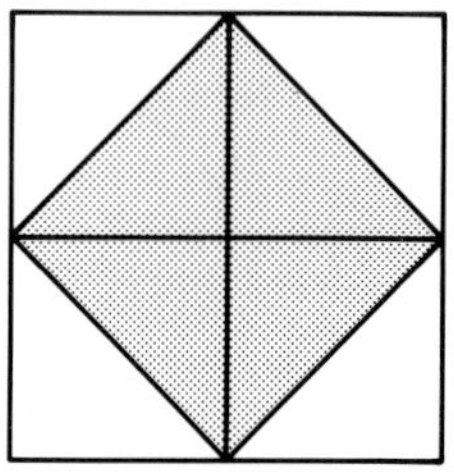

Tiles with patterns that show rotational symmetry

Area of study 17 | P of S 3a | LD 5

TESSELLATION

C79

Commentary

The children will already have met tessellation in the sense of their being involved in pattern making and fitting together, for example, squares to make polyominoes. It is at this Level, however, that they need to be able to determine what will tessellate and this is achieved through an understanding of symmetry and angle properties. They will also be able to use transformation and translation ideas.

In order to tessellate regularly it is essential that the 2-D shapes used make a 360° at their junction.

Semi-regular tessellations can be made using more than two regular shapes, for example, a triangle and a square.

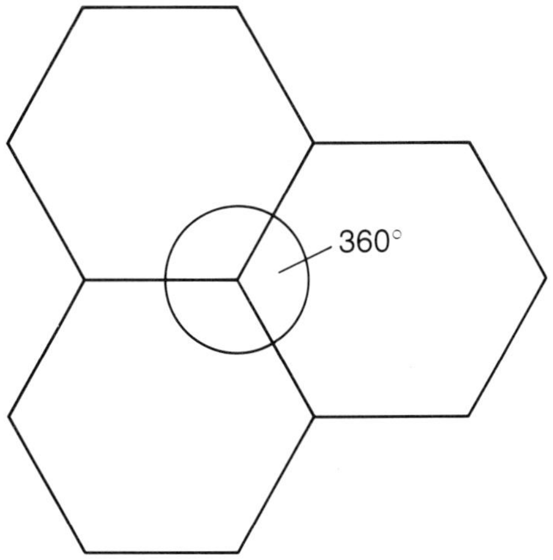

Basic 2-D shapes can be altered by cutting and pasting but, provided appropriate translations and/or reflections and/or rotations are used, these will still tessellate.

The artist M C Escher (1898–1972) made extensive use of tessellation in his work and there are many posters and books which reproduce this work. Some are well worth acquiring.

Link this work to work in art and design and make use of the children's efforts in display.

Activity 1: Developing tessellations

Using what the children already know about regular 2-D shapes get them to explore which of these will tessellate. See if they can suggest where tessellation occurs in nature (for example, bee-hives) and man-made objects (for example, chicken wire).

Get the children to design and make both regular and semi-regular tessellations using squares, equilateral triangles, hexagons and pentagons. Can they find other regular shapes that will work?

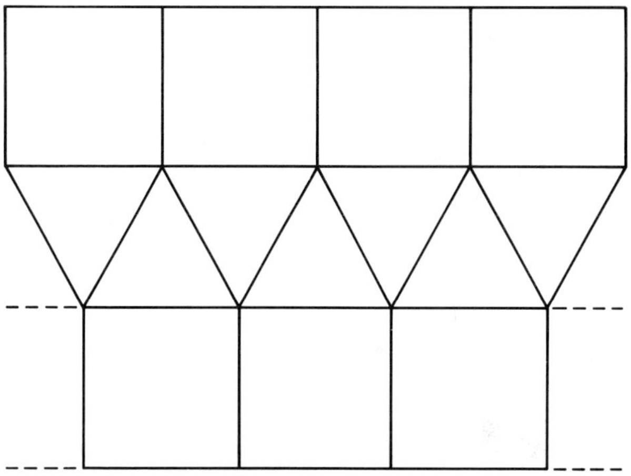

Translation

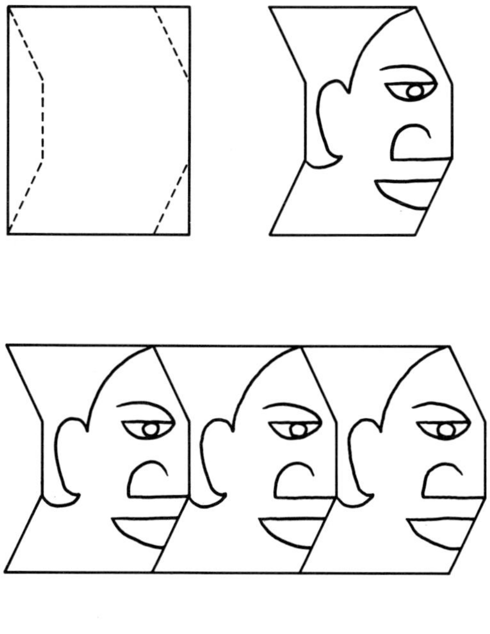

Rotation

For example, about mid-points of the sides.

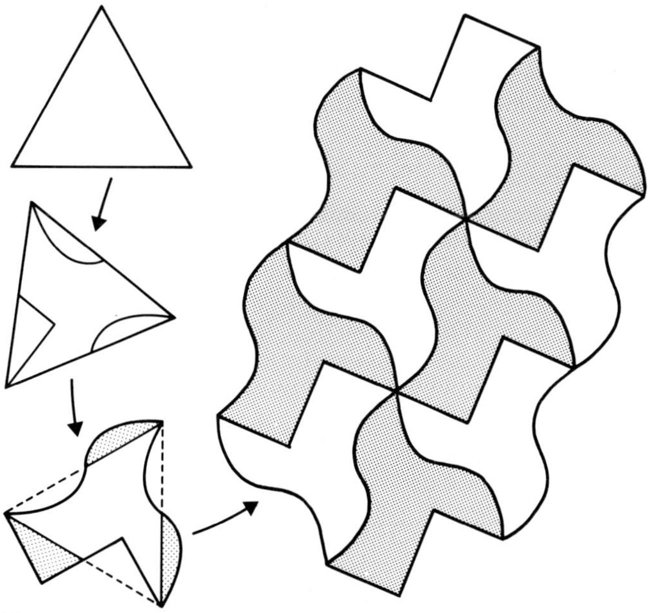

Activity 2: Extending tessellations
Choose one of the regular 2-D shapes to start with and use cutting and pasting together with reflection, rotation and transformation to produce a range of patterns and designs.

Copymaster 79 is a record sheet for the children to record the process from regular shape to complex tessellation.

Activity 3: Computer software
There are a number of packages available which support tessellation work. You can also make use of some of the tiling packages as well as turtle graphics.

Programme of study: Shape, space and measures

Pupils should be taught to:

■ 3. Understanding and using properties of position and movement

b use co-ordinates to specify location, *eg map references, representation of 2-D shapes*;

Area of study 18 | P of S 3b | LD 4 | RC5 | C80

LOCATION

Commentary
Exploring the idea of location gives good opportunities for you to establish the degree of understanding that the children have with regard to measurement, angle, and the translation of 3-D shapes to 2-D representations. Ideas to do with scale and ratio will also come in here to be followed up at later Levels.

Activity 1: Creating a map
Using large squared paper let the children invent their own map. It need not be a treasure island! Other ideas include a city centre, the school library, their room at home, a space station or wildlife park. Show the children how to number and letter the squares. The kind of notation they use does not need to be orthodox at this stage, but you will need to show them some examples.

Resource copymaster 5 gives large squares.

Activity 2: Angles and distances on the map
Using the map the children created in Activity 1, let them put on some features, using angles and distances, to work out locations. For example, if they have drawn a city centre, they can locate the cinema, central park, reference library and museum according to the distances they decide upon and then add a 'mini-guide' saying, for example, 'The library is 500 m north-west of the bus station.'

Copymaster 80 is a map of an imaginary city. It should not replace the children's own efforts, but they may liked to do this one at home or in addition to their own maps.

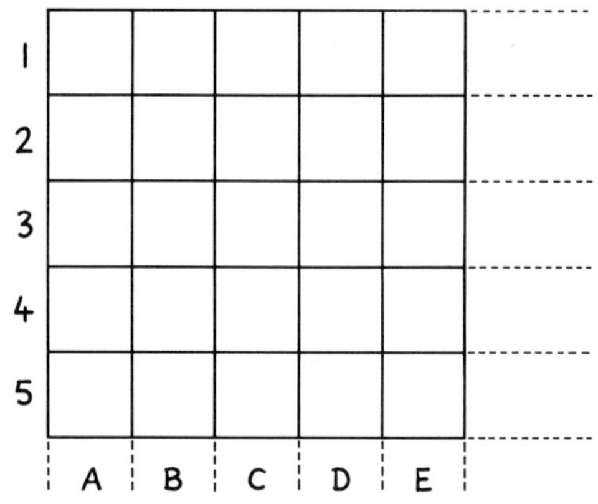

A sample map grid

Activity 3: A look at ordnance survey maps
Look at some real maps with the children and give them some grid references of some important features. Let them go on and work out grid references, angles and distances for themselves and challenge you and the other children with their references and directions.

Link this work to work in Geography. If there is a local orienteering club or society get someone in to talk about this sport.

Activity 4: A treasure trail
Let the children, in groups, create a trail around the school, which is interpretable only by using map references, angles and distances on a scale map you yourself have drawn and photocopied. Let other groups of children follow it a group at a time. Offer the trails as a resource to other classes and as a challenge to the other teachers.

Area of study 19 | P of S 3b | LD 5 | RC1, 3, 4

SHAPE LOCATION

Commentary
Look at Number, Areas of study 26 and 27.

In using all four quadrants the children are making use of what they already know about negative numbers as well as categorisation within Handling data.

The children should learn that a figure can be described using negative or positive co-ordinates or a combination of both.

Activity 1: Shape location
Let the children inspect shapes drawn to span all four quadrants on squared paper and identify them by their co-ordinates. Then let the children try 'translating' co-ordinates into shapes on squared paper.

Resource copymasters 1, 3 and **4** are squared papers.

Programme of study: Shape, space and measures

Pupils should be taught to:

■ **3. Understanding and using properties of position and movement**

c use right angles, fractions of a turn and, later, degrees, to measure rotation, and use the associated language.

Area of study 20 | P of S 3c | LD 2

MOVEMENT AND ANGLE (INCLUDING RIGHT ANGLES)

Commentary
It is important that the children come to see that the concept of angle is to do with rotation. In measuring angles we are actually describing the movement of a line about a point. Whilst the children will need to come to the measurement of angle using degrees (and minutes) at a later stage it is vital that they see angle as dynamic not static.

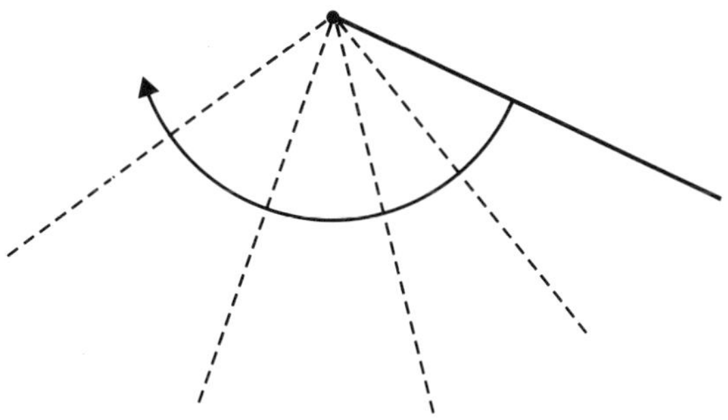

Activity 1: Types of movement
During a PE lesson get the children moving about the room, first in one direction (*translation*), maybe stopping and starting at the sound of a clap, and then turning at the sound of a clap (*rotational movement*).

Move this discussion to an art session, where the children can do a series of prints, first using translation and then rotation. Display the children's efforts. If you have the facilities, set alongside the print work some shots of the children during PE.

Activity 2: Angles discussion
If the children have looked for right angles in 2-D and 3-D shapes and worked on angle in PE they will be ready for you to discuss angle as movement. Show the children a play clock-face, kitchen or fireplace tongs, scissors, a hand puppet crocodile, a pair of spectacles and other examples of things which use angle to operate and where the angle can be varied. Of particular

interest are items where one arm of the angle can be held still, while the other moves, such as the arms on a pair of spectacles or the hinge on a door.

Let the children demonstrate the movement that makes the angle in all these items. You can name them as *acute* (up to 90°), *obtuse* (91°–180°) and *reflex* (180°+), if you feel the children are ready for these words.

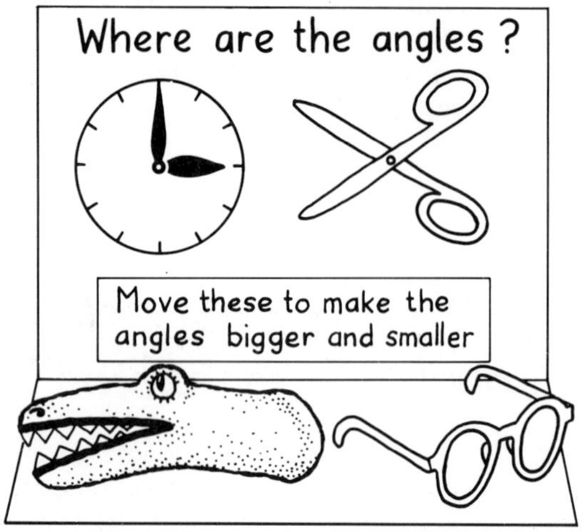

Activity 3: Right angles exploration
Have fun in some PE lessons, creating maze-like pathways around the hall. Thus, the children can make their way from one side of the hall to the other, or to the centre of the hall, without bumping into anyone else, and using right angles to change direction. Once they have invented a track, see if they can repeat it. If so, they can draw it on paper and construct a maze path for a marble or small figure to move through. Display the results.

Activity 4: Angles using turtle geometry
If you have a programmable robot get the children to program it to traverse an obstacle course or find its way through a maze. If you have a LOGO software package available, let the children experiment in drawing shapes and pathways across the computer screen by moving the turtle.

Area of study 21 | P of S 3c | LD 4

ANGLE

Commentary
By the time that the children have reached this Level they should have established a good understanding of angle and rotation. Here they need to consolidate that experience through the recognition of particular characteristics of given angles and the acquisition of appropriate language to describe those angles.

Activity 1: Angle vocabulary
Show the children a number of angles, in the 'real' world, on paper and in regular 2-D and 3-D shapes. Name the kinds of angles and then quiz the children about naming other examples.

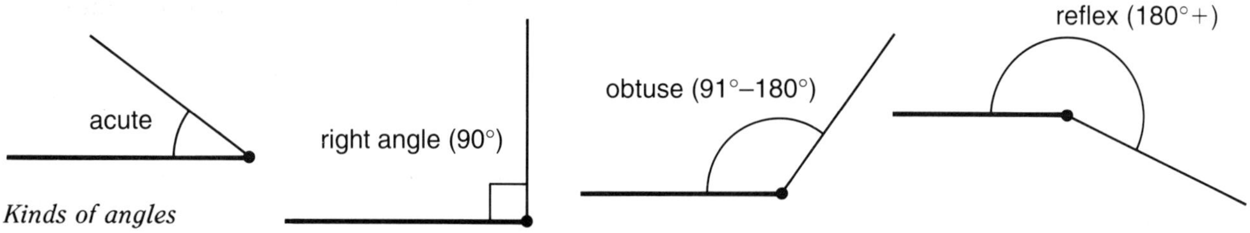

Kinds of angles

Area of study 22 | P of S 3c | LD 5

MEASURING AND DRAWING ANGLES

Commentary
The importance of drawing angles accurately is clear to children when they try to replicate 2-D shapes or nets of 3-D shapes on paper. At Level 4 the three processes which the children will have to be able to engage in order to construct accurately a named 3-D shape were mentioned. These are the construction of appropriate 2-D shapes, the physical construction of the 3-D shape, and the translation of a 3-D shape into its 2-D net (and vice versa). It is at this Level that all these skills should come together to allow accuracy in drawing.

Activity 1: Drawing equipment
Revise and extend the children's skills in using protractors and compasses, to which they were introduced at Level 4.

Activity 2: Practice shape nets
Using their skills with rulers, protractors, compasses and squared paper, let the children draw up some typical layout nets for the construction of regular shapes.

Activity 3: Construction challenges
Let the children put their plans done in Activity 2 to the test by inviting them to design, make and decorate a gift box, a nest of boxes, or an unusual box like a pyramid or prism shape. They must first decide on what they are going to attempt and then submit a rough design sketch to you. You should then give them parameters, such as maximum and minimum dimensions, which they have to operate within. This sort of approach supports and reinforces your work in technology.

Programme of study: Shape, space and measures

Pupils should be taught to:

■ 4. Understanding and using measures

a choose appropriate standard units of length, mass, capacity and time, and make sensible estimates with them in everyday situations; extend their understanding of the relationship between units; convert one metric unit to another; know the rough metric equivalents of Imperial units still in daily use;

Area of study	P of S	LD
23	4a	2

NON-STANDARD MEASURES

Commentary
Do give the children plenty of practice with non-standard measures. The practice not only brings home powerfully the whole rationale behind the need for standard measures, but it also underlines the need for care in doing measuring and sets the scene for an understanding that we choose units to fit the task at hand.

Historically, standard measures came about after the widespread use of non-standard measures like the hand and the foot. Taking this historical route with children seems to enhance their understanding.

Activity 1: Length
Show the children how people in the past measured with parts of their own bodies. Include discussion of the following, introducing one or two in each teaching session:

- handspans;
- feet;
- strides;
- paces;
- cubits.

Let the children work in pairs and record and display the results they obtain in a variety of measuring exercises.

Let the children also experiment with other 'arbitrary' measures, including perhaps string, leaves, twigs or paper strips, and some they make themselves, for example, a plait of wool or a cardboard lizard.

Activity 2: Area
Show the children that area is a measure of 'cover'. Put a large sheet of newsprint on a desk or table so that it covers it. Draw around the edge of the top surface of the desk with a felt tip. Cut this out and show that the piece of paper is a 'picture' of the area of the desk. Let the children find out how many books, shoes, boxes, reading cards and other things cover the desk. Record all their findings on the piece of paper which depicted the desk top and display this.

Let the children practice finding the area of other surfaces around the room, using units that they find appropriate.

Now show the children a variety of things that emphasise why we need to know about area. These might include the following:

- an aerial map of part of a British landscape;
- a picture of a 'Farmland for sale' board listing areas for sale;
- a dress pattern;
- an advertisement for tablecloths giving their dimensions.

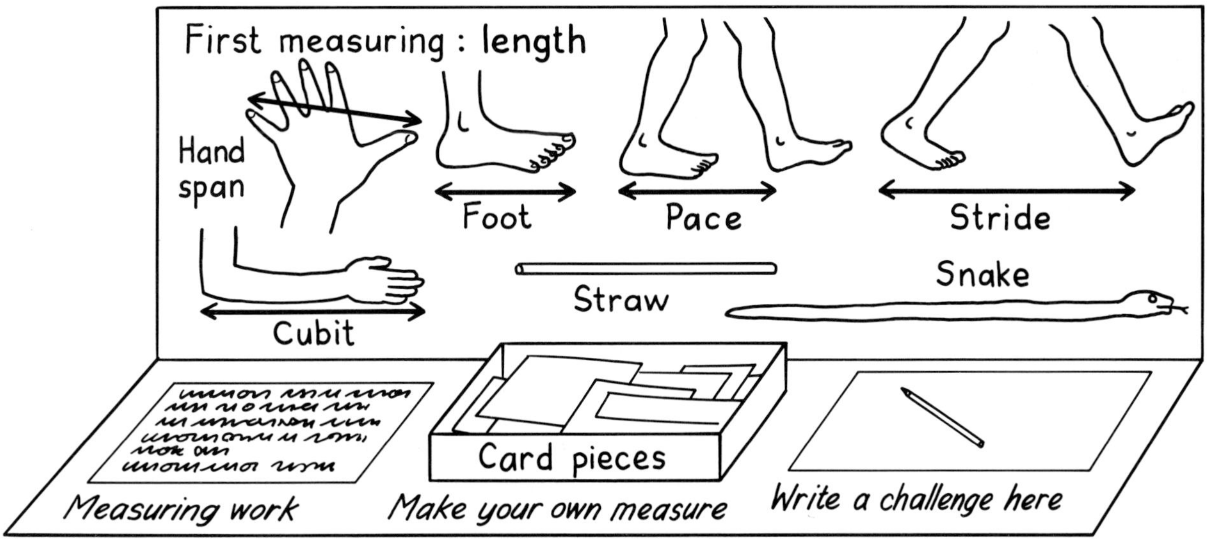

Activity 3: Capacity
With a number of containers of varying sizes and a water tray, sink or bucket of water, let the children experiment to compare capacities. Make sure the collection includes containers made of plastic or other unbreakable material as follows:

- beakers;
- paper cups;
- jugs;
- bottles (from large ones like those that once contained fizzy drinks to small ones used for cosmetics);
- bun and loaf tins;
- egg cups;
- shallow dishes;
- funnels.

Activity 4: 'Weight'
With a classroom balance and a collection of items suitable for weighing, let children make comparisons. The weighing table could have a box with some of the following resources in it:

- supplies of pasta shapes, lentils, twigs, shells, pebbles and other found materials;
- feathers, coal, chalk, wash powder - all well wrapped in clear plastic bags;
- Plasticine©.

Set up a variety of weighing comparisons for the children to work through, for example, 'How many pasta shells balance with the bag of feathers?'

Activity 5: Time
Make some home-made interval timers, like sand and water clocks. Two examples are shown below:

Give the children a series of tasks relating to the timers. Let the children work in twos, so that one child does the timing and the other the task, and then they can swop. Include among the tasks answers to the following:

- How many times can you jump in one drip of the timer? (Watch that the jumping does not disturb the timing interval.)
- How many times can you write your name, count to 100 or recite a poem before the sand runs out?

Activity 6: The need for standard units
When the children have had experience of working with a variety of non-standard units, you can begin to discuss the problems in using these. Let the children compare their results and discuss why there are discrepancies.

Sand clock

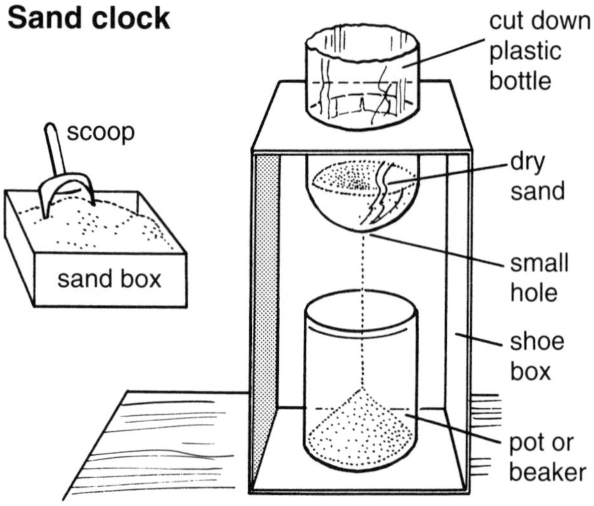

Water clock

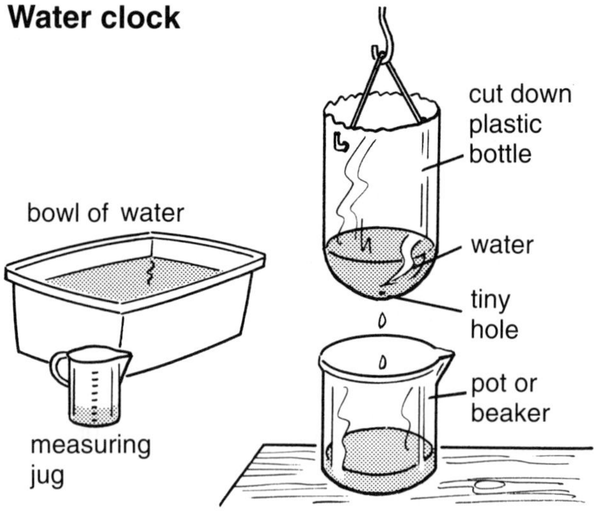

Area of study 24	P of S 4a	LD 2	COMMON STANDARD MEASURES

Commentary
Introduce these common standard measures once the children have had practical experience of the difficulties of using non-standard measures and understand the need for standard units.

Find out which measures are familiar to the children themselves and begin with those. A child who knows what a fish market is, whose dad runs a carpet warehouse or who lives over a pub or sweet shop may already have a good notion of some of the units we use when measuring.

You may find that it is easier to introduce concepts about time using Activities related to minutes and seconds than hours. 'Timing' has thus been introduced at this Level and notions about our daily timetable and telling the time appear at Level 3.

Activity 1: Length in metres and miles
Show the children a metre stick and then let them estimate and measure a wide variety of things in and around school. Remember that the children should be given the chance to choose from a variety of 'tools', including metre sticks, measuring tapes, pieces of string, thick wool or card a metre long, and trundle wheels. Let them measure, for example:

- across the hall, classroom, corridor or playground;

- doorways, notice boards and windows;
- round a pillar, the gym horse or the games shed.

Look at the mileometers in some of the teachers' cars. Draw the dials and discuss the meaning of the figures with the children.

Look at a map of the area of Britain in which the school appears and talk about the distances to, for example, the sea or the nearest major city. Look for 'real' places that occur in nursery rhymes and stories. Let the children find out how far their school is from these. Examples could include Gloucester, York, Sherwood, Banbury and Harlech.

Activity 2: 'Weight' in kilos and pounds
Collect some supermarket packaging which held, for example, 5 kg of potatoes, 1 kg of oranges or 1 kg of sugar, and 1 lb bags which held nuts, biscuits, beans or pulses. Weigh each child on some bathroom scales. Discuss what we weigh in pounds and kilos and introduce the idea of equivalence.

Area of study 25 | P of S 4a | LD 3

ESTIMATION IN MEASUREMENT

Commentary
The ability to make estimates is as important as knowing the four operations in mathematics. With the impact of technology in classrooms and high streets we need to assess, more than ever before, the order of an answer/payment/debit or bill, just so that we can detect operator or technical mistakes in calculations.

Estimates are *not* guesses, and workbooks that imply so are misleading to you and the children you teach; rather estimates depend on information. If we know nothing about a particular concept in mathematics we will not be able to make estimates. Estimation is therefore grounded in understanding which must be gained through, at best, first-hand experience.

Estimation skills are not always generalisable. For example, with practice a child may be able to estimate reasonably accurately how many pencils there are in a bundle. We would expect this skill to transfer to a bundle of crayons, but could not say whether it would transfer to stamps on the page of an album or coins in a purse. In other words, to be good at estimation in a wide variety of situations, children need to have experience of a wide variety of situations!

When estimating measures begin with those units that are most familiar to the children. These will vary according to the life experiences of the children you teach. The child of a sweet shop owner will probably know what a quarter pound of sweets looks like and children who have played with watering cans and buckets may have a notion of a gallon. Practical experience is probably the only way to get a 'feel' for what a measurement looks like and it is only then that we have the cognitive 'picture' to make sensible estimates. Thus the children who make estimates wide of the mark are those who need most subsequent practice of measuring.

Activity 1: Starting estimation
Let the children handle a collection of small items, for example, toy farm animals. Tell them to pick up, maybe five, then six, then eight of these. Then without the children seeing how many there are, assemble a set of, for example, six toys, and cover them. Tell the children that they will get a quick look at the toys and then they will be asked to write secretly how many they estimate there are. Play this until the children are giving estimates of the right order (this may be straight away). Then go through the same process with another batch of items from the classroom. Choose things such as:

- shoebags;
- crisp packets;
- metre sticks;
- coins;
- exercise books;
- marbles.

Activity 2: How many?
Run a little estimation quiz, showing the children pictures of sets of between three and ten items. Discuss those they found difficult, for this will help them develop strategies for making reasonable estimates with bigger numbers. For example, they may say things like 'It is easier if the things are laid out. . . . I have to take a good look before I get it right. . . . If they are things I have counted and worked with before then I make better estimates.'

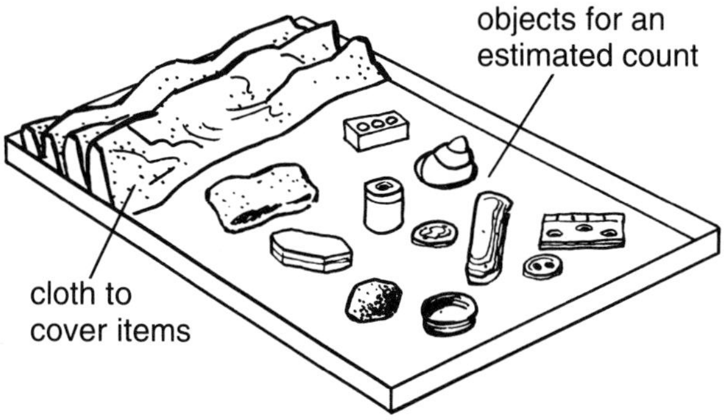

Activity 3: Estimate and measure
Give the children a variety of estimates to make in and around the classroom. This may include, for example:

- the length/height of the door, blackboard, register, bookshelf, broom or chair leg;
- the 'weight' of the teddy, cushion, door stop, sticky tape, crayon pot, teacher's shoe, Kathleen, Nadine's coat, Chris's shoebag or Samir's pencil box;
- the capacity of teacher's cup, the watering can, a paint pot, a flower vase or a yoghurt pot.

Let children record their estimates, so that you have some 'hard data' against which actual measurements can be checked. Try to give them the chance to make the estimates independent of one another. The measuring could be done by choosing a different child to do each measuring task and having you and the group look on.

Area of study 26 | P of S 4a | LD 3

METRIC UNITS

Commentary
At Level 2 the children will have been introduced to common imperial and metric measures. They can now begin to work with the other metric units in general use, like the gram (g) and the centimetre (cm).

Now that the children will attempt measurement in small units it is even more important to stress the need for care.

Activity 1: Length
Give the children a variety of measuring tasks, keeping different units of measurement to different sessions. The following are the units to cover and some measuring tasks which may be appropriate in and around your classroom:

- metres/yards – the hall, cloakroom, classroom;
- centimetres/inches – crayon, paper, shoebag;
- miles and kilometres – compare using the display from a car speedometer, and with your help, the scale distances on local maps.

The tools they will require for this measuring include the following: metre sticks, trundle wheels, tape measures and school rulers.

Activity 2: Capacity
Make sure the children have plenty of practical opportunities in filling and emptying containers with liquids. Conservation of liquid is often hard to grasp and, because of limited practical experience, many adults cannot estimate and approximate with liquids. Did you know, for example, that a seven inch diameter shallow sponge tin holds a whole pint of liquid? The risk of 'mess' is a common reason why children's opportunities are limited in school. If necessary, dress the children in their PE kit which can be dried off afterwards!

Using a variety of containers, some of which state the volumes of their original contents, let the children fill and empty, transfer, approximate and estimate. A selection of containers may include, for example, a milk bottle, juice cartons, fizzy drinks cans, cooking oil bottle, washing-up liquid bottle, water bottles, litre juice cartons, kitchen jugs, egg cups and baking tins.

Give the children tasks which involve measuring:

- pints, half pints, quarter pints;
- litres.

Combine the knowledge they have gleaned in this Activity with what they learn in the next to enable them to carry out some baking in school.

Activity 3: 'Weight'
Look with the children at a variety of scales and balances, and discuss their uses. Include here bathroom scales, kitchen scales and a classroom balance of the type that has two cups and a crude balance point.

Using the appropriate scales, weigh some of the children, a full bag of sugar, and washing powder or cornflakes. Discuss the kinds of balance required to weigh letters or the ingredients of medicines in a pharmacy.

Look with the children at what these 'weights' (pounds, half pounds, quarters and kilograms, grams) look like in, for example, apples, conkers or polystyrene chips.

Area of study 27 | P of S 4a | LD 3

TIME

C81, 82

Commentary
The Babylonians worked with a system based on 60 (sexagesimal). This system is at the root of our degrees in a circle (360) and in seconds in a minute and minutes in an hour (60).

Children need activities which will communicate the passage of time in the sense of change, growth and dissipation, and a sense of the time it takes to do things or for something to happen.

Activity 1: The language of time
Make a collection of books relating to telling the time and obtain a play clock-face. Tell the children about all the language attached to telling the time. Your discussions should include the following:

- face, hands, hour hand, minute hand (include movement and pendulum if appropriate);
- o'clock, half-past, quarter-past, quarter-to, hour, minute, second.

Some of these concepts will only be fully understood as children start to do the Activities below, and do timing and time-telling.

Activity 2: Telling the time
Use the pattern of the school day to show the children their daily 'timetable'. Using the classroom clock or one you have borrowed, have frequent time checks for a week or so, until the children can 'read' the time from the position of the hands on the clock-face.

Let the children record their activities for a typical day on a 'timesheet'.

Introduce children to the idea of the 24-hour clock and show them a digital clock or watch. Practice converting 'conventional' times into 24-hour clock times and ordinary clock-face displays into digital displays. Create a display or time corner, where all the topics of discussion and the books can be set out.

Copymaster 81 is a timesheet the children can fill in and copymaster **82** is a sheet for conventional (analogue) to digital time conversion.

Shamra's timesheet

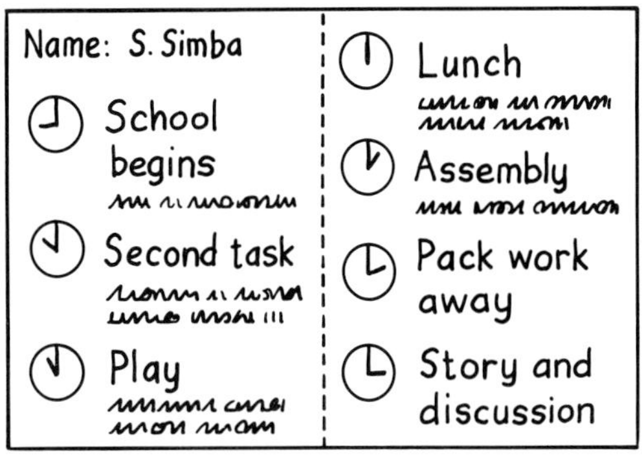

Activity 3: Timing in minutes and seconds
Try letting the children, working in pairs, use timers to track the number of times their partner can do a given job in a minute. A list of tasks may include:

- writing a name;
- counting to 100;
- jumping up and down;
- playing a tune on the recorder.

When they have all had a turn at these kinds of Activities you can check their estimates of a minute by asking them to sit still and quiet, with their eyes closed, and raise their hand when they think a minute has passed!

Timing seconds is more of a challenge. Ask the children whether they can try some of the following in, say, 10 seconds:

- state full name, address and telephone number;
- play 20 drumbeats or 30 shakes of the maracas;
- hop to the other side of the room.

Area of study 28 | P of S 4a | LD 4

ESTIMATION AND MEASURES

Commentary
We have already made much of the need to engage children in an understanding of estimation. This area of work reinforces that need. Children have to come to see that there is a clear and constant relationship between measures that are applied to the same event, providing that those measures are within the same system.

Offering children the opportunity to evaluate their estimated measurements against their classmates' estimates and the 'actual measure' (that is the measure obtained with the degree of accuracy you and the children agree upon) is a skill which is important. In everyday life we are regularly asked to make estimates, for example, of how long a journey or a job will take, or whether a bookcase will fit along a wall.

Activity 1: Estimate experts!
By now, if the children have had plenty of practice at previous Levels they should be better at estimating than some of the adults around them. Test their expertise by giving them an 'around the school estimate quiz'. In their absence, take measurements of all the items in the quiz. Get the children to record their answers. You can set up the following kinds of tasks:

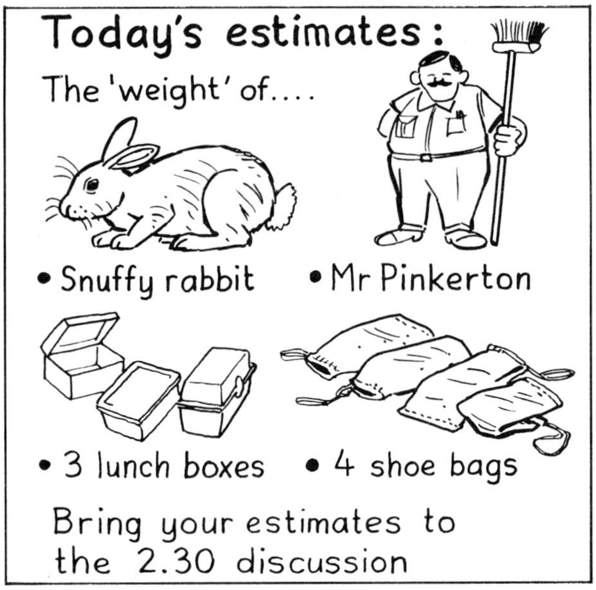

- Coloured string, ribbon, curtain track, skipping rope, tagliatelle, french stick loaf, toilet roll – how long?
- Window, doorway, cupboard, school sign, picture, chart, display board, hall — how wide?
- Milk in jug, juice in glass, amount to fill a straw, water down the loo at each flush, water required for teachers' coffee break – how much?
- 'Weight' of head teacher, school rabbit, contents of ten lunch boxes, cakes made in class 4A – how heavy?
- Length of assembly, to walk across the playground, to stop a football game, to start up the video – how long?

Area of study 29 | P of S 4a | LD 4

RELATIONSHIPS BETWEEN UNITS

Commentary

All systems of measurement have divisions and sub-divisions. They all use the concept of the number line. However, different systems have sub-divisions that are differing fractions of the unit used. For example, 3 feet to the yard, 1000 millilitres to the litre, 10 millimetres to the centimetre, and 60 seconds to the minute. Children need to come to understand:

- how different measures are divided internally and whether a measure is therefore appropriate given the level of accuracy required;
- the reasons for there being different standard measures for the same measurement exercise.

Activity 1: Let's measure

Give the children a variety of measuring tasks and let them try these in, for example, metres, centimetres and millimetres; litres and millilitres; kilogrammes and grammes; and minutes and seconds.

This Activity will serve to emphasise the point that while we can measure things using 'large' or 'small' units, we choose units that are appropriate for the 'order' of result we expect.

Activity 2: On the record

Investigate, from a fact list or a current edition of *The Guinness Book of Records*, some measures that will appeal to the children. Here are some examples:

- *length* – the height of the Empire State building or Nelson's Column, the M1 motorway, the coastline of Britain;
- *'weight'* – elephants, whales, men and women, babies etc.;
- *capacity* – size of the local reservoir, amount of water in the town swimming pool;
- *time* – the human heart beat per minute, insect wing beats, fastest moving animals, lunar month and year, athletics records.

The children can convert the units in which these are expressed into smaller or larger ones. For example, the CN Tower in Toronto (tallest building in the world, built 1976) is 553 m high. What is that in cm? The largest land mammal is the African elephant, weighing up to 7 tonnes; how many kilos is that?

Area of study 30 | P of S 4a | LD 5

EVERYDAY IMPERIAL UNITS AND THEIR METRIC EQUIVALENTS

C83

Commentary

Despite efforts to the contrary by legislators we still use imperial measures in our everyday life in the UK. So pints of milk, miles from A to B, quarters of sweets and acres of ground are all part of the children's experience. However, equivalent metric measures are often now given and in some parts of our life there has been a complete move to metric units. It is important, therefore, that the children appreciate what has happened to our measures and have a grasp of the rough equivalents in imperial and metric units.

Activity 1: Researching imperial and metric units

Make a collection of data to do with imperial and metric measures. This collection could be derived from:

- supermarket and other shop packaging;
- athletics and other sports;
- estate agents;
- car manufacturers' publicity information;
- ironmongers, hardware and DIY stores.

Use the information to produce a class book which allows other children to find out imperial and metric units and equivalents in a whole range of dimensions and situations.

Activity 2: Other interesting measures

There are a lot of measures (not all of them metric) which are in common use and can be used to further stimulate the children's interest in standard measures and equivalents. For example, the use of fathoms and chains at sea, and the use of degrees Fahrenheit (as well as degrees centigrade or Celsius) on weather reports. Collect these and other examples, and add them to the data from Activity 1. Use all that you have for a display in the school hall or foyer for children from other classes and parents.

Create a school data base from this information on measures. The information is invaluable when the children are working on Handling data.

Activity 3: Measures and jobs
Invite the children to find out the measures that their mums or dads use commonly when at work, the kinds of job they do and the situations where measures are particularly important. Where their parents are unemployed, the children can look at the common measures used around the home. Collate and display all the information gleaned from this Activity.

Copymaster 83 is a reply sheet, for children to take home, about the measures their parents use at work or at home. (It will require a covering letter explaining to parents why you would like the information and that you are just as interested in the measures they use to fill the lawnmower or buy paint as those they use in a factory or office.)

Activity 4: Graphs
The children can plot straight-line conversion graphs for the purpose of reading off imperial and metric equivalents. Start with a kilometres–miles conversion (the children should be encouraged to discuss exactly how much information they need to draw such a graph). Once drawn, the children can check their conversions against those to be found in motorist's maps. They might then like to draw other graphs for conversion of measures of their choice. (This work can be linked to work on negative numbers at this Level.)

Area of study 31 | P of S 4a | LD 5

CONVERTING ONE METRIC MEASURE TO ANOTHER

Commentary
This work should capitalise on what the children already know about place value, decimal fractions and number bases.

Activity 1: Bags of sugar
Bags of sugar are now retailed in 1 kg bags. Use this fact, and the fact that a bag of sugar is real to children, to help them become absolutely confident about metric equivalents. As a group, find out some facts to do with the weights of some things in kilos. These will include men, women, cars, ships, cows, elephants and so on. Make a 'bags of sugar' line which puts all of these things, and more, in order of magnitude. How can these different objects and animals be easily labelled? How does the kilo relate to other metric weights such as the metric tonne? Using a gram 'weight' work down from your bag of sugar looking at the weights of, for example, small mammals, birds, books, cartons of yoghurt and so on.

The children can do a similar Activity working with other metric measures such as millilitres and litres.

Programme of study: Shape, space and measures

Pupils should be taught to:

4. Understanding and using measures

b choose and use appropriate measuring instruments; interpret numbers and read scales to an increasing degree of accuracy;

Area of study 32 | P of S 4b | LD 3

COMMON MEASURING TOOLS

Commentary
In conserving such physical attributes as length, capacity and 'weight' we are asking children to understand that, for example:

- a piece of string has a length whether laid out straight or rolled up;
- that a pint of milk is that whether it is in the bottle or poured into a shallow baking tin;
- that Plasticine© has a 'weight' whether in a ball or rolled into a sausage.

To understand conservation we all need lots of practical work through which we can see and 'feel' the constancy of certain attributes.

Activity 1: Length, width and breadth
Using a number of sessions to avoid confusing the children, show them a variety of common measuring tools, including the following:

- a yardstick;
- a metre stick;

- a tape measure and spring rule;
- school rulers.

Let the children experiment with these measures, and make their own card strip metres and strings 1 m long.

Give the children a circle of paper on which they can record the figures that appear on the mileometer dial in one of the teacher's cars, and discuss the meaning of the figures. Look at local signposts to see how distances are measured.

Activity 2: Capacity
Look with the children at a variety of cartons, cans and bottles to find out how we measure the liquids we buy. Remember to include containers that held things like cooking oil, ketchup and washing-up liquid as well as milk and juice. Give the children little challenges, in some sessions using imperial measures and in some metric. For example, let them find out how many 5 ml spoonfuls there are in a bottle which once held cough syrup, and how many $\frac{1}{4}$ pint drinks there are in a bottle of milk.

Activity 3: 'Weight'
Kitchen and bathroom scales can begin the discussion. Weigh a variety of foods, such as a pack of sugar and a pack of corn flakes. Weigh some of the children. Discuss the use of pounds and ounces, and kilos.

Area of study 33 | P of S 4b | LD 4

CHOOSING AND USING MEASURES

Commentary
Here is a point at which the children's degree of mastery of mathematics will be self-evident.

Make sure the children know and act on the knowledge that we make choices about instruments and units when measuring, and that there are implications in the choices we make.

Activity 1: 'Real-life' decisions
Point out to the children that when we are choosing what to measure with, we are already aware of the range of the likely measurements, what it is we are measuring and how accurate we have to be. In the light of this discussion see if the children can say which kinds of measuring instruments are necessary in a number of situations that may be familiar to them. For example:

- What does mum or dad use to measure flour and milk for cooking?
- What do we need to draw a 5 cm margin on a page?

Activity 2: Investigations
Invent some projects which are of interest to the children and ask them to speculate about the range of measuring instruments they would be likely to need to see it through. For example:

- Decide what size of tank to buy for some new pet fish for the school. The fish will be happiest with a water volume amounting to at least $\frac{1}{2}$ litre per fish and a depth of at least 30 cm to swim in. There are to be six to eight fish in the tank. How many fish would be advisable in a tank with proportions that fit the requirements and which looks good?

- A home-made propagator, made from a plastic box which once held ice cream, is to have a plastic sheet 'roof' fitted. The propagation tray inside will require a depth of 4 cm of potting compost.
- How do we measure up for football or netball pitches?
- If the teacher likes to have one part of the room free of desks and tables, and have the children sitting in groups but able to see the board, and leave access to doors and cupboards generous, then how can she work out the best seating plan?
- Devise a storage system for the mathematics resources in class, making decisions about the sizes and shapes of the containers.
- How long does it take for all the school to assemble in the hall? Are all classes taking the quickest route to get there?

If you wish, the children can, with your help, carry through some of these investigations. Real and valuable data can be accumulated which can then be used in other settings, including AT5. Record and store these in a data file or computer data base.

Programme of study: Shape, space and measures

Pupils should be taught to:

■ 4. Understanding and using measures

c find perimeters of simple shapes; find practically the circumferences of circles, being introduced to the ratio π; find areas and volumes by counting methods, leading to the use of other practical methods, *eg dissection.*

Area of study 34 | P of S 4c | LD 4

PERIMETER, AREA AND VOLUME

RC1, 3–5 | C84

Commentary
The children will already know that an essential characteristic of named shapes is that they have clear boundaries. Indeed the word 'perimeter' may already be a part of their vocabulary. However, it may be that some children are confusing perimeter and area. At this stage we need to be working at these distinctions as they will be important when the children come to be looking at 3-D equivalents in volume.

The children should continue to be supported in their learning by the use of practical materials. What is important is a real understanding of the qualities of perimeter, area and volume rather than the memorising of formulae for these. Opportunities come at Level 5 in AT3 Algebra to make general statements about relationships between area and perimeter.

Activity 1: Pacing and tracing
To commit forever to memory the idea of perimeter being all the way round the edge let the children run all the way round the edge of the playing field or playground. Measure the perimeter using a trundle wheel and work out how many perimeter runs the children did as a class!

Draw straight-sided shapes on squared paper and trace around the perimeter with fingers. Count the number of squares all the way round.

Activity 2: Measuring round
Set out some 2-D and 3-D shapes, and invite the children to say how they would go about measuring the perimeters. Experiment with lengths of string and rulers.

Activity 3: Areas of irregular shapes
This Activity is also used in AT2 Level 4. Using a set of irregular objects, such as leaves and hands, trace around them on squared paper. Count the number of whole and part squares each takes up. How do you decide what to do with the part squares? Get different children to compute their answers and put up the range for all of the children to discuss. This work can be used to reinforce some of the ideas to do with accuracy which are to be found in AT5 Handling data.

Resource copymasters 1 and **5** are large squares. Small squares are on **resource copymaster 4** and the graph paper is on **resource copymaster 3**. On **copymaster 84** a number of pictures have been drawn. Children can find the areas of these in squares.

Activity 4: Mosaic play
Using a piece of squared paper as a background and small sticky paper squares cut to match the background in a variety of colours, let the children create as many little men, flowers or another shape as they can which have the same area.

Resource copymasters 1, **3**, **4** and **5** are various squared papers.

Activity 5: Geoboards
Using geoboards, give the children the opportunity to explore many of the shape ideas they already have. Of particular relevance will be explorations of area, perimeter, tile design and nets.

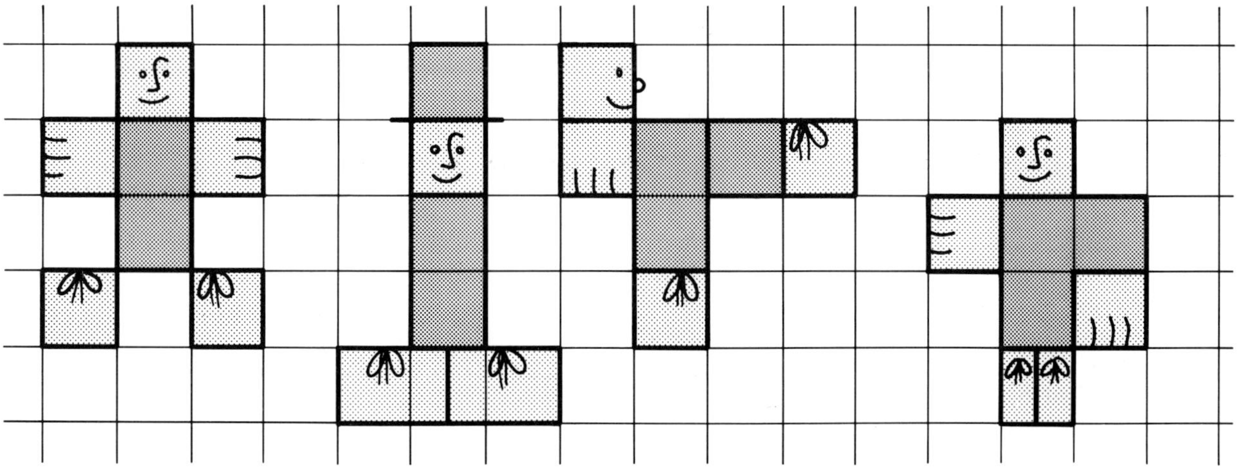

Area of study 35 | P of S 4c | LD 4

AREAS OF PLANE FIGURES

C85, 86

Commentary
It is at this stage that the children should be starting to use general statements (formulae) to establish the areas of squares, rectangles, triangles and related plane shapes.

Once the children understand the computation of area of rectangles then this can be used to develop a formula for triangles. This, in turn will allow the development of formulae for other plane shapes.

Do this work in close association with AT3 Algebra.

Activity 1: Rectangles and squares
Remind the children that at Level 4 they counted squares to find the areas of rectangles. Show them that a rectangle that is, say, two squares wide and six squares long, comprises 12 squares and that we do not need to count the squares to find the area – we can multiply breadth by length. Using geoboards or squared paper let the children try this for a number of rectangles to prove the point.

Together with the children you should then be able to agree the following:

$$A = L \times B$$

where A is the area of a rectangle, L is the length of the longer side and B is the breadth (or length of the shorter side). It is but a simple step from here for the children to appreciate that the area of a square (a special form of rectangle) is computed in the same way. You can link this to what the children already know about square numbers.

Copymaster 85 invites the children to find areas and missing dimensions.

Activity 2: Triangles
Using what the children now know about the area of a rectangle use geoboards to construct a series of rectangles of different areas. The diagonal of each of these rectangles clearly divides the rectangle into two halves each of which is a triangle.

You can then discuss the possible formula for a triangle. This may lead, however, to some children equating the length of a side of a rectangle to the length of a side of a right-angled triangle. It is necessary that they come to see that it is the vertical height of a triangle which is the important dimension. You can illustrate this through paper cutting and folding of other triangles to make right-angled triangles. It is *always* the vertical height that is important. The children should come to see, through these explorations, that the area of a triangle can be obtained from a half of the vertical height multiplied by the length of the side from which the vertical height is measured.

Copymaster 86 invites children to find areas and missing dimensions.

Activity 3: Other plane shapes
Using what the children now know about rectangles, squares and triangles invite them to explore other plane shapes, such as the hexagon. As the children can now find the areas of basic shapes, you can show them how to divide the hexagon and thence find its area.

Area of study 36 | P of S 4c | LD 4

VOLUMES OF SIMPLE SOLIDS

Commentary
At this Level the children should be utilising their knowledge that containers take up space and can be filled with smaller objects or liquids. The children should also exercise their knowledge of nets.

Wherever possible, link this work to Number, Handling data, and work in science.

Activity 1: Cuboids and cubes
Remind the children of their work at Level 4 and show them how they filled boxes with cubes to determine volumes. Repeat this experiment with a small box and show the children that the number of cubes along the length multiplied by the number along the width multiplied by the number high gives the same total as physically filling the box.

Let the children test this out for a number of boxes. Help the children to write the general formula:

Volume = Length × Width (or Breadth) × Depth (or Height).

Activity 2: Triangular prisms
Using the children's knowledge of the area of a triangle build up the concept that a triangular prism can be imagined as a stack of triangles and that multiplying the area of the triangular face of the prism by its height will give the volume. This can be reinforced by reference back to the relationship of the rectangle and triangle in area. Two right triangular prisms placed together would make a cuboid.

Area of study 37 | P of S 4c | LD 5

CIRCUMFERENCE OF A CIRCLE

Commentary
In working with circles it is necessary to introduce the idea of one of the most famous of our mathematical constants, *pi*. Approximations of pi have been available for centuries. It was known to the ancient Babylonians, Greeks, Chinese, Hindus and many others. Pi is an irrational number which means that it is not possible to compute its resolution. Commonly, we use only a few figures after the decimal point but, in fact, mathematicians have so far computed over 130 million digits of pi. So the use of 22/7 is more accurate than the customary 3.142. The symbol π was first used about the year 1700.

Activity 1: Measure up!
Assemble a collection of card circles and cylinders. Invite the children to measure their circumferences and the diameters of the circles and circular faces of the cylinders. The circumferences may be measured with a piece of string and a ruler, or by making a mark on the circle and, starting at the mark, rolling it along a line until the mark comes around to the start. The line traversed can then be measured.

The diameters can be measured by estimating the centre of the circle or circular face and laying a ruler across the centre line. An alternative way of measuring the diameter of the circular faces of the cylinders is to rest the cylinder between two books or blocks on the edge of a desk or table. Allow the books to stand upright so that they just touch the cylinder. The distance between the two books can be measured along the desk edge.

Let the children compare the circumference and diameters and find the ratios between them.

Activity 2: Pi
Using the data the children collected in Activity 1 let them draw graphs of the circumference and diameters. The lines of the graphs should follow similar directions, depending on the accuracy of the measurements. If the children take a variety of readings from their graphs they should arrive at the idea that circumference is three-and-a-bit times the diameter.

Tell the children that the name of this constant is pi and its symbol is π.

$$\text{Circumference} = \pi \times \text{Diameter}$$

so

$$\pi = \frac{\text{Circumference}}{\text{Diameter}}$$

$$\pi = 3.142 \text{ (approximately).}$$

Area of study 38 | P of S 4c | LD 5

AREAS OF CIRCLES

Commentary
This extends the work the children have done on the areas of quadrilaterals and irregular 2-D shapes as well as building on what they know about π and the circumference of circles.

Activity 1: Using squares
Using the counting squares method is generally unsatisfactory for the area of a circle although an approximation can be obtained if a circle is carefully drawn on squared paper using a pair of compasses. Try this with the children as a preliminary Activity. They can assess their accuracy once they have the formula to work with. They should make a note of their results and the radius of the circle in order to use these later.

Try counting squares for a square which exactly contains a circle and a square which exactly fits inside the same circle. The area of the circle must lie somewhere between the two. Could other polygons be used?

Activity 2: Cutting and sticking
Using a coffee filter paper, science filter paper or a circle cut from plain paper get the children to fold the circle in half, half again and again – four folds is probably as much as will be possible. Open out the paper and mark alternate segments with a cross. Then cut the paper into all of its segments. Assemble the pieces to make a rectangular shape with the crosses all at the same side.

From their work on the area of rectangles the children should see that we can get a good approxi-

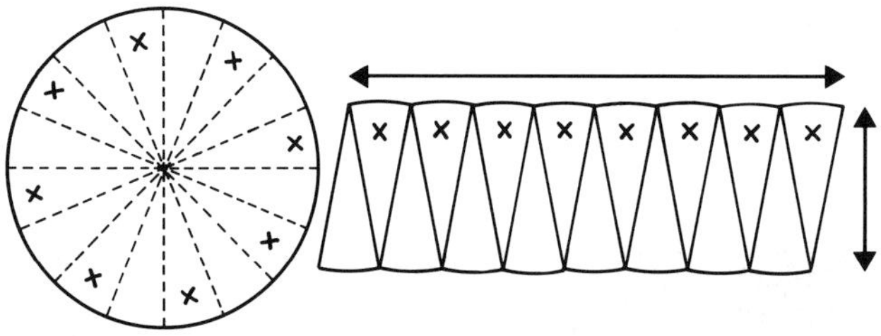

mation of the area by multiplying the length of the side with the crosses on by the length of the short side. These sides correspond, of course, to half the circumference and the radius respectively.

This gives a formula:

$$\text{Area of circle} = \tfrac{1}{2}\text{(Circumference)} \times \text{(Radius)}$$

Now, through discussion of the calculation of circumference ($\pi \times$ Diameter) which the children should already know, guide them through this piece of logic:

$$\tfrac{1}{2}\text{Circumference} = \tfrac{1}{2}(\pi \times \text{Diameter}) = \pi \times \text{Radius}$$

and, putting this into our derived formula obtained from the rectangle we get:

$$\text{Area of circle} = (\pi \times \text{Radius}) \times \text{(Radius)} = \pi \times \text{Radius}^2$$

or, as we often state it, πr^2, where r represents radius.

Area of study 39 | Extension activities

ENLARGING

Commentary

In enlarging 2-D or 3-D shapes it is important to make use of what the children should already know about similarity and congruence. An *enlargement* is always similar to the original shape and the dimensions of the enlargement will be larger by the same ratio in all directions.

There are a variety of ways of enlarging shapes. These include the use of co-ordinates, grids, precise measurement and computer or mechanical aids. The children will already have experience of transformation and translation using co-ordinates, and should have good constructional and measurement skills.

There are many links which can be made through this work. These include area, translation, graphs, scale and ratio, and the use of the computer.

Activity 1: Maps and models

Using maps and scale models discuss with the children the ways in which enlargement and reduction are related. Use this discussion to create the set of ideas which they need to employ in carrying out enlargements.

Activity 2: Rectangles and boxes

Get the children to draw a series of different-size rectangles in the first quadrant of a graph so that a straight line can be drawn from the origin through the top right corner of each of the rectangles.

Using both measurement and co-ordinate descriptions look at the ratio relationships between the rectangles. Follow up this work by making a collection of as many sheets of paper as you can that are identified by size in the A series, for example, A2, A3, A4 and so on. All of these papers will be related in the ways in which the

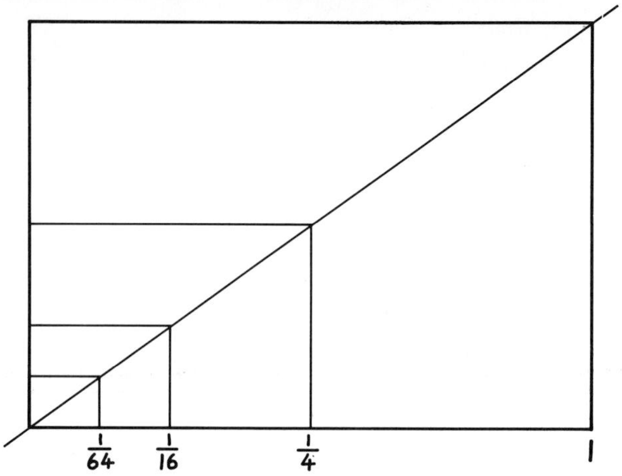

rectangles are formed. Get the children to check this out. If you wish you could extend this work into a consideration of this type of sizing with old and present systems for paper, and in other areas where sizing by dimensions is important.

Using a set of Russian dolls as the stimulus collect boxes which will fit one inside another. Can the children produce nets of open-top boxes which are larger by a given factor but in the same ratio? Get them to make some of these and decorate them to produce a set of 'magic' boxes.

Activity 3: Using grids

You can enlarge a drawing by the use of square grids. Using OHP transparencies make two square grids, one a stated enlargement of the other. Use the smaller grid to cover a picture or drawing and the larger as a guide to the location of an enlarged reproduction of the drawing.

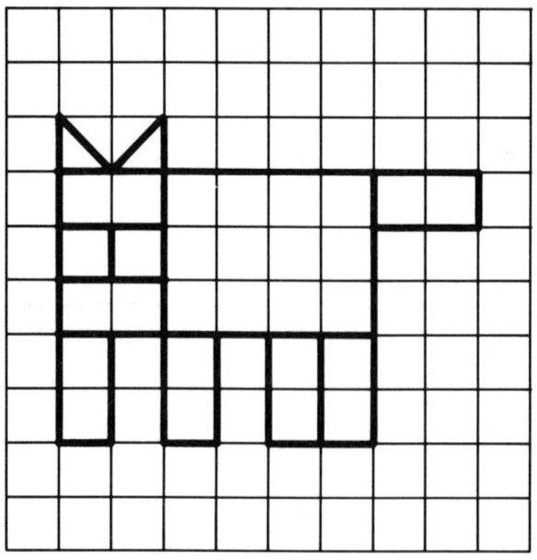

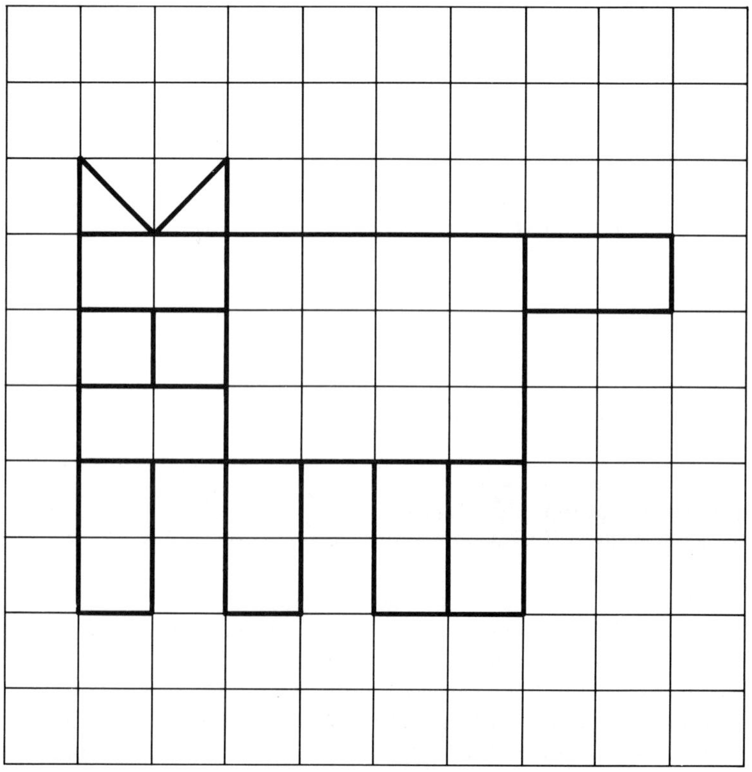

Activity 4: Pantographs
Pantographs are mechanical devices for enlargement. Try to acquire one or, using constructional materials, build one with the children.

Get the children to explain how the pantograph works. Can they build different versions which will give different enlargements?

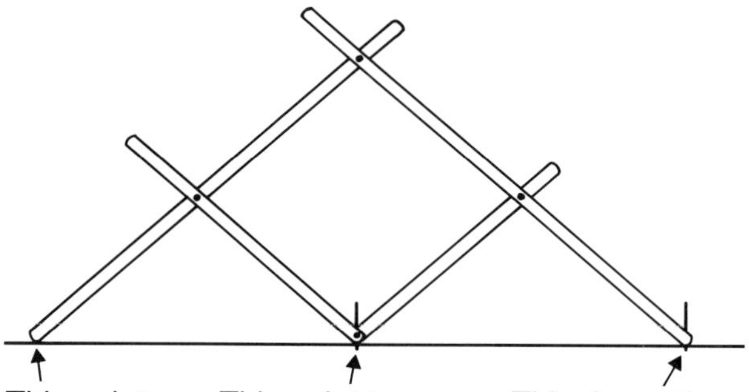

Activity 5: Photographs
Find out about the enlargement of photographs – from the negative size to a print and from a print to a large print. Ask a member of the local photographic society or someone from a local camera or development shop to come in and speak and/or demonstrate.

Activity 6: Robots and computers
See what the children can find out about the use of robots to carry out manufacturing and other processes. To what extent is the movement of a robot engineered in relation to scale, distance and size of the job?

Using turtle graphics and drawing packages find out how to carry out enlargements of drawings and shapes.

Area of study 40

QUADRILATERALS

Commentary
Quadrilaterals are plane figures having four vertices joined by lines. The internal angles of quadrilaterals can be acute, obtuse or reflex.

At this Level the children should be able to name all of the common quadrilaterals and explain their characteristics, including statements about their symmetry, similarity, and side and angle relationships.

Activity 1: A collection of quadrilaterals
Make a collection of as many quadrilaterals as you can and discuss their characteristics. From this discussion get the children to work in pairs to suggest ways in which the quadrilaterals might be grouped. Convenient ways of grouping include symmetrical properties, sorts of angles and whether or not their sides are parallel.

The shapes should include a kite, trapezium, rhombus, square, rectangle, parallelogram and some asymmetrical quadrilaterals. Quadrilaterals with different sorts of angles should also be present. Use this Activity before moving into tessellation.

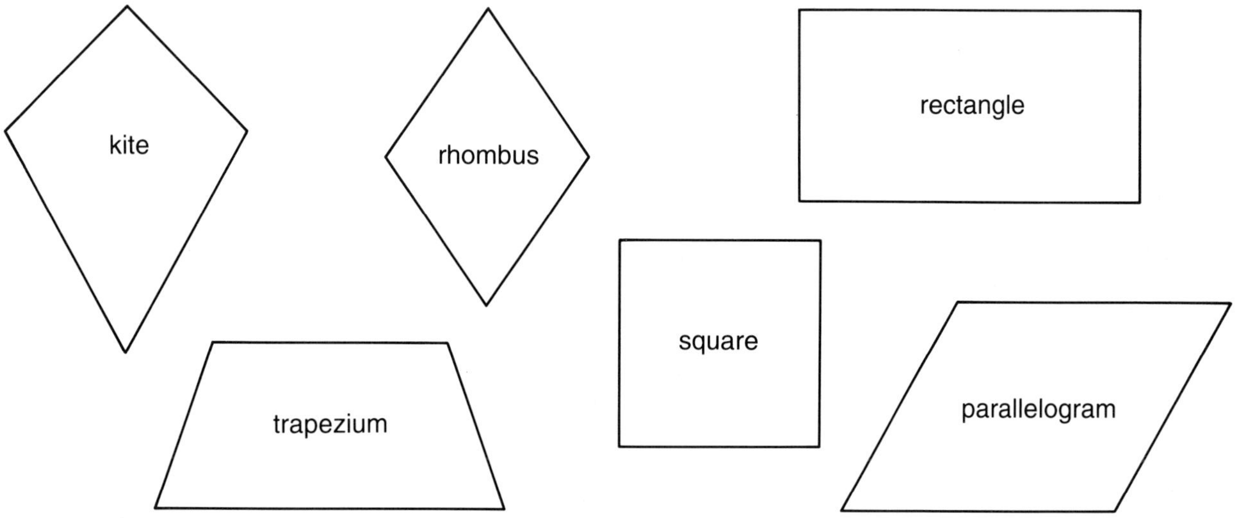

Area of study 41

COMPUTERS

Commentary
By now the children should be very familiar with using computers, including turtle graphics and drawing and painting packages. They should, therefore, be able to use the technology as a resource for the investigation of mathematical ideas and relationships.

Transformation can be viewed as being to do with a study of the effects of movement on shapes and points. This links closely to the idea of translation. *Translating* is a transformation through a movement in a pre-determined direction. Such movements are indicated by lines which are called *vectors*. The use of vectors can be found in science in the description of the effects of a force or number of forces on an object.

Activity 1: Generating and transforming 2-D shapes
Let the children do Activity 3 in 'Tessellation' before they tackle this.

Using the computer, try producing a rectangle and then making it lean to produce a parallelogram. Try rotating a circle to form an oval. Produce a pattern by translation, enlargement and reduction. Use these and similar investigations to generate a discussion about the nature and meaning of transformation.

Area of study 42

BEARINGS

Commentary
In using bearings you are determining the position either of the observer or of the thing observed. Building upon the work the children have done in using co-ordinates and scale, as well as work in geography, it is possible to work in quite a sophisticated way with the use of bearings.

Activity 1: Using angle and distance
Using a fixed line (school wall, boundary fence, marking on the playground) get the children to devise ways of measuring the angle from the base line to a named object. Having obtained the angle they then need to measure the distance to the object in order to fix its position on a scale drawing.

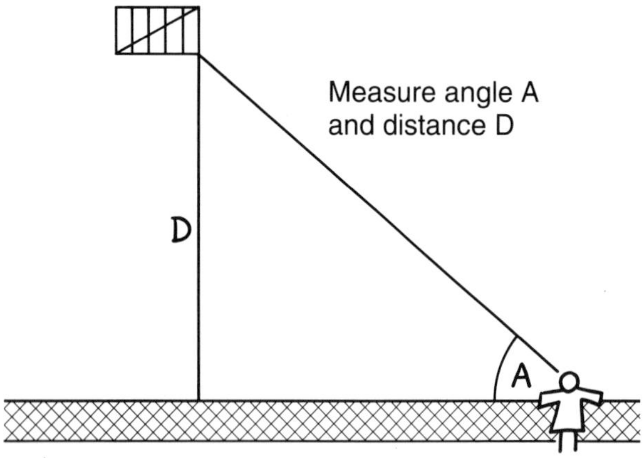

Fence is base line

Ideas for making an angle indicator are given in the following two Activities.

Activity 2: Using two angles
Again using a fixed base line, place two children at a known distance apart from each other on this base line. Get them to take bearings on a fixed object and use the distance apart, together with the bearings, to produce a scale drawing from which they can calculate the distance each of them was from the object, and the distance of the object from the nearest point of the base line.

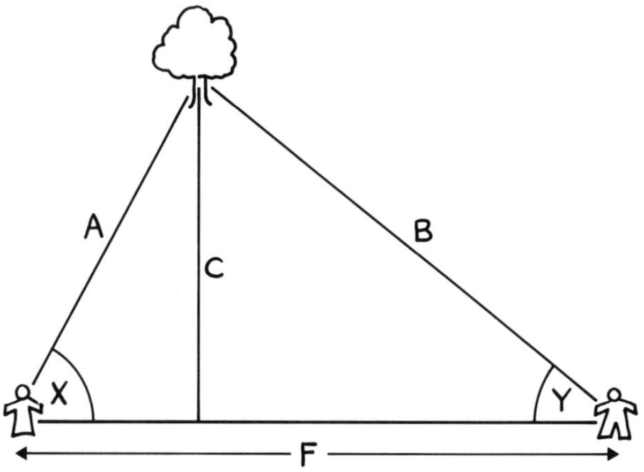

F is known.
Measure angles X and Y.
Find A, B and C.

Use this Activity to discuss navigation and the taking of bearings on a vessel from the shore. Now reverse the procedure and have a child as 'navigator' taking bearings on two objects which are a known distance apart. Use this to extend the discussion of navigation and, with the help of the children, assemble a collection of books about navigation at sea, both ancient and modern.

Activity 3: Bearings over time
It is often the case that navigators do not have two objects with which to take bearings. In this case, they have to take bearings on one object with a time interval between which allows them and/or the object to move. Sightings taken of the Sun and stars are of this type although with celestial and astronomical charts, and a knowledge of the time of day, it is possible to make use of just one reading – the other being provided by the charts. Find out more about these methods including ideas to do with longitude, latitude, international date and time lines and zones, Greenwich Mean Time and great circles. Invite a local sailor or pilot into school to talk about navigation with the children.

Area of study 43

NETWORKS

Commentary
A *network* is a set of points (vertices or nodes) which are connected by lines. Our everyday use of networks includes maps so it is important to have a range of maps which will give the children practice in interpreting and traversing networks.

In exploring networks we are centrally concerned with *traversability*. By this is meant the ability to travel through a network without retracing steps or going over a line more than once.

The investigation of networks also relates to ideas to do with *topology* – the study of shapes which remain constant in relation to their components even if you twist or bend them. So, for example, the drawings of different knots in anglers' guides or camping books are topological drawings. No amount of bending or twisting will change a sheepshank into a clove hitch.

Activity 1: Looking at networks
Let the children pore over a variety of maps. The class collection could include some of the following:

- city centre maps;
- bus maps;
- a London Underground map;
- layout maps like those that form part of the guide to houses open to the public, zoos and art galleries;
- computer games of the *Dungeons and Dragons* type.

Offer the children challenges, such as tracing the route from swimming pool to station, or park to school, or Paddington to Mornington Crescent! Concentrate on finding the shortest routes from one place to another.

Using an appropriate map, identify a delivery schedule and see if the children can find the shortest route for making the deliveries. Can they deliver the goods without crossing their own paths?

Activity 2: The Königsberg Bridge problem and traversability
Leonhard Euler (1707–83), a Swiss mathematician, worked on the Königsberg Bridge problem. The ancient town of Königsberg is built on two islands in the River Pregel. The islands and banks are connected by seven bridges.

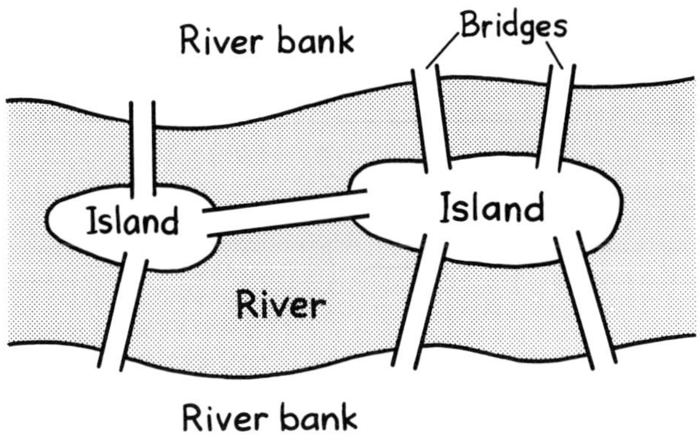

The citizens used to try to walk the town and bridges without retracing their steps to finish at their original starting point. They never managed this.

Let the children explore the problem that the citizens set for themselves. However, do not discuss any possible ways of resolving the problem before the children have tried the next Activity.

Copymaster 87 is a map of Königsberg with its bridges.

Activity 3: Traversing simple networks
In order for a network to be deemed traversable it must be possible to trace a route which uses every path in the network, but only once. Get the children to try out some networks to see if they are traversable. See if they can work out a general rule which will allow them to predict whether a particular network is traversable or not. The rule is that there must not be more than two junctions or nodes which have an odd number of paths arriving or departing from each node. Where is the best starting point for a given network? And what is the finishing point?

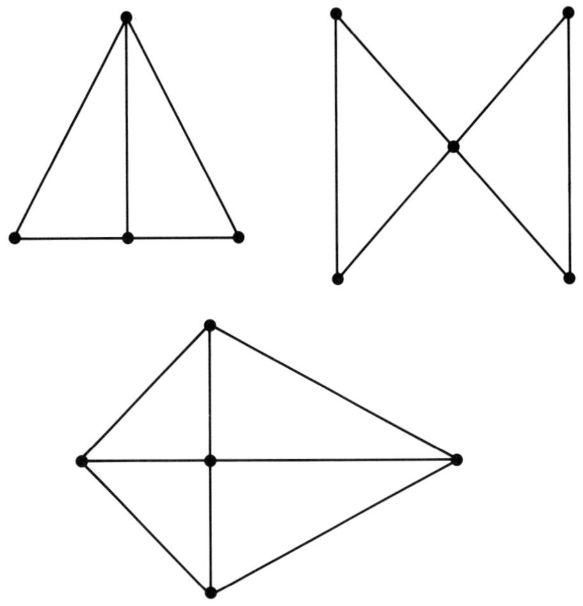

Now return to the Königsberg Bridge problem. Could the town become traversable by building more bridges? Or demolishing bridges?

Extend these Activities by using, for example, computer games which involve pathways and get the children to invent some exploration networks of their own.

Copymaster 88 has some networks for the children to try.

Activity 4: Mazes
Mazes and labyrinths date from ancient times. Many early ones are *unicursal* (have only one route to the centre). Show the children how to draw one of these. The six steps overleaf show how.

Then let the children draw some *multicursal* maze puzzles for their classmates to solve. If they wish they can work in groups to produce 'tiles'. They need to make a number of each design of tile including 'through routes', 'crossroads', 'blank ends' and 'junctions'. The tiles can be laid in a variety of configurations to make mazes. Some sample tiles are shown overleaf.

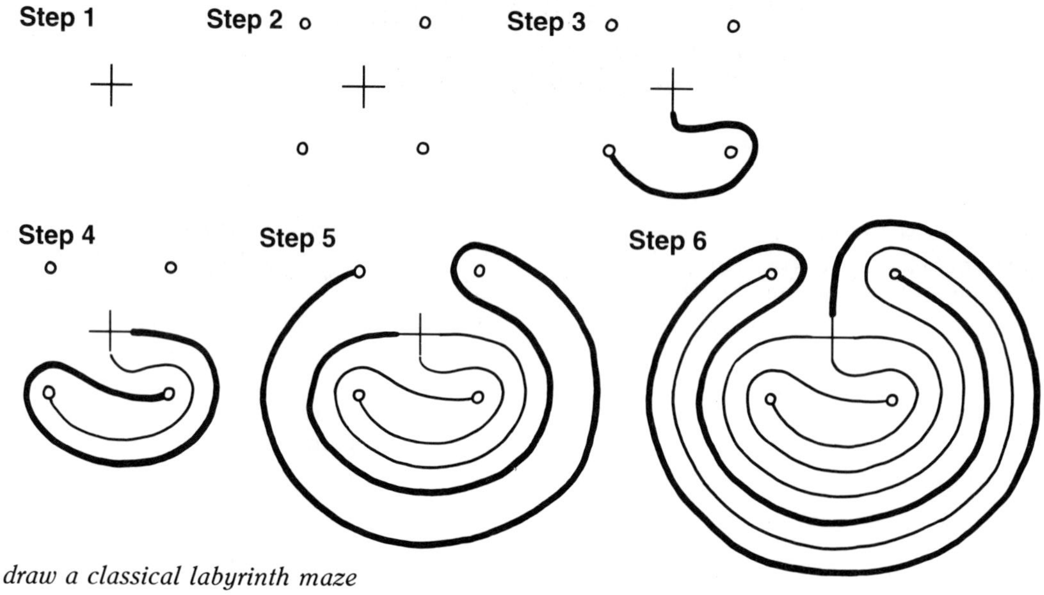

How to draw a classical labyrinth maze

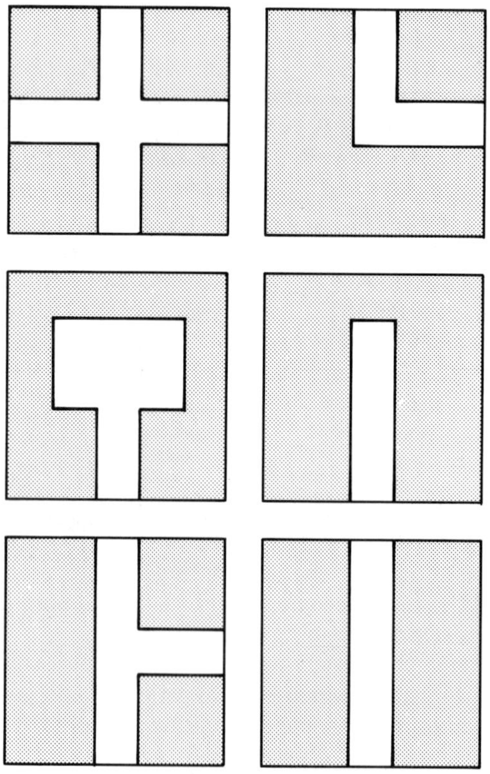

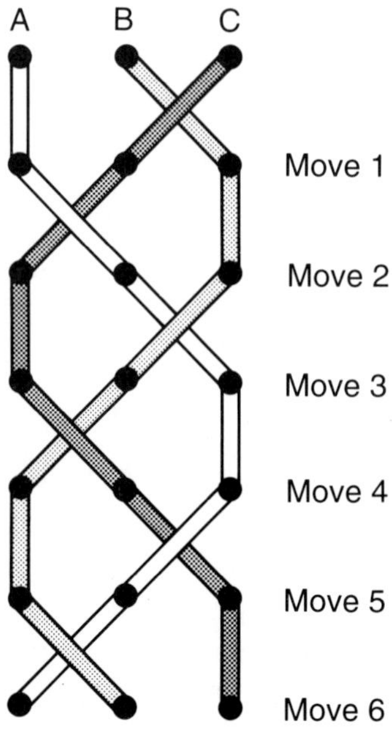

Activity 5: Plaits and knots
With the help of the children create a resource box of pictures and information about plaits and knots. Include, for example, sailors' knots and Celtic knots. Practise making and drawing the knots and working out the pathways taken by the ropes or strands in the design. Opposite is the continuous strand idea present in Celtic knots.

Look with the children at how the number of strands used in a plait changes the number of moves necessary to return to the start. A suggested layout for this kind of work is set out here.

Handling data

INTRODUCTION

It is on the basis of data that we manage our lives. Much of our decision-making is based upon the assembling of data, its interpretation and the prediction of likely events based upon that interpretation. The extent to which we make decisions that are reasoned and reasonable has much to do with the quality, scope and analysis of data. On the other hand, we can leave it all to fate! From these statements you will gather that we see data handling as being an important area of application in mathematics.

Many, if not all of us, have a range of superstitions which can affect our decision making. We all know about lucky heather, not walking under ladders, Friday 13th and what happens if we spill the salt! It is interesting how powerful, at times, is the sense that the coin will come down heads or that the fruit machine will pay out the jackpot at the next spin of the reels. But if we examine probabilities using mathematical techniques our sense of luck is questionable. Whilst it is nice to dream, and none of us would want to deprive children of their ability to immerse themselves in myths, legends and jolly exciting stories, it is equally important that we give children the tools that will enable them to distinguish between sensible choices and sheer fantasy. Traditionally, we have not done very much on the probability and chance aspects of data handling in the primary sector. The National Curriculum changes that.

Besides examining the basis of much of our data collection in terms of its validity another important facet is the discipline of data collection. As in science there is a need to organise the format and scope of any data collection activity and then have the persistence to carry through that data collection without starting to interpret what is being collected too soon. Leaping to conclusions on the basis of partial data is not acceptable and this is one of the often difficult things that we need to draw out of our data handling work. Additionally, of course, it is important to help the children to see that different sources of data may need tapping in different sorts of ways and this is also part of a planned data handling activity. The form in which data comes will affect the ways in which it can be analysed and interpreted.

Presenting data in understandable and clear forms is the final piece of the jigsaw as to construct meaningful pictorial representations needs the author of the work to have understood that data. It is also the case that the choice of representation must be sensibly linked to the type of data and its organisation.

Data handling is a complex activity characterised by the need to plan, the need to be patient and persistent, and the need to have a wide repertoire of techniques and methods of presentation at your fingertips. The early work in data handling sets out to establish important foundations in all of these things.

Resourcing Handling data

You need data! You can get it second-hand, by looking, for example, for lists, tables, frequency charts and block graphs already available. Though these are important they do not replace the first-hand data that the children as researchers collect in school.

Programme of study: Handling data

■ 1. Pupils should be given opportunities to:

a formulate questions about an issue of their choice, and consider them using statistical methods;

b access and collect data through undertaking purposeful enquiries;

c use computers as a source of interesting data, and as a tool for representing data.

For this first part of the Programme of study we have set down examples drawn from the body of the book.

a Area of study 12 **b** Area of study 4 **c** Area of study 8

Attainment target 4: Handling data

This attainment target does not apply to pupils in Key Stage 1.

Level descriptions

■ Level 2

Pupils sort objects and classify them using more than one criterion. Where they have gathered information, pupils record results in simple tables, block graphs and diagrams, in order to communicate their findings.

■ Level 3

Pupils extract and interpret information presented in simple tables and lists. They construct bar charts and pictograms, where the symbol represents a group of units, to communicate information they have gathered, and they interpret information presented to them in these forms.

■ Level 4

Pupils collect discrete data and record them using a frequency table. They understand and use the mode and median. They group data, where appropriate, in equal class intervals, represent collected data in frequency diagrams and interpret such diagrams. They construct and interpret simple line graphs. They understand and use simple vocabulary associated with probability, including 'fair', 'certain' and 'likely'.

■ Level 5

Pupils understand and use the mean of discrete data. They compare two simple distributions, using the range and one of the measures of average. They interpret graphs and diagrams, including pie charts, and draw conclusions. They understand and use the probability scale from 0 to 1. Pupils find and justify probabilities, and approximations to these, by selecting and using methods based on equally likely outcomes and experimental evidence, as appropriate. They understand that different outcomes may result from repeating an experiment.

Handling data

How the Areas of study in this book fit the Programme of study and Attainment target 4: Handling data level descriptions. Points in the Programme of study		Areas of study and 'best fit' with level descriptions			
		Level description 2	Level description 3	Level description 4	Level description 5
■ 2. Collecting, representing and interpreting data	**a** interpret tables used in everyday life; interpret and create frequency tables, including those for grouped discrete data;	1, 2	3	4, 5	
	b collect and represent discrete data appropriately using graphs and diagrams, including block graphs, pictograms and line graphs; interpret a wider range of graphs and diagrams that represent data, including pie charts, using a computer where appropriate;	6	7, 8, 9, 10	11, 12, 13	14, 15, 16, 17, 18
	c understand and use measures of average, leading towards the mode, the median and the mean in relevant contexts, and the range as a measure of spread;			19, 20	
	d draw conclusions from statistics and graphs, and recognise why some conclusions can be uncertain or misleading.				21
■ 3 Understanding and using probability	**a** develop understanding of probability, through experience as well as experiment and theory, and discuss events and simple experiments, using a vocabulary that includes the words 'evens', 'fair', 'unfair', 'certain', 'likely', 'probably', and 'equally likely';			22, 23, 24, 25	
	b understand that the probability of any event lies between impossibility and certainty, leading to the use of the scale from 0 to 1;				26
	c recognise situations where probabilities can be based on equally likely outcomes, and others where estimates must be based on experimental evidence; make or approximate these estimates.				27, 28, 29

Programme of study: Handling data

2. Collecting, representing and interpreting data

Pupils should be taught to:

a interpret tables used in everyday life; interpret and create frequency tables, including those for grouped discrete data;

Area of study 1 | P of S 2a | LD 2

SORTING AND CLASSIFYING

Commentary
Sorting is carried out on the basis of the characteristics or attributes of a collection of items. Children need to understand that within a complete or universal set of data there are likely to be sub-sets which can be defined and identified on the basis of stated attributes. Sorting and classifying helps with all mathematical activity as well as similar activities in other areas of the curriculum.

As well as taking responsibility for sorting the children should also be making decisions about how to record their results. Their repertoire of recording methods can be extended.

Activity 1: Concrete sorts
Let the children bring in some collections they have and talk about how they sort and identify them. Use some classroom collections that are sorted according to criteria. For example:

- books;
- crayons;
- counting and measuring apparatus;
- paper;
- exercise books.

Activity 2: Inspecting sorts
Look at some collections that are laid out in an order and discuss the merits of the sort. For example, you could look at a stamp collection, a list of English kings and queens, the plan of a museum or art gallery, or the signs above the aisles in the supermarket, along with some of the products sold there.

Activity 3: Make and record a sort
Provide the children with a pile of old magazines and catalogues. Let them work in pairs and cut out a collection of pictures. Invite the children to sort the pictures out and stick them to a large sheet of paper, in a way that makes it easy for everyone to see what is in their collection and how they have sorted it. Let all the children look at the results of this work and discuss differences and similarities in the approaches used.

Then show the children some ways of sorting that they may not have thought of. These include Venn diagrams and folding or partitioning paper.

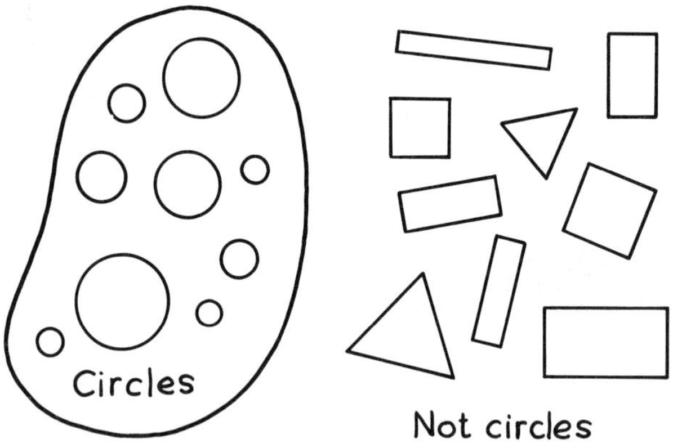

A Venn diagram

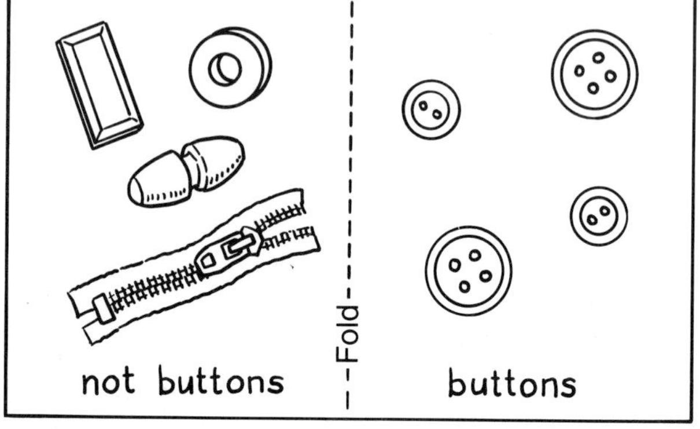

A button sort

Area of study 2 | P of S 2a | LD 2

CARROLL DIAGRAMS

Commentary
Classifying objects on the basis of two different criteria permits the use of a simple matrix for displaying the data. This offers opportunities for the future in that many simple classification keys are based on such distinctions and the use of matrices in mathematics is an important development of some mathematical ideas.

The Carroll diagram is named after Lewis Carroll who was a mathematician as well as the author of the *Alice* books.

Activity 1: Looking at sorting on two criteria
Take a large piece of paper and draw two lines across it to divide it into four segments. Show the children a mixed collection of coloured shape templates. Sort the shapes in front of the children, into, for example, red or not red. Place these piles in two of the boxes and label the boxes.

Now sort the piles again into, for example, three sides or not three sides, and let them take up the remaining boxes. Identify the individual sets with labels.

Activity 2: Making a Carroll diagram
Let the children assemble some items for sorting and transfer their own sorts to Carroll diagrams.

To enliven the Activity and enable the children to commit this important process to memory, let them do sorts with their own collections of keyrings, small toys, teddies, shells, stamps, postcards or photographs.

For future use begin a resource box for sorts. Add to it things such as postcards, souvenirs, little toys and mottoes from crackers, tickets like those for trains and entrance to places of interest, and foreign coins.

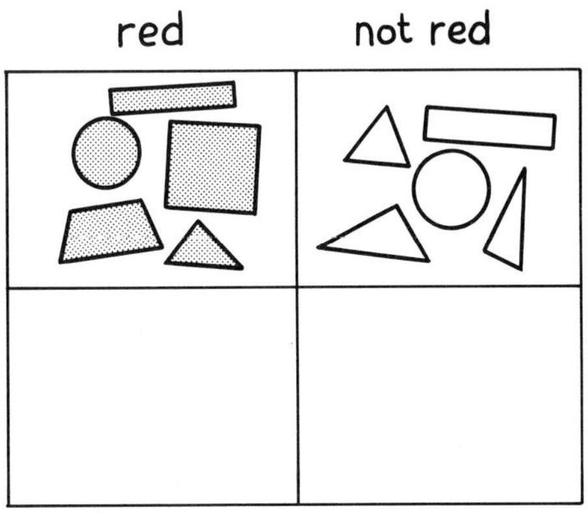

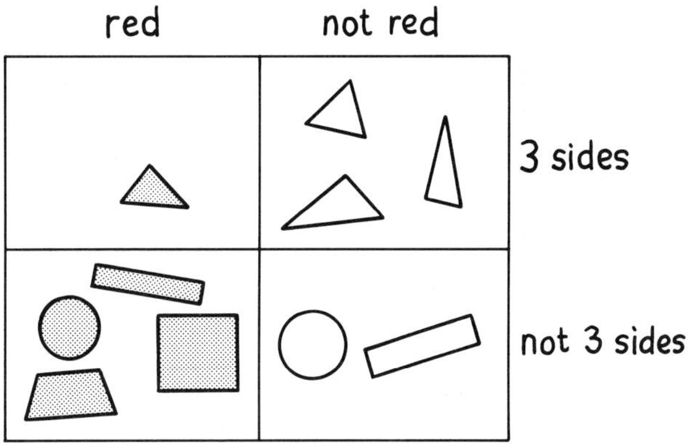

A Carroll diagram

Area of study 3 | P of S 2a | LD 3

TABLES AND LISTS

C89, 90

Commentary
The ability to read from tables and lists is one of the basics for all of the population. This, then, is important work in helping to empower the children for their future decision-making needs.

Activity 1: Looking at lists
Collect a variety of lists as a starting point for discussion.

Here are some possible inclusions:

- shopping list;
- register;
- Christmas present list;
- supermarket checkout receipt;
- book index;
- telephone book.

Discuss with the children why we make lists, and the ways in which lists order information, for example, alphabetically or in order of being checked.

Activity 2: The benefits of lists
Carry through a classroom drama in which a group of children are asked to assemble about 20 named resources from around the room without having them written in a list. Set two children to time the operation. Now give the same task to the group, using an ordered list of different items. Let the children see if the timing differs and discuss the group's experiences. This may provide a good basis for an assembly all about managing yourself and your work in school.

Activity 3: Compiling lists
Present the children with some data which they can set in a list in a variety of ways. Here are some suggestions:

- names of birds and diet;
- foods that might complete a menu;
- shopping list with shops where goods may be found;
- names and addresses;

- bus and train timetables
- recipes
- food labels (ingredients and nutritional value)
- book titles;
- television programme listings.

Copymaster 89 has some jumbled data on it from which a number of lists might be extracted.

Activity 4: Looking at tables
Show the children some tables in common use. Examples might include the following:

- calendar;
- food nutrition details from packaging;
- class timetable.

Working in groups, show the children how to interpret the tables, and discuss the benefits of recording two linked sets of information in this way.

Give the children some information for them to set out in table form.

Copymaster 90 has two sets of data which can be set in table form.

Area of study 4 | P of S 2a | LD 4

TALLYING AND FREQUENCY TABLES

C91, 92

Commentary
Tallying is an ancient method of recording. Tally sticks in which notches and symbols are carved have been used for thousands of years. Indeed it is only in the last century that they went completely out of fashion for certain types of accounting.

Grouped data means that the data is recorded as numbers of items within predetermined class intervals. Class intervals are discussed in 'Drawing frequency diagrams' below. The kind of data you choose for frequency table work does depend on the location of the school and classroom, and the number of children engaged in the group. If the data has to be collected spasmodically avoid having the children wasting time waiting, when nothing is happening. You also want a fair rate of data input to keep up the children's motivation. Thus, predicted occurrence should be your guide to deciding what information to collect.

Activity 1: Designing a data collection sheet
You cannot design a sheet on which to collect data without first having some idea of the kind of data you wish to collect. Decide on the kind of data the children are going to work with. They may have their own ideas, but here are some suggestions:

- How many times do six of your friends eat chips in a week? Does consumption vary from day to day?
- How many times does the classroom door open in an hour? Which classes do the people using it belong to?
- How many times does the word 'is' or 'and' appear in a short book? Is the word evenly distributed?

See how the children decide to set out the information and then, if necessary, show them how to set out one kind of information along the bottom and another along the side.

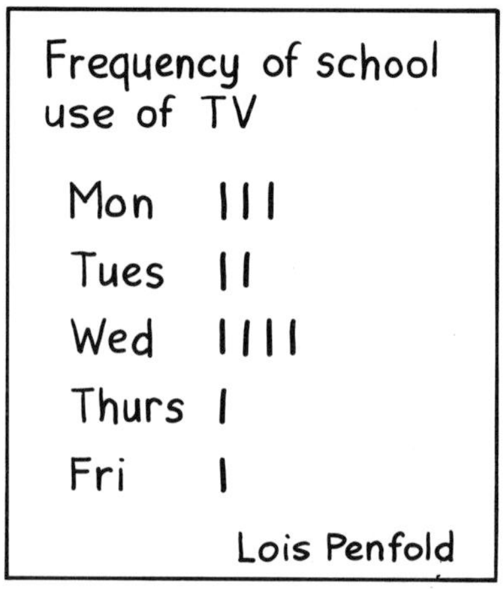

Activity 2: Constructing frequency tables
Using some data the children have collected, help them to create a table, using a tally. Display the children's work. Keep this work as a class resource for subsequent groups of children whom you teach.

Copymaster 91 is a 'blank' for a tally record and could be used for data collection before it is transferred to a 'fair' copy of the children's own devising.

Activity 3: Interpreting frequency tables
Collect some frequency tables for the children to look at. They may be sets of information that children in other classes have collected or of your own invention.

Copymaster 92 presents two frequency charts which you can use for discussion. They should not replace first-hand data the children have collected themselves.

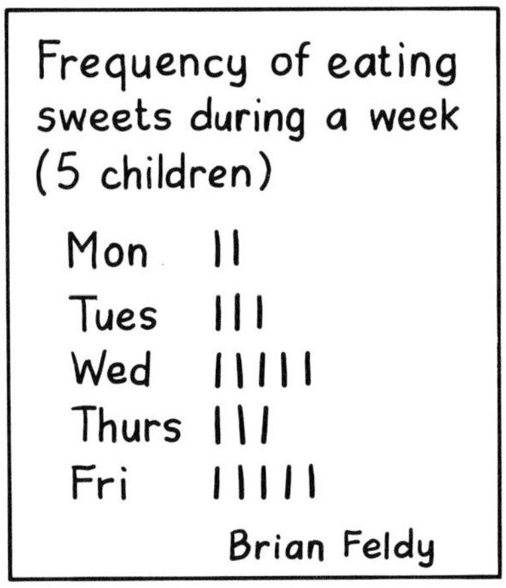

Activity 4: From data collection to frequency table
Invite the children to collect some appropriate information and present it in tabular form. Two examples of data are:

- holiday locations of classmates in the last two years;
- how often classmates' parents use the local shop.

Get the children to group the data as appropriate when they come to present their findings.

Activity 5: Historical perspectives
There is often much to be gained by engaging in work on the history of mathematical ideas, processes and methods. An investigation of tallying in different places and at different times is one such opportunity.

Area of study 5 | P of S 2a | LD 4

TREE DIAGRAMS

Commentary
Tree diagrams have their roots (!) in set theory and logic. The intention is that the children sort items and objects by rigorous analysis of attributes and a series of yes/no type questions. These tree diagrams are closely related to Carroll diagrams.

Activity 1: Tree sorts
Give the children equipment from the classroom which is appropriate for sorting and some less-conventional collections for sorts. Show the children how to set out a number of decision points to create a tree. An example is set out opposite.

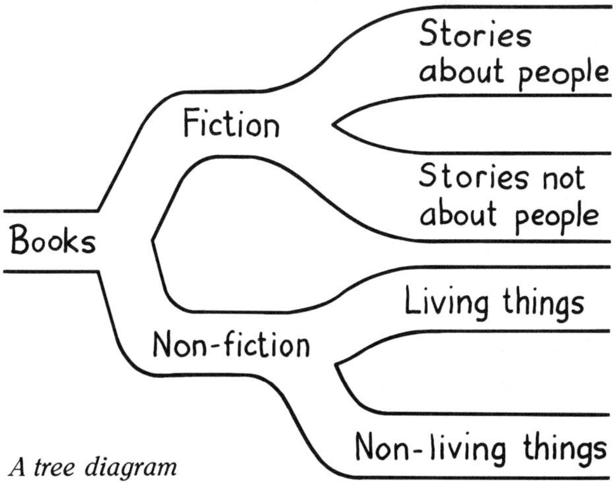

A tree diagram

Programme of study: Handling data

Pupils should be taught to:

■ 2. Collecting, representing and interpreting data

b collect and represent discrete data appropriately using graphs and diagrams, including block graphs, pictograms and line graphs; interpret a wider range of graphs and diagrams that represent data, including pie charts, using a computer where appropriate;

Area of study 6 | P of S 2b | LD 2

BLOCK GRAPHS

RC5 C93

Commentary
The characteristics of block graphs are that:

- each column is discrete;
- the blocks are all visually clear;
- each column has its own label;
- they allow a mix of numbers on one axis and labels on the other

Activity 1: Constructing a block graph
For the children's first attempt at a block graph use some information about themselves that is so familiar it will not 'get in the way' of an understanding of the information layout. Here are some suggestions for a kind of data that may be suitable:

- favourite dinners;
- favourite television programmes;
- favourite colours.

Using data the children have collected or data from the school data bank, create a block graph while the children look on. Use large squared paper and sticky shape counters or *Multilink* to represent entries on the chart. When you have created it you can ask the children questions about the graph, to be sure that they have understood what you have done. An example worked through may look like this:

15 children were asked to say which pets they have

Data:

- 4 have a cat;
- 5 have a dog;
- 2 have guinea pigs;
- 3 have rabbits;
- 2 have a budgie;
- 4 have fish;
- 3 have hamsters;
- 1 has gerbils;
- 3 have no pets.

The vertical (y) axis will be named 'Number of children' and numbered 1–5. The horizontal (x) axis will have a column for each kind of pet.

Resource copymaster 5 is a sheet of large squares which may be suitable for producing block graphs.

Activity 2: Interpreting a block graph
When you and the children have created a block graph like that set out in Activity 1, ask them questions to assure yourself that they have understood. If you used the example above, the questions to ask include, for example, Which is the most popular pet? How many people have a budgie? How many people altogether have a dog and/or a cat?

Copymaster 93 has a block graph drawn on it, for the children to interpret. This is an example and children should have a chance to inspect and interpret plenty of block graphs in the course of their learning.

Activity 3: Block graphs from start to finish
Let the children work in pairs (if this is appropriate) to assemble some data for a block graph, deciding on what goes along each axis, and then draw it up. If this exercise goes well they can ask their classmates problems associated with their graphs.

Area of study 7 | P of S 2b | LD 3

CARD DATA BASES

Commentary
In getting the children to create card data bases you are allowing them to understand the attributes of data bases generally. They will have to learn about:

- attributes which can be used as categories;
- the idea of a field for the entering of information;
- ways of sorting using different fields;
- storage and access;
- regular maintenance of a data base.

Activity 1: Putting information in a data base
Create a card data base that will be of use to the children in your class. If you command the same resources for several years the data base can be updated by subsequent classes of children. In any case, a data base can be passed on to another teacher. You are the best judge of what will best serve the children. You may, for example, like to keep the following on a data base:

- topics that are often covered, listing the location of books and other resources in school;
- the class library;
- a sample of pets;
- school software.

Show the children how the information is classified and what kinds of information are stored. Let each child complete some entries.

Activity 2: Getting information from a data base
Using the same data base, or one created by another class or centrally within the school, let the children access it. You can create challenge cards depending on the kinds of information stored. For example, if the data base is about wild animals, it may be possible to ask children to discover all the big cats that come from Africa, what a lemur eats or what is the smallest land mammal.

Area of study 8 | P of S 2b | LD 3

COMPUTER DATA BASES

Commentary
This work should build onto the work done with card data bases.

Before you use a data base with the children, evaluate its possibilities and limitations, including, for example, how many categories of information are allowed and how many characters can be carried.

There are opportunities of enlargement of a data base by collaboration with others. For example, a joint venture with another school would enhance each of the school's data bases.

The school has a responsibility with regard to the use of data on a computer. It is therefore essential that there is a consistent school policy on data bases.

Activity 1: Putting information in a computer data base
Use an appropriate software package to let the children produce a data base. They may choose any topic which interests them. It would be useful to you if they do not limit it to something topical that may be of little interest to subsequent children in the school, but even then it may have historical purpose. Past crazes such as the *Teenage Mutant Hero Turtles* and *The Simpsons* can be matched with those that feature in ten years' time! Other possibilities include:

- trees;
- dinosaurs;
- famous people;
- cartoon characters;
- television programmes;
- hobbies and sports.

The list is without end.

Activity 2: Getting information from a computer data base
Using the data base the children have created or one you have borrowed from another school, let the children access it and meet challenges you set for them. They should not only be able to call up individual items of information, but also obtain counts for categories of information.

Area of study 9 | P of S 2b | LD 3

BAR CHARTS

C94, 95

Commentary
Bar charts differ from block graphs in that the blocks are replaced by continuous bars. The lengths of the respective bars are the means by which the charts are interpreted.

Review Level 2 and look at what the children have already done about bar charts.

Activity 1: Understanding bar charts
Look with the children at a number of bar charts and discuss the way the information is presented. Quiz the children until they can access the information appropriately and explain what they have done.

Copymaster 94 has two bar charts on it which can be used as a basis for discussion. On **copymaster 95** children are asked to add more data to the chart.

Activity 2: Constructing bar charts
Using information that the children themselves collect let them make bar charts. Keep their charts and data to use with other groups of children. Easy starter charts can be made if you invite each child to list the names of nine of their classmates with their own name, and then ask each named person one of the following questions:

- What size shoes do you wear?
- How many brothers do you have?
- How many sisters do you have?
- What colour is your hair?
- What colour are your eyes?
- Try writing with these four things (quill, Biro, fountain pen, felt tip). Which do you find the easiest to write with?
- What languages are spoken by members of your family?

Area of study 10 | P of S 2b | LD 3

PICTOGRAMS

C96, 89

Commentary
Pictograms are pictorial representations of data. The pictures used in pictograms are intended to identify numbers of items rather than single items. Pictograms are commonly employed in newspapers and on television as they offer attractive visual possibilities.

In using pictograms the children are gaining further insights into counts, frequency and the grouping of data.

Activity 1: Interpreting pictograms
Show the children a pictogram and help them interpret the use of the symbol and 'read' the data. Search out some pictograms for the children to practise on from sources available to you. These include:

- newspapers;
- data bases created by other children.

Copymaster 96 presents two pictograms for the children to discuss and interpret.

Activity 2: Constructing pictograms
Having done Activity 1 the children should be able to create pictograms when given appropriate data.

Example situations which may provide appropriate data may include the following frequencies:

- number of outdoor playtimes in a month;
- number of times cabbage is served at school dinner in a month;
- number eating crisps in a week (sample of 20 children);
- number of drinks consumed in a week (the children in the sample keep and submit a tally);
- the number of comings and goings through the main school door in a morning (exclude school start and end of session).

Copymaster 89 is a tally sheet for information collection.

Area of study 11 | P of S 2b | LD 4

USING A DATA BASE

Commentary
The key word in data base activities at this Level is *interrogation*. The children must be given the chance to interrogate a data base to get information which they can then use.

There are now several commercially-produced data bases which, depending on your particular computers, can be purchased as resources in the same way that books are resources. The advent of the CD–ROM will surely accelerate the numbers and kinds of data bases that children can access.

Activity 1: Inserting data
The work the children have done at previous Levels will be invaluable here, for the school should now have at least one data base to work on. Let the children have the opportunity of adding to this pool of information. They should have sufficient practice to know how to set up and run the program, what form the information should take (that is how many characters per item and so on) and how to insert it appropriately.

If you wish to start a new data base on which children tackling Level 4 can work, you will need to review the kinds of information accessible to the children on data bases already. These may have been set up by other classes or by the children you now teach in previous years. Some suggestions which may not yet have been tackled by these children include the following:

- local buildings;
- different countries (in support of Geography AT2);
- varieties of garden flowers and vegetables;
- facts about 2-D and 3-D shapes (in support of AT4).

Activity 2: Interrogating a data base
In addition to letting the children add to the data base, you can ask them to access it and obtain items of data and counts. If you have commercially-produced data bases then also make use of these.

Invite a local businessperson, shopkeeper, store manager or higher education lecturer to share the ways in which they make use of data bases in their work, for example, customer lists, stock-taking and replacement, and the development of learning packages.

Activity 3: Interpreting data
So that it is not a sterile exercise, let the children use the information they access on computer in combination with other data sources. They could write it up in a report, make it part of a topic folder or part of a multi-media presentation for the class or school.

Imagine an assembly in which a pupil from 30 years ago told of school life then, children were able to act out a school day using data from the school log and other school records about the timetable, and individual school log entries were read out. Some of this data could be put into computer data bases or spreadsheets and the printouts made available on a display. Add to this some old school photos and memories of staff from that time (to whom the children wrote as part of the topic) and something memorable and worthwhile emerges. Video the whole event and use the film as a data source for another group of children.

Area of study 12 | P of S 2b | LD 4

CHOOSING A RESEARCH ISSUE

Commentary
In identifying issues which are appropriate for research activity there are a number of factors which need to be taken into account. The research issue should be:

- manageable by the children in terms of realistic opportunities for data collection;
- amenable to the collection of sufficient data to draw some conclusions;
- resourcable.

Activity 1: Identifying issues
This is a chance to really let the children decide what they would like to do. Discuss what the children like to spend time on, what their hobbies are, what their thoughts and feelings are about topical issues, and their preoccupations. They may of course want to discuss bedtimes and pocket money endlessly, but if not the following list gives some suggested topics that might be raised in discussion or that you may offer as possibilities to get children thinking:

- threatened wildlife;
- helping the Third World;
- children's television;
- soap operas;
- educational television;
- film categories;
- women working;
- men working;
- how children are treated by adults.

However, do give the children the chance to raise their own possible topics of interest first.

Activity 2: Making the issue manageable
Once children decide which issue they are going to address, they will need your help to make it manageable. They need to decide the following:

- *What* exactly they are going to find out.
- *Where* the information will come from (people, television, books, organisations, etc.).
- *Who* – if they are going to ask people then *how many* are they going to get replies from. Will they use an *interview* or written *questionnaire* method.

All this information could form a *research proposal*. The children could make their own folder for their investigation.

You will then need to tell the children about some more skills. For example, here are some interview skills:

- Ask only one thing in a question. (Answers to 'Do you like green or prefer black?' are unclear.)
- Make sure the question does ask for the information you need. ('Have you lived here long?' is no good if you want to know *how* long.)
- Ask people for their help and tell them how long the interview will take before you start.
- You will not be able to write as quickly as people speak, so either limit the number of 'open' questions; use a questionnaire rather than an interview; or record the interview on tape.

Area of study 13 | P of S 2b | LD 4

INTERPRETING AND CONSTRUCTING BAR-LINE GRAPHS

RC3,4 | C97

Commentary
Block graphs and bar graphs should have set the scene for the introduction of line graphs and children should realise that line graphs are suitable for data that is 'continuous'.

When the numbers of items are great it is sensible to group the data. This is commonly done by adopting predetermined groups with given ranges, using class intervals. For example, if the children were collecting information about the amount of pocket-money that Year 5 children receive they might organise the data in class intervals of:

0–49p
50–99p
£1–£1.49
and so on.

Activity 1: Talk about graphs
Look at a number of graphs the children have already produced and point out that the data in them is discrete (that is one 'result' is separate from the next). Show the children how a graph of, for example, outdoor temperature against time of day can be drawn as a continuous line.

Show the children what bar-line graphs look like and explain that they are useful for clearly indicating the size of a category or number as well as the precise point at which this lies on a graph.

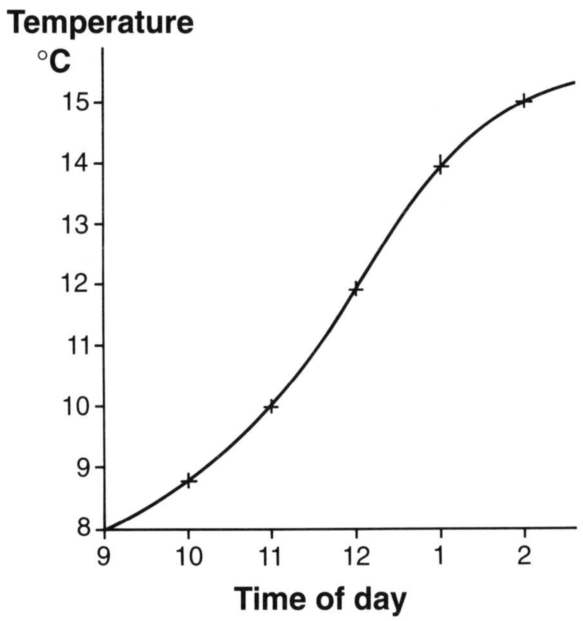

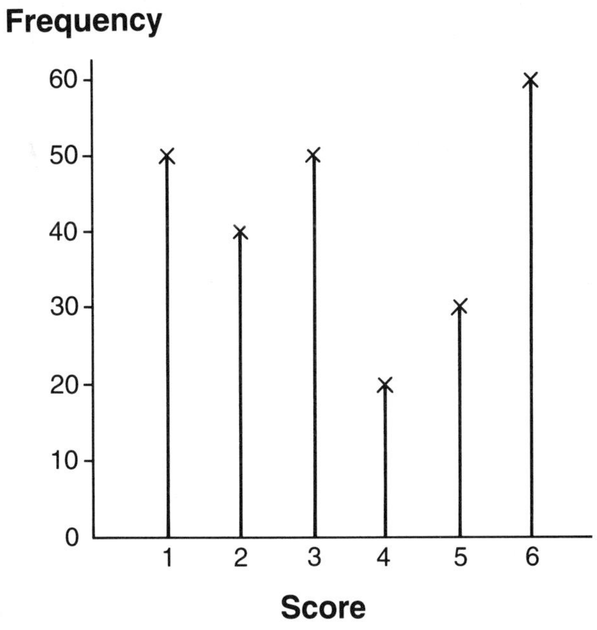

Activity 2: Drawing graphs
Give the children some sample data from which to produce line graphs. Here are some examples:

- $2\times$ table – (x-axis) 0–10 number of times, (y-axis) 0–20 product;
- centimetres to inches conversion – (x-axis) inches, (y-axis) centimetres;
- circumference and diameters of circles – (x-axis) diameter, (y-axis) circumference. See AT4 Level 5.

Resource copymasters 3 and **4** are graph paper sheets.

Activity 3: Drawing frequency diagrams
With their past experience the children should now be able to scrutinise data and work out class intervals suitable for a frequency diagram.

Sample data suitable for grouping is to be found on **copymaster 97.**

Area of study 14 | P of S 2b | LD 5

DRAWING CONCLUSIONS THROUGH USE OF A DATA BASE

Commentary
By now the children should have had plenty of practice in using data bases. It will help you, the teacher, and the children themselves if they take a little time to evaluate their experiences so far.

Data bases have appeared regularly through the Levels but with a somewhat different expectation on each occasion. This mirrors a particular sort of model which can be broadly described as developmental in respect of: data logging → accessing data → evaluating patterns → synthesis of ideas.

At this Level the children should be evaluating patterns in data and drawing conclusions. They will be starting to synthesise the specific ideas. In order for this to happen view the work at this Level as both a consolidation of what has gone on before and an opportunity for you and the children to create new challenges from known material.

Activity 1: Data base fluency
A discussion or, more formally, a check-list should reveal answers to the following:

- Do you know the name of your school's software package which contains a data base?
- Do you know how to load and access the data base package?
- Have you attempted to put information into data bases?
- What were the data bases about?
- Have you retrieved information from a data base?
- Have you had the chance to write up your findings?
- What form did your writing take – a story, report or spoken presentation?
- If you could create your own data base what would it be about and what sort of information would it contain?

Base the Activities you make available to the children on their fluency. The work should culminate in a set of challenges related to a data base held on disc.

Activity 2: Themes and topics
Locate computer data base work within a selected topic or theme. Some examples are:

- a school resource bank – containing everything for every conceivable part of the curriculum and topic;
- family data – do make sure this is entered in coded fashion so that the anonymity of the families is preserved;
- oral history – interview the adults in school and ask the children to talk to adults at home about life and times past; create a file each for the 1940s, 1950s, 1960s . . . and so on;
- compile a diary of events from the school log book – again preserving the anonymity of individual staff and children, but introducing categories of events like closures, staff changes and building improvements.

Area of study 15 | P of S 2b | LD 5

OBSERVATION SHEET DESIGN

C98

Commentary
In order to make sensible collections of data which allow ready and unambiguous collation it is vital that the children learn the importance of designing appropriate recording devices. An observation sheet is one such device and must be organised in such a way that the act of recording does not actually inhibit or distract from the act of data collection.

Activity 1: Design
The design of the observation sheet will depend on the kind of information the children are going to collect. They will be able to decide what to observe, but here are a few additional suggestions:

- the constituents of their school meal, chosen by one in two of the children staying to lunch on a given day;
- the times of arrival of children coming through the school gate on a typical morning;
- the kinds and locations of building materials found in school buildings and those visible from the school compound;
- the kinds and numbers of mini-beasts (for example, insects) found in one of the school flower beds.

Activity 2: Data collection and collation
Using an enquiry of the children's own choice, and the observation sheet they designed in Activity 1, let them attempt to get their information down on paper and afterwards determine how they will present it. If their first study goes well it can be placed in a folder and added to class data resources.

If children require further practice invite them to redesign their observation sheet and collect a different kind of data. The class data bank should swell considerably as a result of the children's efforts.

Copymaster 98 is a report form allowing the children to evaluate their efforts.

Area of study 16 | P of S 2b | LD 5

PIE CHARTS

C99

Commentary
Pie charts are a good way of seeing how a section of data relates to the whole. Pie charts, for this reason, are commonly used in newspapers and company statements. They are highly visual and readily accessible.

Pie charts are not easy to construct by hand, but the use of computers has made the process much easier. The reasons for this are to do with the computations involved in working out proportions of a circle and the accuracy of measurement required when the angles have been worked out. With real data it is often the case that the angles are not precise.

Activity 1: Interpreting pie charts
Use sample pie charts from newspapers and books to show the children how data can be set out in this way. Set some challenges relating to pie charts of the kind 'What percentage . . . ?'

Some hypothetical pie charts are set out on **copymaster 99**. Give the children some challenges using these.

Activity 2: Constructing pie charts
Using data gleaned in other Activities ask the children to create pie charts. Do this both by hand and using the computer.

Activity 3: The use of pie charts
Invite in some people who make use of pie charts and other types of pictorial representation of data to talk about why they use them and how they choose between one type of representation and another. Examples of organisations to approach are:

- advertising agencies or the local newspaper;
- county council treasury departments;
- statistics departments in the LEA;
- the local further or higher education institution.

Area of study 17 | P of S 2b | LD 5

THE RESEARCH PROCESS: USING OBSERVATION

C98

Commentary
Observation does not mean recording all you see, but recording all those items relevant to the study in hand. The children therefore need your help before they begin data collection, in really refining what it is they are looking for.

Link this work to what the children are doing in Technology.

The research process has been divided up and compiled as a list of Activities. Depending on the size of the investigation, the children may be able to do Activities 1 and 2 in one session.

Talk to the children about bias and how to avoid it by showing them examples. Thus, if you want to make the case that accidents occur at the playground entrance, you do need to look at what happens at other locations in the playground too.

Activity 1: Deciding issues
The children may at this Level be able to identify the issues that are topical and manageable within the school or the school community. Here are a few suggestions showing the type of enquiry which the children and the other people involved in the research will see as worthwhile for investigation. They are:

- A study of the school playground environment – Is it secure? Is it safe? Is it attractive? Is it stimulating? How can it be improved?
- Creating a play area for pre-school children, involving visits to playgroups and nurseries to look at what children play with and on, and observations about the safety factors to consider.
- A study of shopping areas to see whether they are 'friendly' to people with prams and buggies, people in wheelchairs and the elderly.
- A study of buses/taxis available in the locality – What is the take-up rate? What are the limitations of the transport considered? How could it be improved?

Activity 2: Planning data collection
Having decided on an issue for study, the children will need your help in deciding what data to collect and how to go about collecting it. Let them draft some lists of the following:

- locations needing to be visited;
- the most important things to look for;
- how to avoid bias in data collection;
- the timing of the project;

- the times of data collection;
- administration problems and expenses, for example, how do we get to the point of data collection and who will supervise?

The children can then design their observation sheet and divide the kinds of observations they want to collect amongst the groups doing the research.

There is a sample observation evaluation sheet on **copymaster 98**.

Activity 3: Analysing results
Help the children to be systematic in their analysis. 'Rules' that you may like to discuss include the following check points:

- Am I looking at one kind of data at a time?
- What do the counts and figures I have included mean? In other words, a report communicates results to others so it must make sense to people who know nothing about the research.
- Have I presented the findings neatly and clearly?
- Have I drawn conclusions that fit the data?
- Is there evidence of bias?

Decide with the children what form the presentation of their results should take and what their next steps should be.

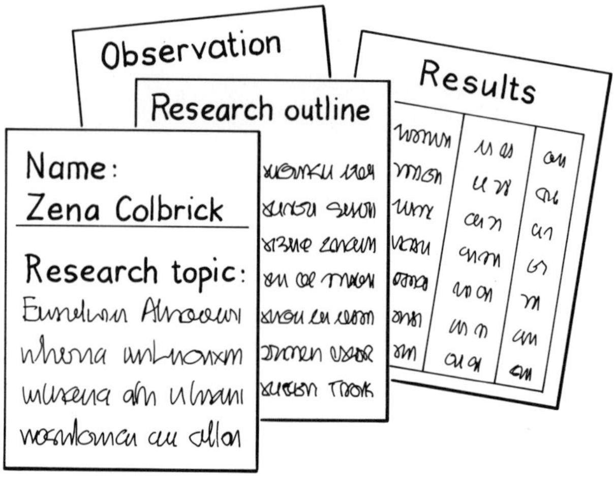

Area of study 18 | P of S 2b | LD 5

THE RESEARCH PROCESS: USING QUESTIONNAIRES

Commentary
Give the children some of the vocabulary of the researcher, including a discussion of open/closed questions, multiple choice questions and response 'scales' of the type:

YES completely satisfied	YES reasonably satisfied	neither satisfied nor dissatisfied	NO slightly dissatisfied	NO completely dissatisfied

Alert the children to possible bias in question wording.

Activity 1: Piloting and refining
Help the children to create a questionnaire. For this 'practice' Activity the data and topic could be imaginary. For example, the topic may be about the sightings of UFOs, a children's parliament or vegetarianism declared as law. Help the children to devise a number of questions. Include some of each of the following:

- Closed questions, that is with a predetermined answer – for example, 'Have you ever seen a UFO? Yes/No.'
- Open questions, that is inviting a new reply every time – for example, 'How would you feel if/How did you feel when a spaceship landed in your garden?'
- Multiple choice questions, with a choice of predetermined answers, and where, depending on the question there may be more than one reply – for example, 'Which of these things would you like to do? Travel in space/go to the moon/spend time on an interplanetary station.'
- 'Scale' answers – for example, 'How much would you like to go into space? Very much – Quite like it – A little – Wouldn't like it.'
- Biased questions – for example, if you say 'Surely you wouldn't . . . would you?' or 'Everybody does . . . do you?', then this is pressing the person asked into a certain kind of answer.

When the children have made up some questions, and discussed the problems in question design, invite them to make up a ten-question questionnaire and try it on their friends and teachers.

Activity 2: Following up on observation
With the experience they may have gained in Activity 1 let the children devise a questionnaire to help in a research project of their choice. This may be one of those discussed in 'The research process: using observation'. For example, if the children have watched under-fives at play and have some recorded observations, they may now decide they want to send a questionnaire to playgroup leaders. Remind the children about the skills used in the wording of questions and about possible bias.

Programme of study: Handling data

Pupils should be taught to:

2. Collecting, representing and interpreting data

c understand and use measures of average, leading towards the mode, the median and the mean in relevant contexts, and the range as a measure of spread;

Area of study 19 | P of S 2c | LD 4

MEDIAN AND MODE

Commentary
Three averages that we use are the *mean*, *median* and *mode*. In reading about average the children should appreciate the importance of knowing which sort of average is being talked about.

The *median* is the middle value in a set of results. If there is an even number of results the median lies between the middle two. The *mode* is the result that occurs most often. The *mean* is the average which is in everyday use. The mean average is obtained by dividing the sum of a set of results by the number of results.

Whilst sets of hypothetical data can be given to children in order to give them practice in finding the median and mode the concepts will be internalised more readily if the data are real and meaningful.

Activity 1: Median
Let the children open up six packs of cheese biscuits and count the contents before they share them out for eating. (If possible, keep the biscuits for Activity 2 and keep the results for a discussion of 'Mean and range' below.) Let the children record how many biscuits there were in each pack, starting with the least. Thus, if the results are:

20 21 22 24 24 24;

then show the children that the median is between 22 and 24 (i.e. 23).

Let the children set one another tasks involving finding the median. The children themselves may be able to think of ways of doing this. Here are some examples:

- a number of Smarties® tubes with a variable number of sweets, 1p coins or buttons in them (median contents);
- a picture of a number of children of different ages, with their ages marked (median age).

Activity 2: Mode
Using the results of the cheese biscuits counts in Activity 1, show the children that the mode (24) is the most common result.

Let the children work out the mode for some of the tasks they set up in Activity 1.

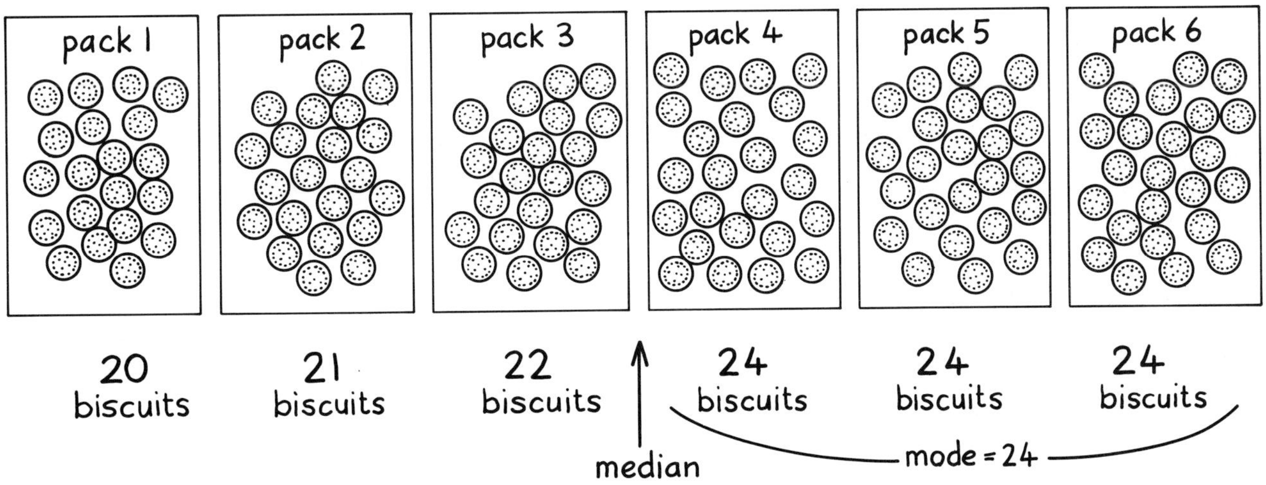

Area of study 20 | P of S 2c | LD 4

MEAN AND RANGE

Commentary
The *mean* is the average with which we are familiar. The *range* is the difference between the lowest and highest of a list of results.

Activity 1: Mean
Using the data collected in the cheese biscuits data count under 'Median and mode' or using another collection of packs of biscuits let the children assemble the numbers of biscuits in each pack. Help them to find the average number by summing all the biscuits and dividing by the number of packs. Point out that the average in this case has to be a number of whole biscuits. With other samples of data the mean average can be found more accurately to perhaps two decimal places.

Activity 2: Range
Using the data from Activity 1, let the children find the difference between the lowest and highest number of biscuits contained in a pack. Ask the children to assemble some data from which their friends can detect the range. The following examples may set the children going:

- population figures for capital cities;
- distance away for a number of stars (light years);
- amount of pocket-money members of the class get per week;
- hours of sunshine from records from the local weather station.

Programme of study: Handling data

■ **2. Collecting, representing and interpreting data**

Pupils should be taught to:

d draw conclusions from statistics and graphs, and recognise why some conclusions can be uncertain or misleading.

Area of study 21 | P of S 2d | LD 5

STATISTICAL CONCLUSIONS

Commentary
Children's capacity to detect different ways of interpreting statistics and graphical data will be directly related to the breadth and extent of their experience. It is therefore important to set up a 'press cuttings' squad to assemble a bank of data for discussion and interpretation.

Activity 1: Discussing data and conclusions
Using data or graphs taken from the national or local press, or television programmes like BBC's 'Children's Newsround', discuss the outcomes with the children and ask them to propose all the possible conclusions one could draw from the data.

Use also data the children themselves have collected, and work they have done in other Areas of study, for example,

Area of study 4: Tallying and frequency tables
Area of study 6: Block graphs
Area of study 9: Bar charts
Area of study 13: Interpreting and constructing Bar-line and Line graph

Programme of study: Handling data

■ **3. Understanding and using probability**

Pupils should be taught to:

a develop understanding of probability, through experience as well as experiment and theory, and discuss events and simple experiments, using a vocabulary that includes the words 'evens', 'fair', 'unfair', 'certain', 'likely', 'probably', and 'equally likely';

Area of study 22 | P of S 3a | LD 4

BEGINNING PROBABILITY

Commentary
Assessing probabilities seems to be fundamental to human survival! You need to know what the chances are that a car will hit you, a dog will bite, or a hot drink scald your tongue before you take a risk. In all these examples you do need prior knowledge, if not experience, to make realistic judgements. It is rather like estimation.

Many small children seem very adept at judging positive probabilities (as the look on the face of a two-year-old at the sight of a chocolate bar shows!). Parental protection prevents their contact with the negative kind. Probability is not about what is nice and what is nasty, good or bad, but simply the likelihood of something occurring.

You need to arm the children with sufficient facts and experience (which may be at second hand for not every child needs to be bitten by a dog before they know that dogs may bite) so that children can begin to assess probabilities of all kinds.

Activity 1: Possibilities in daily routine
Once children have had practice in going through the routine of a school day many times, they will be able to assess the probabilities that PE will be on Wednesday or that assembly will follow playtime. You can begin their experience of making these assessments by discussing with them the idea of 'probability' and 'chance'. There are also aspects of their daily routine at home which they can tell you about. Questions like, 'What do you do first when you get up?' or 'What does mum say as you leave the breakfast table?' may produce answers like, 'I always put my slippers on' or 'Most days mum reminds me to clean my teeth.' These are statements about probabilities.

Activity 2: Predicting outcomes
Show the children a coin and a die. Ask them what will be the outcome if you toss the coin or roll the die. Discuss their answers with them. They should be able to predict that the coin will show either a 'head' or 'tail', and that the die will show a number from one to six. Discuss with the children the possible outcome of a human pregnancy, litter size in cats and dogs, what kind of seed will grow on a plant, and similar events. Put the results of the discussions in a class book or on a chart.

Activity 3: Testing outcomes
You can let the children do some simple experiments to demonstrate outcomes. The problem is that in a small number of trials your results may not show the pattern predicted, so do bear this in mind. Let the children flip a coin a fixed number of times (say 20) and using rubber stamps bearing pictures of 'head' and 'tail' let them stamp them in two columns.

Put a number of blocks or beads of two colours into a bag (perhaps 4 red and 4 green). If the children take out a bead a fixed number of times (about 10) returning the bead to the bag after each 'go', they can record the colours obtained.

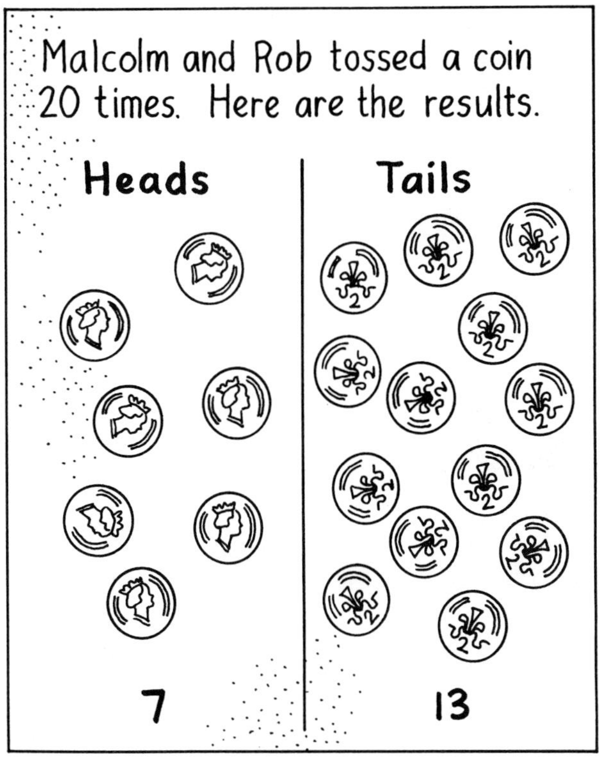

Area of study 23 | P of S 3a | LD 4

OUTCOMES OF EVENTS

Commentary
Some of the work expected here demands quite sophisticated thinking. There is much research to show that children (and even some adults) assign aspects to chance events which logic tells us cannot be there. Placing a bet on a horse would not be an attractive option for some people if they did not believe that four times a winner means next time a winner or that the outsider has a good chance of winning! However, research also shows that young children can be educated to assess degrees of uncertainty and chance. If you are prone to illogical estimations of chance yourself, keep your opinions from the young mathematicians in your care!

Activity 1: What is certain?
This is not an easy point for discussion! While nothing can really be said to be certain, there are plenty of things that we depend on which for practical purposes are certain. Examples that you can give the children may include the following:

- day following night;
- there are clothes there when we open the wardrobe;
- the cheese shop sells cheese.

See what the children regard as virtual certainties. Is it virtually certain that you will tell Gary off before the day's out?

Activity 2: What is impossible?
This is an opportunity to tap the children's prodigious imagination. Invent a whole host of impossible happenings, put them in a class book and let the children enjoy reading them. For example, it is impossible that the dinner ladies are made of marzipan, that celery can talk, that the sun disappeared forever 10 minutes ago, that aliens will come to stay for the weekend, that human beings will all talk like Mickey Mouse tomorrow, or that cats all secretly speak Spanish. If you offer them a few equally ridiculous suggestions they will soon fill a book for the book corner, which they will pore over and relish.

Activity 3: Degrees of uncertainty
When you have talked of things that are 'certain' and those that are impossible, discuss the idea that all other happenings have some uncertainty attached. Talk about some of the events in everyday life and how likely it is that they will happen in the opinions of the children. Such statements could include:

- I am quite likely to get up at seven o'clock tomorrow.
- It is uncertain whether there will be chocolate pudding for tea.
- It might rain before the weekend.
- There may be a general election before the end of the year.
- We may be doing mathematics when the fire practice bell goes off.
- Somebody may fall and hurt their knee at playtime.

Area of study 24 | P of S 3a | LD 4

THE CHANCES ARE ...

C100

Commentary
Children have lots of experience of chance through the games that they play, both board games and many playground games. But, in common with many adults they are prone to having the mental equivalent of lucky four-leafed clovers! To get to grips with the idea of likelihood is, therefore, important. Statistics is a branch of mathematics which is of great significance in our present world – so many decisions are now taken on the basis of trends and projections.

Activity 1: Comparing the 'likelihood' of events
Using the children's experience at Level 2, discuss which happening in a pair of events is more or less likely. There may be disagreement among the children about these decisions and individual estimates are equally valid so long as they can be justified.

Here are a few suggested comparisons:

- The head teacher will come into the class before play/the clock will stop before play.
- There will be no Easter eggs in the shops until a week before Easter/May trees will blossom in June.
- Four class rubbers will go missing today/there will be more children going home to dinner than stay at school for dinner tomorrow.

Activity 2: A 'likelihood' line
When the children are adept at making the comparisons you have tried in Activity 1, give them a list of events and let them try to place the most likely at the top and least likely at the bottom. This is to give them the idea that events have 'degrees of uncertainty'.

You could devise a chance 'scale' which illustrates the concepts you are trying to explain. You could, for example, use words like 'almost certainly will happen', 'very likely to happen', 'likely to happen', 'unlikely to happen', 'very unlikely to happen', 'almost impossible'. Compile a list of statements which the children can place in order of the likelihood of their happening. You can include things like:

- I will wear shoes tomorrow
- There will be salmon sandwiches in my lunch box
- The weather tomorrow will be similar to the weather today
- My teacher is going to be a Hollywood film star when she retires.

Copymaster 100 presents a list of possible happenings and the children are asked to say where they fall along a scale from 'extremely unlikely' to 'very likely indeed'.

Area of study 25 | P of S 3a | LD 4

EVENS AND FAIR

Commentary
Fair is an important concept in the discussion of probabilities. *Fairness* means control of variables so that any possible outcome has a chance. A weighted coin or die is unfair because the weighting prevents certain outcomes. One of the difficulties that we have with the idea of fairness is that it is so commonly used to describe a wide range of human activities where the variables are often complex and not controllable in the way that mathematics and science experiments are. Exploring our concept of 'fair' is useful in coming to a mathematical definition of what is 'fair'.

Activity 1: What are 'evens'?
Explain to the children that, if there are only two possible outcomes, the chance of each is the same as the other each time, so we call this evens (provided it is fair). If there are more than two outcomes, the chance of each particular outcome is *still the same each time* but is less than evens, and diminishes as the number of possibilities rises. Do remember that if you decide to put this to the test, a small number of trials may not produce a convincing result. If, for example, you toss the coin 20 times and it is 'heads' on 18 of those occasions, this does not actually support the 'evens' discussion! This does not shake the principle, however. Let the children try coin tossing and let them offer explanations for the pattern of results they obtain (which may not be evens). For example, the coin may be weighted in some way to favour one side, it may be unevenly worn or it may not be tossed without bias. Tell the children that if these (and other explanations they may have) do not account for a result that is not 50 per cent heads, then they may need several hundred throws before the evens pattern emerges in the results.

Activity 2: Chances that are not evens
To highlight the point about what constitutes evens talk about other common situations where the chances may be greater or less than evens. Here are some examples:

- throwing a 6 on a conventional die – one in six;
- landing on a particular square in hopscotch or snakes and ladders;
- getting three plums together on a fruit machine;
- pulling out an ace from a pack of shuffled cards – $\frac{4}{52}$ which equals 1 in 13.

Activity 3: Fair/unfair in games
A game is not fair if the players do not have the same chance of winning. The children should be able to spot which of these games are fair and which are not:

- Two people trying at the coconut shy, one stands 2 m nearer to the nuts than the other.
- Two people play *Snakes and Ladders*; player 1 rolls one die; player 2 two dice and sums the dice totals before moving that number of steps.
- Two people play *Snap* with hands dealt evenly from a complete pack.
- Four people play *Happy Families* and only one player can look at any time at everyone else's cards.

Activity 4: Using fair/unfair
Sportsmen and women utilise the idea of what is fair in setting rules for games and competitions. Scientists try to devise fair tests of their hypotheses. Use what the children now know to explore, at this stage, their developing concept of fairness in everyday life and how this relates to mathematical investigations.

Programme of study: Handling data

Pupils should be taught to:

■ 3. Understanding and using probability

b understand that the probability of any event lies between impossibility and certainty, leading to the use of the scale from 0 to 1;

Area of study 26 | P of S 3b | LD 5

PROBABILITIES

C101

Commentary
At Level 3 the children were introduced to the idea of an evens chance and the likelihood of events. At this Level these basic ideas are explored more fully.

We have grouped all of the requirements of probability and chance together here as the concepts are so closely related and interdependent.

Activity 1: Estimating probabilities
Discuss a whole range of possible events and invite the children to say which are more likely and what their reasons are for saying so. Now that the children have begun to work on probabilities they should be able to help to create a set of sample events. Here are some suggestions:

- The classroom door will be jammed when someone tries to open it tomorrow morning.
- Someone in the class will have a cold next week.
- The head teacher will wear yellow socks on Friday.
- Dennis the Menace will retire this year and leave the *Beano*.
- Bugs Bunny's antics are based on those of a live rabbit.
- 90 per cent of boys born in Britain tomorrow will be named Jeremy.
- Tall girls grow into tall women.
- More people in the class are right-handed than left-handed.

Activity 2: Probability scales
Let the children establish that something which they assess as impossible (for example, all noses will turn green in the night) fits at the 0 end of a continuum and something which they regard as certain (for example, that the register will be taken tomorrow) lies at the other end of the same continuum, at the point we designate 1. The children can then set events of their own choice at various places along the line. They will note that the mid-point of the line represents evens (a 50 per cent chance of something specified happening).

Copymaster 101 is a probability scale to which the children can add their items.

Activity 3: All possible outcomes
Try telling the children about an event and asking them to come up with all the possible outcomes. If, for example, you throw a die, the possible outcomes are one, two, three, four, five or six. What are all of the possible combinations of two dice if you want to throw a total of nine?

If you want a meal at lunchtime the possibilities are a school dinner, a packed lunch or to go home for lunch. Here are some more examples:

- What are the possible outcomes among a litter of five kittens – how many could be male and how many female?
- If you send for red shorts by mail order and the wholesaler has run out of red in your size, but has stocks of your second choice colour then what are the possible outcomes?

Programme of study: Handling data

Pupils should be taught to:

■ 3. Understanding and using probability

c recognise situations where probabilities can be based on equally likely outcomes, and others where estimates must be based on experimental evidence; make or approximate these estimates.

Area of study 27 | P of S 3c | LD 5

PROBABILITIES AND OUTCOMES

C102

Commentary
The idea of experiment is important here. It is necessary for the children to appreciate that experiments should be repeated and that the outcomes of experiments are not necessarily identical. They should have encountered this in repeated readings and observations in their science work.

Activity 1: Simple experiments
Again it is possible to use simple activities to get at important ideas. Use coin-tossing once more as a starting point. With a group of children get them each to toss a fair coin ten times and record the outcomes individually. Then pool the results, but list each outcome separately for all to see. Who had the most

heads? Tails? An equal number of heads and tails? What if we add all of the heads and tails from the group? Is this nearer to a prediction of the 50–50 split? Try again for another ten throws. This Activity could also be carried out with a die – listing all outcomes from 1 to 6 inclusive – or with a spinner.

Copymaster 102 gives children a structured sheet on which to record coin and die throws.

Area of study 28 | P of S 3c | LD 5

DECIDING ON TYPES OF EVIDENCE

Commentary
In some cases, such as the tossing of a coin, it is possible to make a prediction through logical analysis, but in other situations there are so many or unknown variables that it is necessary to collect data before a prediction for the future can be made.

Activity 1: Challenges
Give the children a series of challenges where they have the opportunity to decide what evidence they need to make an estimate of probability and how they can assemble that evidence. Here are some examples:

- What is the probability that the next person coming through the classroom door will be aged eight?
- What is the probability that it will rain before next Saturday?
- What is the probability that sales of books at the school book fair will exceed 200 books?
- What is the probability that oranges will be on the school meal menu on Monday?

The children can record a table of challenges with evidence needed and methods suggested to accrue evidence.

Challenge	Evidence I need to estimate probabilities	How I could get the required evidence

Area of study 29 | P of S 3c | LD 5

WHAT ARE THE CHANCES?

Commentary
At this Level the children should be starting to make general statements about probability using what they have learned in Number as well as Handling data.

The children should be familiar with a 50–50 chance and that this can be expressed as a one in two ($\frac{1}{2}$) chance. Use this knowledge to extend into other probabilities of this type.

Activity 1: What is equally likely?
Discuss with the children a number of situations in which all possible outcomes are equally likely. See if the children can generate some examples. Possibilities include:

- heads or tails at the toss of a coin;
- spinning a 1 or a 2 on a hexagonal spinner with three 1s and three 2s on it;
- taking a blue bead, or a yellow bead or a red bead from a bag with six red, six yellow and six blue beads in it;
- taking a spade card or a hearts card from a pile made up of the same numbers of spades and hearts cards.

When you are sure the children are confident about what 'equally likely' means, move on to Activity 2.

Activity 2: A formula for equally likely
Show the children that the likelihood of the example events from Activity 1 happening is:

$$\frac{1}{\text{The number of events}}$$

and that this holds for all situations in which the possible outcomes are equally likely.

RECORD SHEET

Class(es) ______________________ **Name** ______________________

	AT1 Using and applying mathematics	AT2 Number and algebra	AT3 Shape, space and measures	AT4 Handling data
Extension activities				
Level 5				
Level 4				
Level 3				
Level 2				